Contracts &

Fifth Edition

Liability

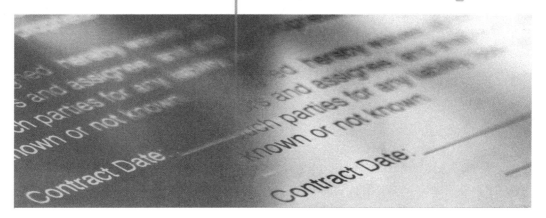

David Jaffe / David Crump

A Service of

NAHB

BuilderBooks™
National Association of Home Builders
1201 15th Street, NW
Washington, DC 20005-2800
www.builderbooks.com

Contracts and Liability, 5th edition
David S. Jaffe
David N. Crump, Jr.

Doris M. Tennyson	Senior Acquisitions Editor
Jenny Stewart	Assistant Editor

BuilderBooks at the National Association of Home Builders

ERIC JOHNSON	Publisher
THERESA MINCH	Executive Editor
DORIS M. TENNYSON	Senior Acquisitions Editor
JESSICA POPPE	Assistant Editor
JENNY STEWART	Assistant Editor
BRENDA ANDERSON	Director of Fulfillment
GILL WALKER	Marketing Manager
JACQUELINE BARNES	Marketing Manager

GERALD HOWARD	NAHB Executive Vice President and CEO
MARK PURSELL	Executive Vice President Marketing & Sales
GREG FRENCH	Staff Vice President, Publications and Affinity Programs

ISBN 0-86718-558-9

Printed in the United States of America

Library of Congress Cataloging-in-Publication Data

Jaffe, David S.
    Contracts and liability / David S. Jaffe, David N. Crump, Jr.— 5th ed.
        p. cm.
    Rev. ed. of: Contracts and liability for builders and remodelers / David S. Jaffe. 4th ed. c1996.
    ISBN 0-86718-558-9 (pbk.)
    1 Construction contracts—United States.   I. Crump, David N.   II. Jaffe, David S. Contracts and liability for buildersand remodelers.
    III. Title.
        KF902.Z9C695 2003
        343.73'078624—dc22

                              2003015954

Disclaimer
This publication is designed to provide accurate and authoritative information in regard to the subject matter covered. It is sold with the understanding that the publisher is not engaged in rendering legal, accounting, or other professional service. If legal advice or other expert assistance is required, the services of a competent professional person should be sought.

From a Declaration of Principles jointly adopted by a Committee of the American Bar Association and a Committee of Publishers and Associations

For further information, please contact:
BuilderBooks™
National Association of Home Builders
1201 15th Street, NW
Washington, DC 20005-2800
(800) 223-2665
Check us out online at: www.builderbooks.com

12/03 Armen Kojoyian/SLR/DRC, 2000

ABOUT THE AUTHORS

David S. Jaffe is Staff Vice President of Construction Liability and Legal Research for the Legal Affairs Area of the NAHB Advocacy Group. He is the author of several other NAHB publications, including *Warranties and Disclaimers for Builders* and *Warranties and Disclaimers for Remodelers.* He regularly advises the builder and remodeler members of NAHB on contract and liability issues and on other aspects of construction law. He is a regular speaker at NAHB educational programs on contract and liability topics and trends related to the building industry.

David N. Crump, Jr. is Director of Legal Research for the Legal Affairs Area of the NAHB Advocacy Group. He administers NAHB's Legal Research Program that provides legal information and research services for NAHB members.. His experience entails more than a quarter century of legal practice. His former positions include those of municipal attorney and trial court judge. He is a frequent speaker at NAHB educational programs on a wide variety of legal issues.

CONTENTS

FIGURES

Chapter 7 Inspections

Chapter 8 Design-Build Contracts Used by Remodelers and Custom Builders

Chapter 9 Contracts With Other Team Members

Chapter 10 Liability and Contract Enforcement

Appendix

1

THE NATURE OF A CONTRACT

THIS BOOK IS ABOUT contracts for builders, remodelers, and developers—people who use contracts everyday. These individuals are skilled in the construction trades and they are constantly contracting in the course of their businesses. However, they may not totally understand what contracts are, why they are important, what needs to be included in them, or what procedures are involved.

You wouldn't try to build a house without a blueprint because it has too many elements to consider. Overlook one feature of construction and the project could become a disaster. Misinterpret the procedures of construction and the walls could come tumbling down. The same is true with the many facets of a business relationship. Think of your building contract as the blueprint for the business relationship with your customer. You need it to:

- Define the project
- Determine costs and the method of payment
- Set down the rights and responsibilities of each party
- Provide a means to resolve any disputes

Without a well-drawn contract, your relationship with the customer could become a nightmare, and no matter how skillful and professional you are at construction, your business undertaking could fail and your profits disappear.

A well-drawn contract should reflect all the terms agreed upon between the builder, remodeler, or developer and his or her customer. Okay, you say, but why not just use a form that provides all the "standard" clauses? The answer to that question is that every business relationship has unique aspects. A standard form is not going to cover all the necessary details and it may even contain language that is inappropriate for your specific project. In addition, state laws and local regulations differ. Therefore, a well-drawn contract cannot be a one-size-fits-all standard instrument. Well-drawn contracts do have common features, but these features should be amenable to supplementation and modification as needed. You need to take extra care in drafting any contractual agreement to assure that the contract language is right for that particular project.

Subsequent chapters will explain specific contract clauses and provisions, and they will provide examples specific to the homebuilding industry. This chapter explores the nature of a contract and its formulation and interpretation.

PERMANENCE

If a contract serves as the blueprint of your business relationship with the customer, you both will need to refer to it from time to time. If the only repository for the contract terms is the memory of each party, trouble lies ahead. Memory is imperfect. Forgetfulness, inattention, confusion, stress, and even deceit can affect recollection. An oral contract is only as good as the memory (and honesty) of each party. Two conflicting memories will provide no guidance and damage or destroy the effectiveness of the contract as a blueprint. To paraphrase an old maxim, "The oral agreement is worth as much as the paper it is printed on." To provide the permanence needed for effectiveness as a blueprint, the contract must be in writing. By law you need to commit to writing certain contracts involving the sale or transfer of real estate and contracts exceeding one year in time for performance.

CONTENT

A blueprint that omits critical components is of little use. Likewise, a contract that omits important provisions cannot serve as a blueprint. Even a written contract can prove ineffective as a blueprint if it lacks the content necessary to interpret and govern the business relationship. As an absolute minimum, the contract must contain a "mutuality of performance"—a description of the work you are to provide and provisions for payment in return. The contract also should fully state all the remaining terms of your agreement. If it does not do so, you may encounter the same difficulties with permanence as in oral contract situations. Review all the terms with your customer. Are the terms complete? To be valid, a contract must reflect a "meeting of your minds." This phrase means that each party must have the same understanding about the contract provisions. Different assumptions by a builder and a customer about important contract provisions caused by incomplete contract language could result in a judicial ruling that voids the entire contract.

AVAILABILITY

You cannot use a blueprint if it is unavailable for reference. Everyone using a blueprint needs to have access to it. The same is true with contracts. Mutual rights and responsibilities are key components in contracts, and contracts can prevent conflicts with customers over these rights and responsibilities only if the contract is available for easy reference. Therefore, each party should receive a signed original document—not a copy. If one party controls the only original of the contract, a contract's effectiveness as a "peacemaker" is diminished.

CLARITY

A current "plain language" movement works to require simpler language in all consumer contracts. The purpose of the plain language is to make contract provisions perfectly understandable to laypeople and thereby (a) avoid conflicts and misunderstandings over contract provisions and (b) enhance the contract's effectiveness as your blueprint. Contract clauses that contain confusing, repetitive, inappropriate, or even incomprehensible language frequently come from boilerplate forms or they obviously have been copied from other documents. Even typographical errors are sometimes reproduced and used repeatedly in contract after contract. In such circumstances, neither party will have a clear understanding of what such contract provisions say or mean.

Further, if the contract requires enforcement, no judge, jury, or arbitrator is likely to have a clue as to the parties' intention in the use of such language. A principle of contract law holds that decisions involving ambiguities in a contract go against the party who drafted the language or provided the form. To be sure, legal terms and phrases that may be difficult for ordinary consumers to understand sometimes need to be used in the course of a contract's text. But contract provisions need to be understood by both the parties and those outsiders (judges, juries, and arbitrators) who may be called on to interpret the meaning. Where necessary, include in the contract an explanation of such a provision or term used in the contract. Do not heedlessly include obscure language just because it appeared before in some other document.

FLOW

The sequence of blueprint drawings follows a certain logic. They have a flow that permits the user to easily access all necessary information. If the pages are out of order, interpreting the project becomes frustrating and someone could miss a critical feature. The same situation is true of contracts. A well-drawn contract has a logic or flow that permits easy access to and a better understanding of terms. And fewer conflicts arise between the parties. Such contracts frequently include:

- A beginning (date of agreement, identification of the parties, addresses)
- A middle (project description, specifications, consideration, and method of payment)
- A conclusion (warranties, terms of interpretation and enforcement, additional terms, and signatures)

Normally, you are not legally required to follow a logical sequence or placement of contract provisions. But be aware that courts occasionally refuse to enforce certain "hidden" clauses (those in fine print or in unexpected locations, such as the back of a page).

SIGNATURES

A signature on a written contract provides evidence that the signer has accepted the contract terms. That issue could be in dispute if the contract is not signed. Even though an unsigned contract may sometimes be deemed valid, certain contract provisions (such as the payment of interest or the resolution of disputes through arbitration) will not be enforced without a signed, written agreement. All interested parties to the agreement should sign the contract. If a husband and wife are, or will be, the owners of the real estate, both should sign the contract, even if the negotiations took place with only one of the spouses. Otherwise, enforcing the agreement against the nonsigning party may be difficult. Further, the jointly owned assets of the person who signed the contract (jointly owned with a nonsigning spouse) may be beyond the reach of collection on a judgment. For business entities (partnership, corporation, limited liability company), generally one person can sign on behalf of the business. A partner, director, or managing officer has legal authority to sign on behalf of the business. Proof of signature is normally not required for most contracts. If the instrument is to be recorded, however, the document will in most cases require a notary public to attest to the identity of the persons signing the instrument.

Now that you have a sense of the nature of a contract, you are ready to move on to specific provisions. Please keep in mind that the terms, clauses, and forms in this book are simply illustrations. You should have an attorney assist you in the preparation of individual contracts to meet your particular needs. Any suggested contract provision will not and cannot apply to every situation. Contract law can differ greatly from state to state. Even municipal law can effect the terms of a contract. The examples provided are intended only to identify issues and problem situations, to suggest approaches for resolving them, and to explore alternatives. This book is offered as an informational service to builders and remodelers. It is not intended to serve as a substitute for the services of counsel. Builders, remodelers, and developers should have their attorneys prepare documents that meet their specific needs.

2

CONTRACT BETWEEN BUILDER AND BUYER (OWNER)

A WRITTEN CONTRACT RECORDS THE exact terms of an agreement between parties. The contract defines the scope of the work and the price of the product and allocates the risks inherent in a particular transaction between the parties. This chapter of *Contracts and Liability* should help builders and their attorneys write construction contracts that lessen builders' risks.

Many provisions in ready-made contract forms, such as the American Institute of Architects' Document A201, expose builders to considerable liability during the construction process. No boilerplate contract clause is suitable for every situation. Therefore, builders should critically examine every transaction into which they enter to foresee contingencies or events that could impair the transaction's benefits to them. Builders should make sure that each of their contracts is written to provide them with adequate protection from events that may expose them to liability.

Contracts allocate the responsibilities and the risks associated with those responsibilities. Some risks are standard and cannot be assigned or transferred to others. For example, the builder bears the responsibility for and the risks associated with ensuring that a home is built according to plans and specifications. The allocation of other risks and responsibilities is not always so clear. For example, who should buy the builder's risk insurance? Not necessarily the builder.

Builders should not shy away from risks as long as they get paid for taking those risks. The object is to avoid as many risks as possible for the same price.

This chapter examines the purpose of various clauses that might be included in a construction contract and presents sample language that may be used in construction or sales contracts between buyers (or owners) and builders. The explanation for each provision helps readers understand the sample language.

These suggested provisions do not address every contingency, and they do not apply to all construction and sales agreements. Neither does this chapter cover all of the provisions that builders and buyers should consider for a sales or construction contract. For example, parties should negotiate and document who will be responsible for miscellaneous items such as:

- Payment of hazard insurance and utility fees during construction
- Peroration of tax and insurance costs on sale of the property
- Bond requirements, if any
- Payment of impact fees, if any

These and other provisions, if written correctly, may further protect builders against unnecessary liability.

Builders who offer an insured warranty to their customers should redraft or not use those warranty provisions contained in this book that conflict with their particular insured warranty program.

Contracts are legal documents that greatly determine a builder's liability if a home buyer alleges that the builder failed to perform the contract obligations. An attorney experienced in construction contract law should therefore prepare (or at least review) any such documents before a builder signs them. To find such an attorney the builder could contact the local home builders association or the local branches of the Associated General Contractors or the Associated Builders and Contractors.

The sample language presents an option for the reader. Depending on the particular transaction, the reader may choose one or the other, both, or neither of the possible wordings presented.

Warning! The National Association of Home Builders has provided this guide and sample contract language merely to point out the types of provisions of which builders should be aware. These suggested provisions should not be used unless they have been reviewed by an attorney experienced in residential construction law.

This chapter addresses the major sources of potential liability that a builder may face in two different types of construction contracts: (a) a contract with a buyer who owns the lot or land on which the house will be built and (b) a contract to construct a house on a lot owned by the builder under which the house and the lot will be sold together.

The parts of the contract include the agreement, the general conditions, and the plans and specifications. Other documents or clauses may be included in a contract.

THE AGREEMENT

The agreement is the document that the parties sign. All the other documents that make up the contract such as the general conditions and the plans and specifications are named in the agreement as being part of the contract.

The builder's warranties and warranty limitations often also are drafted separately (see Chapter 4, Express and Implied Warranties and Limited Warranty). If the agreement specifically incorporates these other documents, their requirements and limitations will be a part of the agreement. The agreement should specifically and accurately describe the referenced documents by date, number of pages, plan number, name, and any other appropriate information. The requirements contained in the incorporated documents should not conflict with each other or with the terms of the agreement. Examples of contract documents appear in Figure 2.1.

Common sense will dictate which of the following provisions apply to a particular builder's needs.

Caption

The caption is the heading or introductory part of a legal document. It should include the names of all of the home buyers (both husband and wife, for example, if they are buying jointly). The full legal name of each party should appear in all documents in the transaction. If a purchaser is a corporation or other business entity, the documents should include the full name and type of business entity. The names of the parties should be exactly the same in the contract as in all other pro-

Figure 2.1 Examples of Contract Documents

- The agreement includes all the items that can vary from project to project, such as the names and addresses of the parties to the contract, the name and location of the project, the dates for beginning and substantial completion of the project, a list of the other documents included in the contract, a list of the work involved in the contract documents but to be done by others, price of the contract, payments and how they are to be made, and signatures. The agreement includes any part of the contract in which blanks must be filled in.
- Additions are changes to the contract (issued before execution of the agreement).
- General conditions set forth those conditions that do not vary from one contract to another, such as settling disputes, grounds for terminating or suspending the contract, and procedures for making changes in the work. They spell out responsibilities not assigned by other parts of the contract (such as insurance and bonds). They also cover ownership of the drawings, specifications, and other documents.
- Specifications describe the work to be done, the material to be used, and how it will be used or installed.
- Drawings (plans) are pictorial representations of the project.
- Special conditions are any modifications or additions to the general conditions.
- A warranty is a statement (oral or in writing) that the work will meet certain standards and a promise by the builder to correct deficiencies in workmanship and materials.
- Change orders are modifications to the contract (issued after execution of the agreement).
- A draw schedule describes when payment is due; it is often tied to commencement or completion of certain stages of the work.
- An allowance schedule identifies those items of work that are not sufficiently detailed in the contract documents to enable the parties to determine the actual cost of the item.

---

ject documents. The caption should also provide the location and a legal description of the property (e.g., lot, block, and subdivision).

> This contract specifies the terms between (<u>buyer's name</u>) (the customer) and (<u>builder's name</u>) (the builder) to construct the (home or other structure) on the property located at (<u>legal description of property</u>).

CONTRACT DOCUMENTS

As discussed earlier, a typical written residential construction contract consists of several different documents, and these documents are incorporated in the contract by reference in the agreement. For example, the plans and specifications are usually incorporated in the contract by reference as a matter of convenience. Generally, when a written contract incorporates other documents by reference, a single contract is created that includes the contents of the incorporated documents. To avoid any confusion about which plans and specifications are incorporated, the agreement should specifically and accurately describe the referenced documents by date, number of pages, plan number, name, and any other appropriate information. In addition, the parties should initial each page of the documents at the time of contract signing. They also should initial the drawing(s) and every page of the specifications to avoid (a) an accusation that a different page has been substituted or (b) a plea of ignorance if a disagreement arises between the owner and the builder. Moreover, the prudent builder will include an "order of preference" clause in the contract. This clause specifies whether the plans or the specifications take precedence in case of a conflict between the two. The parties are free to decide the order of precedence when the builder provides the specifications but not the plans. He/she may want the specifications to take precedence in case of a conflict.

> The terms of this contract include the conditions of this contract and, by reference, the provisions in the other documents specifically listed below. The terms of this agreement prevail over any conflicting provisions in the documents incorporated by reference. In the case of a difference, discrepancy between, or ambiguity in the plans and specifications, the parties agree that the specifications shall govern.
>
> The builder shall perform all of the work that is required by this agreement and any documents incorporated by reference below.
>
> Except for written modifications executed by both parties subsequent to the execution of this contract (for example, change orders), the terms of the contract are limited to the provisions contained in this agreement and the other documents described as follows:
>
> (title of document), dated the _____ day of _____, 20_____ consisting of _____ pages;

_____

8

(title of document), dated the _____ day of _____, 20_____ consisting of
_____ pages;

(title of document), dated the _____ day of _____, 20_____ consisting of
_____ pages:

EXAMPLE

"Where the signatories execute a contract which refers to another instrument in such a manner as
to establish that they intended to make the terms and conditions of that other instrument a part of
their understanding, the two may be interpreted together as the agreement of the parties."[1]

PROTECTING OWNERSHIP OF PLANS

Builders who provide their own plans for a house should consider expressly prohibiting buyers
from giving or selling those plans to other potential buyers or builders without permission (or compensation). The best way to protect design plan ownership rights is to register the copyright for
the plans through the Copyright Office of the Library of Congress. For further information on
the registration of copyrights, including forms and instructions, you may visit the U.S. Copyright
Office website at www.loc.gov/copyright.

Similarly, if the buyer provides the plans, the builder should make certain that the buyer owns the
plans because if the buyer does not own the plans, the builder may be sued for copyright infringement.

Sample contract language for circumstances using a builder's plan and also using a buyer's plan
is provided below:

Builder's Plans. The builder has provided the building plans and specifications to be used under
this contract (<u>reference by title, date, author, and number of pages</u>). The buyer has no ownership
rights in the plans and specifications used under this contract, and the buyer will be liable to the
builder for the amount of lost profits and all consequential damages for the reuse or resale of
these copyrighted plans.

The builder makes no representations or warranties about the quality of these plans except
those specifically provided in the limited warranty references in this contract.

Buyer's Plans. The builder agrees to construct the home in accordance with the building plans
supplied by the buyer (<u>reference by title, author, and number of pages</u>). The builder assumes no
responsibility or liability for defects in the design or engineering of these plans. The buyer
warrants that the plans and specifications are adequate and that the builder can rely on them. The
buyer will be liable for any damages caused by defective building plans and specifications,
including but not limited to additional costs caused by delay in substantial completion of the home,
additional costs for materials necessitated by any changes, and additional labor costs, pro rata
overhead, and profit on the additional work.

The buyer represents that (a) the house plans provided to the builder are the result of an original design, (b) the buyer is the sole owner of the design, and (c) the buyer has exclusive rights, including copyright, in and to the design as represented in the structure, plans, specifications, and drawings for the house. The buyer agrees to indemnify and hold the builder harmless from all claims of third parties for copyright infringement or conversion that may be asserted as a result of the builder's construction of the house for the buyer.

TIME OF COMMENCEMENT AND SUBSTANTIAL COMPLETION

The date the work begins should be no earlier than the date of execution of the contract. Instead of a specific date, a flexible starting date may be established by using a notice to proceed—for example, "The work shall commence on the date stipulated in the notice to proceed."

PRACTICE POINTER

The builder should have evidence of the financing approval or ability to pay before commencing work (see Price, Deposit, and Payment later in this chapter). For buyer-owned lots, the builder should require evidence of a valid title and a copy of the current survey, deed restrictions, liens, and easements, if any. These items may help protect the builder's lien rights, may help avoid claims of encroachment or trespass by third parties, and may help identify any potential site or construction restrictions that the builder can avoid.

The contract completion date should be expressed as a number of days (preferably calendar days) from the contract date or notice to proceed and should be based on "substantial completion" of the work rather than on final or full completion. One common definition of substantial completion is when the buyer can use the project for its intended purpose. Another example of a substantial completion date might be the date of the final inspection or the date the Certificate of Occupancy is issued. The contract should clearly define what constitutes substantial completion. Substantial completion should not be pegged to "buyer's satisfaction," which is a subjective standard. A finding that the work is substantially complete entitles the builder to the contract price. Keep in mind, however, that the buyer will be entitled to an offset for expenses he/she may incur in completing any unfinished work or correcting any deficient work.

If construction is connected to an interstate land sale, the builder must comply with time periods for delivery under the Interstate Land Sales Full Disclosure Act, 15 United States Code sec. 1701 et seq. (1982) (see 24 Code of Federal Regulations parts 1700–1730).[2]

The contract should include a provision for extending the time of completion. A sample provision is as follows:

The work to be performed under this contract shall be substantially completed not later than ___(number)___ calendar days from ___(date of commencement)___, provided that if the builder is delayed in the completion of the work by any act of the owner or by the owner's failure to perform under the contract, by adverse weather conditions, by natural or man-made disasters, by strikes, or by such other causes outside of the builder's control, then the time of substantial completion shall be extended by the same period of time encompassed by the aforesaid cause of delay.

CASE STUDIES

Case 1. A contract for the sale and erection of a prefabricated house provided for completion of the house on September 27th. When the purchasers arrived on the scene at 4 p.m. on the specified date, at the builder's behest for a final inspection, the workers were still "slapping on siding, laying floors, bulldozing the yard, hooking up utilities, and so on," and the purchasers refused to accept the house, despite the foreman's assurances that the home would be completed by 5:30 p.m. The court held that the builder substantially complied with the contract on the date specified when only service walk, some grading, and blacktopping were left undone at 5:30 p.m. The court found that no substantial sum was required to complete the items left undone, and the purchasers could have resided in the home at that time.[3]

Case 2. Aleda Construction Co., Inc., sued the Winns claiming that the Winns breached a written construction contract by failing to pay the balance due for the construction of a house. The contract provided for payments to be made at various specified stages of completion and that the funds would be paid "in consideration of the covenants and agreements being strictly performed." Final payment was due when the house was "fully complete (NOT substantially complete) and Aleda supplied the Winns with a final survey and executed Release of Liens." At trial, Aleda's president conceded that (a) several items were incomplete (which he estimated would cost $500) and (b) Aleda had not furnished the Winns with a final survey or a Release of Liens. Finding for the Winns, the court concluded that Aleda had not "strictly" performed and that the house was not "fully" completed.[4]

PRICE, DEPOSIT, AND PAYMENT

This section of the contract specifies and defines the builder's compensation for the construction of the project. It also instructs the parties in the manner and time of payment. To achieve these goals, this section should:

- Include the cost of the work. Some builders charge buyers a total fixed price for the project. Others bill on a cost-plus-fee or cost-plus-percentage basis. The cost-plus contract should specify the percentage or fee required, the guaranteed maximum price (if any), what constitutes costs (see section on costs), how the fixed fee is to be adjusted for change orders, the type of fee schedule, and all anticipated costs and fees, when applicable. In either case, the contract should specify (in both words and numbers) (a) the total price of the construction or sales transaction and (b) the amount of the buyer's deposit to be paid to the builder upon execution of the contract.

- Identify the first and, if applicable, the second mortgage or deed of trust.

- Specify that work covered by change order falls within the general scope of the work contemplated by the contract, and specify a percentage of profit for additional work. Change orders for deductions from the work usually involve no reduction of profit, and this fact should be clearly stated.

- Establish the amount of the deposit and the due dates for all payments. The builder should check applicable state laws regarding escrow accounts (see sample state law in Figure 2.2). Parties often arbitrarily set due dates for payments. The due dates should be mutually acceptable to both builder and buyer. The dates often reflect specific stages of construction. Builders can specify that payments come due at the start of a construction activity rather than at the end. (Example: A payment might come due on the beginning of framing rather than at the completion of the foundation.) The reason for this is that buyers rarely dispute when an activity begins but sometimes question when an activity ends. The contract should account for the time necessary for the builder to prepare an application for payment and for the buyer to make the payment. For instance, the contract might state: "The owner has ten (10) days from the statement date to pay the builder."

Figure 2.2 Sample State Law Regarding Escrow Account

Pursuant to Maryland statutory law (Md. Real Property Code Ann. §10-506 [1988]), a custom home builder must include in each custom home contract an escrow account requirement notice. The escrow account notice shall be on a separate page of the custom home contract, and the escrow account requirement notice shall state:

Escrow Account Requirement

Unless your contract is financed by a mortgage issued by a federally chartered financial institution or a financial institution supervised under the Financial Institutions Article of the Annotated Code of Maryland, or unless all deposits, escrow money, binder money, or any other money paid in advance, or is paid to the licensed broker, to be held in the escrow account of the broker, Maryland law requires that all consideration exceeding five percent of the total contract price that is paid by a buyer to a custom home builder in advance of completion of the labor, or receipt of the materials for which the consideration is paid, shall be deposited in an escrow account and paid out of that account only for certain purposes specified by law. To ensure this, the law requires that your builder may only accept such payment in the name of the escrow account. Thus, you should make out your check to "(*name of builder*), escrow account." Records of payments out of this account must be carefully maintained by your builder, and the builder must permit you reasonable access to escrow account records. Your builder, however, may choose to establish a separate account for your project, which will require your signature for any withdrawals."

- Require interest for late payments. For example, "Payments due under the contract but not paid shall incur daily interest at the rate of _____ percent (_____%) from the date payment is due." The builder should check applicable state laws concerning maximum allowable interest rates (usury). Instead of charging interest on late payments, the contract could provide for a late payment fee similar to liquidated damages. Such a late fee might be included in a cost-plus-fee contract as well as in a fixed-cost contract.

An alternate clause may read as follows in this example:

Buyer hereby acknowledges that late payment by the buyer to the builder of progress payments and final payment may cause the builder to incur costs not contemplated elsewhere in this contract, the exact amount of which will be difficult to ascertain. Accordingly, any sum due the builder under this contract shall be paid within ten (10) days of written request. If full payment is not received within ten (10) days, the buyer shall pay ten percent (10%) of the total amount overdue as a late charge. The parties agree that such late charge represents a fair and reasonable estimate of the costs the builder will incur by reason of late payment by the buyer.

- Specify whether retainage is allowed. Retainage is a percentage of the contract price that is withheld by the owner until completion, such as when the project is substantially completed and all potential mechanics liens have been waived or released. If retainage is provided for, the contract should specify when (under what circumstances) the retainage will be disbursed.
- Require evidence of financing. The builder should be allowed to verify that the buyer has satisfactory financing, including an allowance for subsequent change orders. The buyer should be required to produce evidence of financing before the builder is obligated to start work.
- Satisfy any special state or local requirements. Some states require that the contract specifically identify certain expenses (e.g., Washington state requires that the sales tax be listed separately from the total price).

Fixed-Price Contract. The buyer agrees to buy and the builder agrees to [construct and/or sell] the building [and lot] for the consideration of _____ dollars ($_____), the total price. The buyer will pay _____ dollars ($_____) to the builder as a deposit [if one is required] upon signing this contract. The buyer will make the following interim payments of _____ dollars ($_____):

    (List payments and tie them to a construction activity such as the beginning of drywall.)

    The buyer will make a final payment in the amount of _____ dollars ($_____) to the builder at final settlement [within ___(_____) days of substantial completion].

    Cost-Plus-Fee Contract. The buyer agrees to buy and the builder agrees to [construct and/or sell] the project for the consideration of the builder's actual costs and expenses (as defined in Section _____ of this contract, Costs to Be Reimbursed) plus a fixed fee of _____ dollars

($_____). The buyers will pay _____ dollars ($_____) as a deposit upon signing this contract [or on or before some date other than the date the contract is signed] and will make a final payment (including all costs and expenses plus the fee specified above) to the builder at final settlement [or within ___(_____) days of substantial completion). Substantial completion has occurred when the buyer can use the project for its intended purpose.

   If the buyer requires an addition to the scope of the work, the builder shall account for the cost of these additions separately and shall be reimbursed _____ percent (_____%) of the cost of the changes.

Costs to Be Reimbursed

This section is applicable to cost-plus-percentage or cost-plus-fee contracts. The list below suggests costs that may need to be reimbursed in a construction project, but it may not include all costs to be reimbursed on every job. The builder should include all relevant items and especially every contingency negotiated with the buyer. Builders should check this section against their general ledgers and other accounting records to make sure all appropriate costs are included.

Many contracts will also include a section regarding costs not to be reimbursed. These provisions should be carefully reviewed because, by definition, they exclude some of the builder's actual costs. These items would be paid out of the percentage or fee added to the defined costs and therefore would cut into the builder's profit.

Because of the numerous costs associated with building a home, disputes are likely to occur over costs. Therefore, the parties should take great care in identifying which costs are reimbursable and which are not. Moreover, the actual costs incurred by the builder must be reasonable. Builders should be prepared to show that (a) any money they claim to have paid out for materials and work on the job were necessary and (b) they deducted costs incurred because of the inefficiency or incompetence of their agents or employees.

The term cost of work means costs necessarily incurred in the builder's proper performance of the work contained in the contract documents, including the following items:

- Wages, benefits, and costs of contributions and assessments for workers' compensation, unemployment insurance, Social Security, taxes, or any other costs incurred by the builder for labor during performance of this contract.

- Salary, wage, or hourly rate for supervision by builder. The rate for the builder's time should be agreed on by the parties.

- Salaries for the builder's field personnel to the extent their time is spent on work required by this contract. This payment of salaries includes (but is not limited to) work performed at shops, on the construction site, or in transporting materials or equipment except where such work is not in accordance with the plans and specifications.

- For out-of-town work, the builder's and the builder's agents' reasonable travel and subsistence expenses incurred performing this contract.

- Payments made by the builder to trade contractors for work performed according to subcontracts under this agreement.

- Cost of land and all land development expenditures associated with or apportioned to this project.

- Cost of all materials, supplies, and equipment incorporated in the work and consumed while doing the work; cost less salvage value of such items used but not consumed that remain the property of the builder, including all costs of installing, repairing and replacing, removing, transporting, and delivering the machinery and equipment except in cases in which the builder is in error.

- Rental charges consistent with those prevailing in the area for machinery and equipment used at the construction site, whether rented from the builder or others, including all costs of installing, repairing and replacing, removing, transporting, and delivering the machinery and equipment.

- Small tools (any tool that costs less than _____ dollars [$_____] and consumables are not to be included in the cost).

- Sales, use, excise, or any other taxes related to the work imposed by governmental authorities.

- Impact fees, exactions, royalties, charges, inspection costs, or any other fees related to the work imposed by governmental authorities.

- Permit fees, royalties, or damages for infringement of patents and costs of defending related lawsuits for items specified by the buyer, deposits lost for causes other than the builder's negligence, and tap fees.

- Expenses for telephone service at the site, telephone calls, telegrams, delivery fees, and other similar petty cash items related to work.

- Costs incurred for safety and security at the job site.

- Costs incurred for building code and regulatory compliance.

- All landscaping and backfilling necessary under the contract documents, including the cost of all grading, removing or planting trees, removing snow, frost breaking, water pumping, excavating and related work, delivering the necessary materials to the site, and hauling away excess fill material or trash and debris.

- Builder's risk or other insurance, soil fees and civil engineering fees, performance bonds, and labor and supplier's bonds in an amount equal to 100 percent (100%) of the maximum costs.

- Costs associated with differing site conditions, as provided for in Section ___ of this contract.

PAYMENT SCHEDULES

The builder and the buyer should negotiate a mutually agreeable payment schedule. In the absence of an agreed payment schedule, the builder would not be entitled to receive payment until a completed structure is delivered to and accepted by the owner. Typically, when the owner is financing the project, the method of payment is by means of regular periodic payments from the owner to the builder, documented by invoices. As an alternative, a draw schedule can be established measured from benchmarks in construction activity. Draw schedule payments normally require the approval of both the home buyer and the construction lender. A specified amount (e.g., 10 percent) is often paid up front. The builder then withdraws (with necessary approvals) a stated percentage from the account at successive phases during construction. The lender ordinarily holds a retainage until the structure is accepted by the buyer.

A draw schedule should require the buyer to make or authorize each payment to the builder within a specified number of days after the builder's application for payment. The builder uses the application for payment document, along with various supporting documents, to establish the builder's right to payment. Before requesting final payment, the builder should ensure that all claims have been settled and should obtain signed confirmations from the buyer that, based on the final inspection, the contract requirements have been fulfilled. Alternatively, the contract may provide for inspection by the lender or another third party at certain stages of the construction, with payment due directly from the lender upon satisfactory inspection.

The parties should stipulate specifically who will schedule the inspections and who will pay the inspector. In any case, the contract should specify whether the progress payments provision includes payment not only for the work in place but also for materials and equipment suitably stored at the site or at an off-site location agreed upon by the owner.[5]

A progress payment provision might give the owner the right to withhold a payment under certain circumstances enumerated in the contract. For example, a failure by the builder to pay trade contractors or suppliers might authorize withholding payment. Another progress payment term might provide that (a) the builder can stop work until he/she is paid and (b) if payment is not made within so many days after it is due, the builder can terminate the contract. The following sample language provides for two methods of payment.

Regular Periodic Payment. The builder shall prepare [weekly, biweekly, or monthly] itemized statements for the buyer that specify all costs incurred by the builder in furtherance of performance of the terms of this contract. The buyer will place adequate funds in an escrow account from which payments are made for the cost of the work. Each draw will be based on an application for payment submitted to the buyer by the builder. The buyer will make funds available to the builder within _____(_____) days of receipt of the statement (less _____ percent _____[%] retainage) as provided for in the Notices provision of this contract.

Payments Tied to Construction Activity. The builder shall prepare [weekly, biweekly, or monthly] itemized statements for the buyer that specify all costs incurred by the builder in furtherance of performance of the terms of this contract.

The buyer will place adequate funds in an escrow account from which payments are made for the cost of the work. Each draw will be based on beginning various phases of the work as described below. The buyer will make funds available to the builder within _____(_____) days of receipt of the notice (less ___ percent _____ (%) retainage) as provided for in the Notices provision of this contract.

The buyer agrees to make progress payments as follows:

___ % upon signing the contract

___ % upon beginning of the slab (foundation)

___ % upon beginning of framing

___ % upon beginning of drywall

The buyer shall make final payment to the builder, including the entire unpaid balance of the cost of the work and all other compensation due to the builder, as defined in Sections ___, Price and Deposit, and _____, Costs to Be Reimbursed, of this contract at final settlement [or within ___(_____) days after substantial completion of the work].

LIQUIDATED DAMAGES

A liquidated damages clause provides for the payment of a predetermined amount of money in the event of a breach of contract. Because estimating the actual losses that a builder or a buyer has suffered as the result of a failure to perform on the contract can often be difficult to determine, a liquidated damages clause (meaning that the damages are determined or settled, and are agreed to in advance[6]) can eliminate this problem. A liquidated damages clause must not impose a penalty on either party. It should reasonably approximate the actual losses one party could expect to incur if the other party does not perform. If a court determines that the language of a liquidated damages clause creates a penalty (unwarranted compensation not related to incurred losses), it may void the provision entirely, requiring as a condition of recovery that the nonbreaching party produce competent evidence at trial of all actual and consequential damages that have been incurred as a result of the breach by the other party.

———————

Examples of liquidated damage provisions (agreed to ahead of time) may include the amount that the builder will pay to the buyer if the builder does not complete the contract by a certain date or the amount that the builder may retain (or receive) if the buyer defaults on the contract. A primary purpose of the clause is to compensate for expenses, such as hotel costs a buyer may expect to incur while waiting (during an unauthorized delay) to occupy the home or lost profits a builder may incur (while being unable to engage in other projects) waiting for the buyer to make selections (beyond the authorized period). This type of provision may serve to minimize damages in the event of a lawsuit brought on the basis of a default and can save time and expense by eliminating the need to present evidence at trial of actual damages.

EXAMPLES

If the buyer incurs additional costs as a consequence of the builder's failure to perform the terms of this contract by its stated completion date (for example, housing, moving, or travel expenses), the builder will compensate the buyer in the amount of _____ dollars ($_____) for each calendar day that the project is delayed beyond substantial completion (when the buyer can use the project for its intended purpose [or otherwise defined]). If no actual damages occur, the builder does not pay any.

Delays may occur in a construction project that are beyond the control of the builder. The contract should provide for excusable delays.

The builder will use its best efforts to complete construction of the project before the completion date. However, if reasons beyond the builder's control cause an unavoidable delay in the progress of construction (including, but not limited to, such factors as the unavailability of materials, inclement weather, strikes, changes in governmental regulation, acts of governmental agencies or their employees, acts of God, or the failure of the architect or the buyer to perform their responsibilities under this contract), the builder may request an extension of the date of completion of the project in writing. The request must be made within 30 days of the beginning of the cause of the delay. The buyer shall not recover any compensation from the builder for delay caused by differing site conditions, as defined and provided for in Section ___, Differing Site Conditions, of this contract.

This liquidated damages remedy is exclusive of all other legal and equitable remedies.

Should the buyer fail to carry out this Agreement, at the option of the builder all moneys paid hereon shall be forfeited to the builder as liquidated damages unless the buyer is unable to secure financing as set forth in paragraph ___ of this contract.

CASE STUDY

A husband and wife who breached a contract for the construction of a custom home sought the return of a $5,000 deposit that they had given to the contractor. The contract provided that the deposit was to be forfeited as liquidated damages if the couple breached the contract. The couple argued that the provision was a penalty and therefore unenforceable. Finding for the builder, the court concluded that the amount set as liquidated damages represented a reasonable approximation of the contractor's actual damages and was not a penalty because (a) the deposit amounted to less than four percent of the total anticipated price, (b) the contractor kept the lot off the market from 90 to 120 days, and (c) the contractor had lost $12,500 net profit provided for in the contract.[7]

BONUS FOR EARLY COMPLETION

As a corollary to the liquidated damages clause for a delay in completion, builders can include a bonus provision entitling them to a per diem sum of money for an early finish. The contract should address the question of whether an extension of the completion date also extends the bonus date. Some contracts simply state: "Under no circumstances will the bonus date be extended." However, the language that appears below is more favorable to builders.

Early Completion. Substantial completion of the work before the stated completion date in Section ___ of this contract will result in the buyer paying to the builder the sum of _____ dollars ($_____) for each calendar day between the date when the work is substantially completed and the completion date set by the contract. Unavoidable delays as described above will extend the completion date for the purposes of this per diem payment for early completion.

NOTICES

To take advantage of certain rights provided for in the contract, each party often must give certain notice to the other party. The contract may provide the form of the notice and the time within which the notice must be given. Failure to follow these notice requirements may jeopardize a claim. For example, the contract might provide that the builder is entitled to notice of defective work within so many days of the discovery of the defective work. It might also give the builder several days to correct the work before the owner may declare the builder to be in default of the contract. (See also the sample Notice and Right to Cure Contract provision in Chapter 4, Warranties and Disclaimers). If the owner fails to provide the builder with such notice, the owner may

---

be precluded from terminating the builder. Contracts should include the agreed upon method of furnishing notices and the agreed upon addresses for delivery.

> Any notice required or permitted to be delivered under this contract should be mailed to the parties at the following addresses:

_____	_____
(builder)	(buyer)
_____	_____
(street address)	(street address)
_____	_____
(city, state, zip)	(city, state, zip)

> For purposes of this contract, notice is received when sent by certified mail, postage prepaid, return receipt requested via the United States Postal Service.

RECORDS—STATUTE OF LIMITATIONS AND REPOSE

The builder should document the progress of construction and should retain all records related to the project until there is no longer a risk of liability, that is, until all applicable statutes of limitations have expired. The statute of limitations is the period of time during which a lawsuit can be timely filed. If the statute of limitations has expired, a court can rule that a lawsuit cannot be maintained, regardless of the merits of the claim. The purpose of a statute of limitations is to require that suits be brought during a period of time when witnesses and supporting evidence are more likely to be fresh and available and to provide a final cut-off to potential claims. Statutes of limitation normally begin to run when the contract is signed or when the house is occupied or substantially completed, depending on the type of action. The statutory period of time can run for many years and may be extended in the case of hidden (latent) defects. Courts often rule that statutes of limitations do not begin to run until a hidden defect is discovered or should have been discovered. Potentially, this could mean an indefinite period. A statute of repose is designed to address this situation. A statute of repose is the absolute time limit on bringing a legal action, regardless of when any defect, hidden or otherwise, may be discovered. To be absolutely sure that all the statutes of limitations have expired, a builder may want to retain his/her records for the period set by the statute of repose.

EFFECTIVE DATE AND SIGNATURES

Ideally, to avoid the possibility of nonapproved changes in contract terms or language, all parties to the contract sign the document at the same time. If that is not possible, however, the sample clause below assures that the builder will not be bound by the terms of the contract until the builder (or an authorized representative) has signed.

_____

This contract has no force or effect and will not be binding upon the builder until it is accepted and executed by the builder. This contract shall become effective on the date designated below or on the day it is executed by both parties, whichever is later.

We, the undersigned, have read and understand and agree to each of the provisions of this contract and hereby acknowledge receipt of a copy of this contract.

_____	_____
(buyer's signature)	(name of builder, corporate name where applicable)
	By _____
	(authorized signature)
Date _____	Title _____
_____	Date _____

This contract is dated, and becomes effective:

_____
(month, day, year)

| _____ | _____ |
| (buyer's initials) | (builder's initials) |

If a printed or typed contract has been modified through handwritten or retyped changes and/or additions, each party should initial those revisions to ensure validity. After a contract has been signed, any changes to the work should be documented by written change orders. (See the section on Changes In Work). Any changes or additions to the contract after it is signed will require a written and signed amendment to the contract. (See the Entire Agreement and Severability section presented later in this chapter.)

The buyer and builder should sign at least two original contract documents (duplicate documents that are each signed by both parties). The parties should execute the contract in their proper capacities, as individual buyers or sellers or as partners, officers, or directors of a partnership or corporation that is a party to the contract. The parties should use their complete legal names on all contract documents and any subsequent change orders or contract amendments. If you are signing on behalf of a corporate or limited liability entity, make certain that the contract reflects this fact. Once both parties have signed the contract, they can complete and initial the date-of-contract provision.

GENERAL CONDITIONS

Every construction contract has terms and conditions that apply to all contracts and are not specific to a single project. These general conditions are sometimes included on the same page as the agreement. Some builders include the agreement and the general conditions in one document; others separate the two. The builder should review the general conditions to make sure that they do not conflict with the contract for the specific project.

CASE STUDY

In an action for breach of a construction contract, Grubb claimed that a corporation of which he was a principal stockholder—Double Cousins Company—should have been the defendant in a lawsuit and not Grubb personally. Grubb and Fitzgerald entered into a contract with Cloven, which opened as follows:

> To Double Cousins Company, Agent 1.
>
> The undersigned, herein called the Buyer, offers to buy, subject to the terms set forth herein, the following property:

Then follows a blank space in which had been written by hand:

> House on Buyer's lot according to Plan 5392-R of Architect's York and Schenke of New York.

The contract was signed by Grubb and Fitzgerald, each of whom was identified only as the Seller, and by Cloven, who was identified as the Buyer.

The court concluded that the face of the contract provided substantial evidence that the contract was entered into by Grubb as an individual and that the contract was not between Cloven and any corporate entity. The court found that "The contract refers to the Double Cousins Company only as Agent." Grubb and Fitzgerald signed their names as Seller, respectively, and did not purport to represent anyone other than themselves.[8]

Obviously, no contract can cover every contingency. But the more that the parties identify their respective obligations under the contract, the fewer surprises there will be after the project has started.

FINANCING AND OTHER CONTINGENCIES

If the buyer chooses to use third-party financing, the builder may include a financing commitment from a lender in the contract. The contract should allocate payment of loan application fees and closing costs between the buyer and the builder. The generic term closing costs refers to many fees and expenses. To minimize disputes, the parties should identify and specify who will be responsible for the payment of each cost.

If he/she has not already done so, the buyer should agree to apply for a loan within a certain period after execution of the contract. The contract should specify that if the buyer does not receive a loan, the contract will be terminated and the parties will be released from their obligations under the contract. If the buyer has given the builder a refundable deposit, the contract should specify the conditions under which the builder will return the deposit to the buyer.

A buyer who does not need financing should place funds equal to the total price of the agreement in an escrow account. Similarly, if the buyer needs only partial financing, the balance of the funds due should be placed in escrow.

> The buyer represents that [he or she] has arranged sufficient financing to comply with this agreement. Before commencing work under this agreement or at any time during the progress of the work, the builder may request evidence in writing (acceptable to the builder) of financing for the work. Failure of the buyer to produce the requested information within ____(_____) calendar days of the written request will constitute a breach of contract by the buyer, and the builder may suspend the work. If the buyer fails to provide the requested information within an additional ____(_____) calendar days thereafter, the builder may terminate this agreement. Should the builder suspend or terminate this agreement, he or she shall be entitled to collect or receive payment for materials and labor expended on or for the project, along with a reasonable profit and overhead.

OTHER CONTINGENCIES

Any other contingencies that the parties contemplate should be specifically identified. For example, if the agreement is contingent upon additional appraisals, soil-bearing tests, percolation tests, inspections, or the sale of other property, the contract should specify the time period in which those events or requirements must occur, what will happen to the agreement if the conditions are not fulfilled, and how the deposit money will be allocated.

If the builder sells a lot to the buyer with the understanding that the builder will construct a house on the property, the contract of sale should make the lot sale contingent upon the buyer's execution of a construction contract with the builder within a specified period.

Builders should consult an attorney concerning the specific language for contingencies.

Allowances

The total contract price shall include any allowances mentioned in the contract documents. Contracts frequently provide for allowances for items of work that are not sufficiently detailed in the contract documents to enable the builder to determine the final cost of the item. Their inclusion in the contract establishes that the item is within the builder's scope of work subject to final price adjustment.[9] Allowance items may be of two types: (a) items that remain to be selected by the owner or buyer (such as wallpaper and cabinets) and (b) items of work for which the actual cost cannot be determined until the builder receives additional information regarding the scope of the work or until the conditions are verified or the work is actually performed (such as the cost of well drilling). In the first situation, the builder should closely monitor the owner's or buyer's spending habits during construction and periodically notify the owner or buyer of the balance on each allowance. In the latter situation, the builder must be able to justify the original estimate because if the actual cost greatly exceeds the allowance, the builder may have to deal with an angry customer. Moreover, if the allowance is grossly underestimated, a court may allow the builder to recover only the reasonable costs.

The prudent builder will provide in the allowance clause or in the separate allowance schedule that (a) whenever costs are more or less than allowances, the contract price shall be adjusted accordingly by change order and (b) the change order shall reflect the difference between actual costs and the allowance. The builder should not assume that the owner or buyer understands that he/she is responsible for paying the difference in cost if the cost of an item exceeds the allowance. The builder shall supply items for which allowances are provided within the amounts specified. Those amounts must cover the applicable taxes as well as the builder's cost for materials and equipment delivered to the site. Trade discounts (price reductions) are passed on to the owner, but a discount for timely payment may be retained by the builder. The allowance item should clearly state whether it is for materials only, installation only, or both materials and installation.

To avoid delaying the work, the contract should provide that the owner must promptly select all materials and equipment for which allowances are provided. So long as the builder has no reasonable objection to the selections, the owner may specify the materials and fixtures and the vendors for these items. A builder with actual knowledge concerning potential problems with materials or vendors may have an obligation to inform the buyer of these concerns.

CASE STUDY

As work on a project progressed, the general contractor-landlord failed to notify the inexperienced tenants about how much of the allowance had been used. Therefore, the court ruled that the general contractor-landlord could not recover all the expenses incurred to "finish out" space occupied by the tenants under a lease, even though the tenants exceeded their allowance by $16,270.81. The court held that the landlord was not entitled to recover expenses in excess of the contract allowance from the tenant because in "dealing with neophytes, there was an obligation of fair dealing, which required some notification to the tenants of the status of the allowance balance at a meaningful time."

The court noted that the tenants relied on the landlord to do the job within the allowance, even though they did not communicate that expectation explicitly. Despite knowledge that tenants often have unrealistic expectations, the landlord did not provide effective notice. The court observed that the case presented the classic perils of a failure to communicate.[10]

PERMITS, LICENSES, AND OTHER APPROVALS

The builder is usually responsible for obtaining all permits, licenses, fees, and approvals associated with the construction and occupancy of the project. The builder must be careful, however, about agreeing to obtain all permits and the like. He/she is probably better off identifying in the contract the various permits, licenses, fees, and approvals for which he/she will be responsible. For example, the builder who agrees to obtain all permits probably contemplates obtaining the local building permit and the certificate of occupancy permit but does not contemplate obtaining a wetlands permit or a state water quality certification. However, if the builder agrees to obtain all permits and the owner's lot contains wetlands, the builder may be required to obtain a wetlands permit before he/she may continue with the project. The permitting process can be lengthy (in some cases more than a year) and expensive.

However, if the land is owned by the buyer, then the buyer should be responsible and should bear the cost for obtaining all approvals required by any homeowner's association or architectural review board and further should be responsible for and pay the costs of all land use and environmental permits, including wetlands permits.

> The builder shall obtain and pay for all building and construction permits, licenses, and other approvals necessary for occupancy of permanent structures or changes in existing structures, unless the land is owned by the buyer of the house. If the land is owned by the buyer, then the buyer shall be responsible for and shall pay the costs of all land use and environmental permits and for all approvals of plans and specifications required by applicable recorded covenants or architectural review boards.
>
> Should the builder or the buyer fail to obtain or be denied the necessary permits, licenses, or other approval for which they may be responsible, the other party shall be entitled to terminate this contract on written notice.

INSURANCE AND RISK MANAGEMENT

An agreement to carry insurance coverage is often written into construction contracts. The contract will generally require both parties to buy and maintain insurance for specified injuries or risks and in specified dollar amounts. The contract should clearly state the insurable interest of each party and establish who owns or is responsible for what property, during what period of time, and the type and amount of coverage required.

In new home construction, more often than not the contract requires the builder to obtain insurance. The need for insurance and the exclusions to insurance policies vary according to the type of construction involved, but some common types of insurance include the following:

- Comprehensive general liability
- Builder's risk
- Workers' compensation
- Automobile liability

- Professional liability
- Completed operations
- Umbrella liability

The contract may also require the buyer or owner to obtain insurance. If the builder is building on the owner's land, the builder will want the owner to maintain property insurance that will (a) protect the builder, the trade contractors, and the trade contractors and (b) insure against the loss of work in place or materials on the site. The contract also may require the owner to obtain insurance against loss resulting from injury of third parties (persons not parties to the contract) or to their property.

Builders should consult a construction insurance expert to determine their insurance needs as well as an attorney for specific contract language.

RISK OF LOSS

Builders obtain insurance for numerous risks, but one risk that goes to heart of the transaction is the risk of loss caused by accidental destruction of or damage to the house during its construction. The parties should always obtain insurance to cover such a loss. In addition, their contract should discuss their respective rights and obligations if such a contingency occurs. Many builders would be surprised to learn that if a builder agrees to construct a complete house, the builder generally bears the risk of loss if the house is accidentally destroyed before its completion, and the builder may be required to rebuild the house. Therefore, if a builder wishes to make some other arrangement in the event the partly completed house is destroyed, he/she would be wise to do so in the contract. For example, a well-known builder provides that if the damage covered by property insurance is greater than 30 percent of the value of the contract, (a) the contract shall be terminated, (b) the builder shall be compensated for work completed before termination, and (c) at the owner's option the contractor will negotiate a new contract for the repair and/or completion of the home. On the other hand, if the loss is less than 30 percent of the contract value, the builder will proceed under the original contract but will prepare a change order for the labor, materials, and profit and overhead costs required to repair the damage. The change order is to be paid from proceeds of insurance and the owner's funds.

DIFFERING SITE CONDITIONS

Unexpected site conditions, such as rock or an unexpectedly high water table, can be expensive to work around. The following sample provision protects both builders and owners if unanticipated site conditions are encountered. Builders are protected from having to absorb increased project costs arising from unexpected hidden (latent) site conditions. There is protection for the buyer as well.

The opt-out provision allows the buyer to cancel the contract (after the builder has been paid for all expenses) should the hidden site conditions prove too expensive a proposition for continued construction.

The contract should include a clear definition of differing site conditions and provide for notification, work changes, or contract modification procedures on discovery of such a problem. An alternative to the cancellation provision below could require the buyer to pay the extra costs incurred (plus profit at a specified percentage of the cost). Or, if the builder is building on his/her own lot, he/she may reserve the right to switch the project to another lot. These suggestions could replace the equitable adjustment language below. The definition of equitable adjustment can be confusing. Builders' attorneys should check the case law precedents in their states to see how the term is interpreted by the courts. The term should be used only where it has an identified meaning.

A differing site condition is a physical characteristic of the property that materially changes the construction techniques from those reasonably expected at the time of the contract. Examples of differing site conditions are subsurface or latent physical conditions at the site differing materially from those indicated in the contract or unknown physical conditions of an unusual nature (that are not reasonably foreseeable) on the building site.

Before disturbing any differing site condition, the builder shall notify the buyer of such a condition except in the case of eminent danger to persons or property. The buyer shall investigate the condition within _____(_____) business days. If the buyer and the builder agree that the differing site conditions will cause an increase in (a) the builder's cost of performance of any part of the work under this contract or (b) the time required for that work, the issue will be resolved as follows:

   A. If the total contract price will increase by more than _____ percent (___%) [for example, 10 percent], the buyer may terminate the contract upon paying the builder for all costs expended to date and for the builder's full profits as provided in Section ___, Price, Deposit, and Payments, of this contract; or

   B. The builder and the buyer shall execute a written specific cost adjustment to this contract, including any adjustments in the time for performance required by the differing site conditions.

The buyer's failure to investigate the condition will confer authority upon the builder to complete construction of the project according to the terms in Section ___, Liquidated Damages and Unavoidable Delay, of this contract, and the builder shall further be entitled to [an equitable adjustment or payment of any increased costs necessitated by the differing site condition].

If the parties cannot agree on the existence or consequences of a differing site condition, the terms of this provision shall be arbitrated as provided for in Section ___, Arbitration, of this contract.

_____

ARCHITECTS AND CONSTRUCTION MANAGERS

Sometimes buyers hire architects or construction managers who participate in the construction of their houses. The contract should name the architect or construction manager and designate whether he/she is the buyer's agent.

Warning! A builder should not rely on the directives of an architect or a construction manager unless that person has written authorization to act on behalf of the owner. If the contract provides such authorization, it also should specifically provide that the builder will not be held liable for any actions made in reliance on recommendations of the architect or construction manager.

The architect or construction manager typically is responsible for:

* Processing change orders
* Overseeing the payment process
* Interpreting or obtaining interpretations of plans and specifications pertaining to design considerations

Of course, the architect or construction manager cannot change the obligations of the parties as spelled out in the contract. Sometimes the architects or construction managers have roles in disputes. For instance, the parties could agree that before they can submit a dispute for arbitration or litigation, they must submit it to the architect for consideration as a mediator.

This contract specifies the terms between (<u>buyer's name</u>), the buyer, and (<u>builder's name</u>), the builder, to [sell and/or construct] a home on the property located at: (<u>legal description of property</u>).

[<u>Name of architect and/or construction manager</u>] is the buyer's agent, and the builder may rely on representations, statements, revisions, and approvals made by [<u>architect and/or construction manager</u>] related to the performance of the terms of this contract. The builder will not be held liable for any actions made in reliance on recommendations of [<u>architect and/or construction manager</u>].

CHANGES IN WORK AND CHANGE ORDERS

A buyer does not have the automatic right to order changes in the work unless the contract confers that right. However, most contracts do include a change order clause giving the buyer that right. This section sets up the procedure for writing change orders and explains how the cost will be determined, including overhead and profit. The actual change order is a separate document (Fig. 2.3).

Figure 2.3 Sample Change Order

Change order number _____

Date _____

Project description _____

Project number _____

Description of change (including reference to drawings and specifications revised, new drawings and specifications issued)

_____

_____

_____

Reason for change

_____

_____

_____

Total price prior to this change $ _____

Change in price for this change order $ _____

Total revised price $ _____

Revised schedule of payments:

_____

_____

_____

_____

The estimated completion date provided for in paragraph ___ of the contract is now (date). All other terms and conditions of the contract referred to above remain unchanged.

_____   _____
           (builder)   (buyer)[1]

Date _____   Date _____

---

[1]This form is designed for a single buyer. If more than one buyer is involved, the form should be adapted to accommodate the initials and signature of each of the buyers.

After the contract is signed and work commences, often the buyer will request that changes be made in the design or materials used. Before beginning any new work created by a buyer's request for a change, the builder should require that the buyer execute a written change authorizing the work to be performed and agreeing to any additional payment for the change. A change order is an agreement that should specify (a) the revisions in the work and the price, (b) a revised payment schedule, if necessary, and (c) a new date for substantial completion, if necessary.

If the parties cannot agree on the price of the change order work, the contract could include a provision for the builder to be paid for additional work done on a cost-plus basis. If the contract includes more than one owner or purchaser, getting both owners to sign the change order may be time-consuming. To expedite the work, the contract might provide (a) that either owner may sign the change order as agent for the other and (b) that the signature of one owner is binding on the other owner.

A change order should address all changes from any cause or source that affect the scope of the work, the contract price, and the time for performance and not just changes requested by the owner. Thus, additional work to be performed under a differing site or concealed conditions clause should be handled by a change order. Similarly, any increase in the scope of the work required by a building and/or planning department that is not the builder's fault should be handled by a change order.

The contract should expressly provide that such an increase will be treated as extra work and that the extra work will be done after a written change order is signed by the buyer. Generally, the contract will call for payment of each change order to be made (a) when the work is performed, (b) upon completion of the change order, or (c) before the next draw.

A builder who performs work without obtaining written change orders and who then presents the buyer with a large bill for that work at closing is asking for trouble.

The buyer may request changes in the work within a reasonable scope. The builder will make requested changes additionally or in the alternative on presentation of a written change order signed by the buyer describing the changes to be made, any extra work to be done, and any changes to the contract price or completion date (Figure 2.3).

Change orders must be signed by all parties and become part of this contract. The buyer agrees to pay the builder for changes in the work on the same basis as specified in Section ___, Price, Deposit, and Payment Provisions of this contract. [If more than one buyer is involved, add the following: The buyers agree that either of them may sign the change order and that the signature of one is binding on the other.] The buyer agrees to make requests concerning any changes, additions, or alterations in the work in writing directly to the builder named in this contract and not to the workers, including trade contractors and trade contractors' workers on the job.

If the buyer and the builder cannot agree on a fixed price amount for any change order, then payment to the builder on that change order will be calculated and paid by the buyer on the basis of the cost of labor, materials, equipment, and supervision, plus _____ percent (___%) of such costs ("cost-plus").

CASE STUDY

A builder of low-rent housing who submitted change orders and performed extra work authorized orally by the developer's architect could not recover for the cost of extra work under its contract with the property owner because the change orders were not approved by the owner as specifically required by the contract. The developer who accepted the work was not a party to the contract and did not approve the changes in writing. Fortunately for the builder, the court allowed recovery on other grounds.[11]

MECHANIC'S LIEN

Mechanic's lien laws (construction lien laws in some states) ensure that participants in the construction process get paid for their work by granting them a specific interest in real property that has been improved by their labor or materials. All 50 states, the District of Columbia, and Puerto Rico have such laws. The requirements of these laws vary considerably from state to state. For a builder, trade contractor, or supplier to benefit from or comply with a lien law, the procedures and requirements of the law in the jurisdiction where the real property involved is located must be strictly followed.

The claimant (the person claiming the lien) must provide one or more forms of notice before the lien can be effective. This process is often referred to as perfecting the lien (language that is commonly used in the mechanic's lien statute). To perfect the lien often the claimant must file a formal Claim of Lien. Such a filing must be made within a fixed period after completion of the contract or the last furnishing of services or materials.

When the lien has been perfected, it may be enforced in a lawsuit to compel the sale of the property. The time for enforcing the mechanic's lien varies from state to state but seldom exceeds one year after the date on which the lien was filed.

Some states allow a builder to waive his/her lien rights by signing a lien waiver before beginning work for the owner or buyer. The lien waiver clause typically provides that the builder will not file any liens against the property on account of labor or material or equipment furnished pursuant to the contract. A lien waiver clause offers little, if any, benefit to a builder. Homeowners find such a provision attractive because it ensures that the property will remain unencumbered by liens.

Obviously, builders should be wary of signing any form that has the effect of waiving their lien rights before they receive payment, and they should be sure they can recognize a lien waiver and be on the lookout for such wording because the owner's attorney or the lender may suggest adding it.

> The builder unconditionally waives, releases, and relinquishes all right to file or maintain any mechanic's lien or other claim in the nature of a lien against the real property improved under this contract or the building on account of any labor, material, equipment, extras, change order work, or increased costs.

INSPECTION, ACCEPTANCE, AND POSSESSION

Inspections allow buyers to identify and give builders the opportunity to correct defects in materials or workmanship. Because the buyer or the buyer's agent makes periodic inspections, the builder can document a buyer's satisfaction with the completed home. The builder should keep a record of each inspection for (at minimum) the duration of any statute of limitations or repose (see Figure 7.1, Sample Home Maintenance Instruction Checklist, and Figure 7.2, Sample Punchlist Instruction Letter).

The contract should define possession and determine what steps the parties must make before the buyer takes possession. For example, builders often include provisions for inspection, formal acceptance, and final payment before a buyer can take possession. Some contracts state that (a) the owner or buyer will not occupy the house until final payment of all sums due, including any extra charges, and (b) occupancy of the home shall be deemed acceptance of the work, including defects that could have been discovered upon a reasonable inspection by the owner or buyer.

> "The effectiveness of making time of the essence is dependent upon the expectation and understanding of the parties that their negotiated agreement requiring performance on a specified day and at a specified time will be strictly enforced without resort to litigation to determine whether the defaulting part's non-performance should be excused." *Barlet v. Frazer*, 218 N.J.Super.106, 109 (1987)[12].

The sales contract should state that "time is of the essence" and require the builder and buyer to make full settlement of the terms of the contract by a specific date (Fig. 2.4). The certificate of acceptance is part of the contract documents. The buyer must see this document before the job is finished and have an opportunity to ask questions about it. If the buyer sees it for the first time when asked to sign it, he/she may balk at signing.

> The buyer or the buyer's agent shall inspect the house in the presence of the builder or the builder's representative. During the course of construction, at the option of the buyer, and at final inspection upon substantial completion, the buyer will give the builder a signed punchlist that identifies any alleged deficiencies in the quality of the work or materials.
>
> The builder shall correct any items on the buyer's punchlist that are, in the good faith judgment of the builder, deficient in the quality of work and/or materials according to the local standards of construction. The builder shall correct those defects at its cost within a reasonable period of time. The builder's obligation to correct any defects shall not be grounds for postponing or delaying the closing, nor for imposing any conditions upon the closing not specified in this contract.
>
> Upon substantial completion of construction, the buyer shall sign the certificate of acceptance (attached and incorporated by reference in this contract). The buyer shall not occupy the project before inspecting the home, signing the certificate of acceptance, and making the final payment to the builder.

ACCESS

In the interest of safety and to minimize the buyer's opportunity to communicate with independent trade contractors regarding the means, method, or manner in which they are to perform their work, the contract may limit the time of day during which the buyer may visit the site. Requiring the buyer to schedule visits with the builder may work to prevent injuries that might occur if the

Figure 2.4 Sample Certificate of Acceptance

The buyer certifies that all of the terms and conditions of the contract entered into by the buyer and the builder for the [construction and/or purchase] of property at (address of house) have been met, and the buyer and the builder further acknowledge and agree as follows:

1. While the house has generally been constructed according to basic plans and specifications contained in the contract documents, the buyer understands that the house may not correspond in some respects with those plans and specifications because changes may have been made before or during construction. These changes may be attributed to a variety of events, including changes in topography, construction techniques, building codes, the availability of material, or other events.

The buyer understands that the builder is not obligated to furnish any as-built plans, specifications, or drawings of the house. The buyer also understands that the house may differ in some respects from the models, drawings, maps, pictures, or other depictions of the house the buyer was shown. The buyer acknowledges that minor variations may exist in the outside and inside dimensions, configurations, colors, location, general appearance, and other characteristics. The buyer has had an opportunity to inspect all aspects of the project and has done so or elected not to do so.

2. The buyer has inspected the house and the property on which it is located. The buyer has also delivered to the builder a written list of all items the buyer believes (a) have not been properly constructed or (b) are not in proper condition and has described the specific problems. Except as noted on the list, the buyer accepts the residence and property as is and acknowledges that from now on the buyer will have no claim against the builder for any item that was not listed that could reasonably have been ascertained or observed during the buyer's inspection. The buyer has no objections relating to color, appearance, type or brand of equipment, dimension or size, location, breakage or cracks, or any other conditions that reasonably could have been discovered by the buyer during the inspection.

3. The buyer understands that no warranties are being made by the builder except those appearing in the written limited warranty provided by the builder as part of the contract documents. All statements, representations, promises, and warranties made by the builder or any agent of the builder are superseded by the written limited warranty, and the buyer is not relying on any representations, promises, or warranties except for the written limited warranty that is included by reference in this acceptance document.

The buyer understands that the duration of all implied warranties from the builder, including (but not limited to) the implied warranties of habitability and workmanlike construction, has been limited by the builder to one (1) year from the date of sale or the date of occupancy, whichever comes first.

4. The buyer understands that in exchange for the limited warranty and the other provisions of the contract with the builder, the buyer will have no right to recover or receive compensation for any incidental, consequential, secondary, punitive, or special damages, nor any damages for aggravation, pain and suffering, mental anguish, or emotional distress, nor any costs or attorney's fees. This provision shall be enforceable to the extent allowed by law.

5. The buyer and the builder agree that the claim procedures described in the limited warranty and the arbitration procedures described in the contract shall apply to any claims made by the buyer or the builder, and the binding arbitration provisions of the contract shall be the sole available remedy for any unresolved dispute relating to the construction of the house.

6. The buyer acknowledges satisfaction with the manner in which the sales transaction was closed, including all financial calculations and adjustments. And buyer acknowledges receipt of all closing documents to which the buyer is entitled from the builder.

7. Each provision of this certificate is separate and severable from every other provision. If any single provision is declared invalid or unenforceable, the buyer and the builder understand that all the other provisions will still be valid and enforceable. The buyer and the builder agree that every provision of this certificate will survive the closing of the sales transaction and will not be merged with the deed.

_____   _____
(buyer's signature)   (name of builder, corporate name where applicable)
Date_____   By _____
                                                                              (authorized signature)
                                                                   Title _____
                                                                   Date _____
_____

1. Sample language that appears in brackets presents an option for the reader. Depending on the particular transaction, the reader must choose one or the other, both, or neither of the possible wordings presented. A builder may wish to simplify this certificate of acceptance by eliminating or reducing the language in paragraphs 1, 3, 4, and 5, which largely repeat provisions already covered by sample language in this chapter. This form is designed for a single buyer. If more than one buyer is involved, the form should be adapted to accommodate the initials and signature of each of the buyers.

2. Builders should make sure that this limitation of the implied warranties conforms to any limitation appearing in the limited warranty (see Limited Warranty in Chapter 6 and Representations and Warranty in this chapter).

buyer is free to roam the site unaccompanied. For example, the contract might provide for site visits in the presence of the builder early in the morning or in the evening. Alternatively, the builder may give the owner or buyer free access to the property with the agreement that the owner or buyer enters the property during construction at his/her own risk. Risk of injury because of construction site conditions and hazards should be mentioned in such an alternative provision.

In either case, the contract might provide that the owner or buyer must indemnify the builder against claims, damages, property damage, or bodily injury arising out of the owner or buyer's unaccompanied site visit, but only to the extent it was caused in whole or in part by the owner or buyer's negligent acts or omissions. Obviously, because the buyer or owner is paying for the home, the builder should be sensitive to (and respectful of) the buyer's or owner's right to participate in the building process by visiting the site, asking questions, and commenting on the work. The builder may have more control over the owner's or buyer's access to the site if the builder owns the lot because keeping the owner off his/her own property may be difficult.

> The owners shall at all times have access to the property and the right to inspect the work. However, if the owners enter the property during the course of construction, they do so at their own risk, and the owners hereby release the builder and do hereby indemnify and hold the builder harmless from any and all claims for injury or damage to their person or property, and to the person or property of any agent, employee, or invitee of the owners or of any other person accompanying the owners.
>
> The owners shall not in any manner interfere with work on the job nor with any trade contractor or workers. The owners will not communicate directly with the builder's workers, employees, agents, or trade contractors regarding the means, method, or manner in which they are to perform their work. If the owners delay the progress of the work, causing loss to the builder, the builder shall be entitled to reimbursement from the owners for such loss.

WORK PERFORMED BY OWNER AND OTHER CONTRACTORS

Some buyers and owners reserve the right to perform some of the work themselves or they reserve the right to subcontract part of the work. Some builders strongly believe that the owner should not perform any of the work, and they try to discourage this practice. They may even include such a warning in the contract.

If the owner reserves the right to perform some of the work or to award separate contracts in connection with other portions of the work, the contract must clearly describe the work to be performed by the owner or the trade contractor, including the time within which the work is to be performed.

If the owner enters into multiple contracts with different contractors for work on one project, the owner generally is under an obligation to coordinate and control the operations of all contractors to avoid unreasonable disruption of, or interference with, the operations of the other contractors. If that coordination fails, the delayed performance may be compensable. Finally, if the owner performs certain work or has other contractors perform that work, the builder should expressly provide that the builder is not warranting such work.

MANDATORY CLAUSES

Both builders and remodelers must take care to include any applicable mandatory language in their contracts. Some state laws may require that certain information be included in custom home contracts, new home sales contracts, remodeling contracts, and other consumer contracts. For example, under Maryland law a custom home builder must include in each custom home contract a disclosure concerning the buyer's risk under mechanic's lien laws.[13] Federal law can also impose requirements on contract inclusions. For instance, the Federal Trade Commission requires all builders and sellers of new homes to disclose to customers information about the type, thickness, and R-value of the insulation installed in the house, to wit:

> "If you are a new home seller, you must put the following information in every sales contract: the type, thickness, and R-value of the insulation that will be installed in each part of the house. There is an exception to this rule. If the buyer signs a sales contract before you know what type of insulation will be put in the house, or if there is a change in the contract, you can give the buyer a receipt stating this information as soon as you find out."[14]

Because new legislative and regulatory action can impose changed requirements from time to time for mandatory contract language and information, because there may be exemptions and particular applications, and because such requirements can vary from jurisdiction to jurisdiction, it is important to consult with a local attorney concerning what, if any, mandatory contract clauses apply to your type of contracting and to your location.

ESCALATION CLAUSE

If a party agrees to perform work for a fixed price, that party bears the risk of an increase in the cost of compliance because of an increase in the cost of labor or materials during the project. In other words, a party will not be excused from completing the work covered by the contract just because it turns out to be more difficult or burdensome to perform. The ongoing saga of the increase in lumber prices is evidence that an increase in the cost of materials during the project can significantly increase the cost of compliance of a fixed-price contract.

The parties can provide in the contract that if a contract price increases because of any price increase in labor or materials or because of additional work required by the building department or other governmental agency, before or during construction, the owner will pay the builder the increase upon proof of such an increase. In addition, the parties might agree that if a price increases more than a particular percentage, the owner has the option of paying the increase or terminating the contract after reimbursing the builder for all work completed before notice of termination.

CASE STUDY

In this case, the Hudsons sued D and V Mason Contractors, Inc., for breach of contract to construct a house when the builder refused to complete the Hudsons' house for the agreed-upon price of $17,400.00. The building company contended that it was excused from performing because of a scarcity of labor in the building industry and an increase in (a) the interest on construction financing, (b) the points the builder was required to pay on the mortgage, and (c) construction costs.

The builder relied on a provision in the contract that made the builder's ability to complete the house dependent on conditions similar to those existing at the time the contract was signed. The contract gave the builder the option to cancel the contract if the builder was unable to promptly obtain the labor and materials required for construction as needed. The builder could also cancel the contract if any present or future rules, regulations, or restrictions by the federal, state, or municipal governments prevented the builder from completing the project.

Finding for the owners, the court cited the general rule that a court cannot alter a contract merely because it will create a hardship. The court noted that contractual provisions attempting to qualify an undertaking in the face of increased cost considerations must be specific with reference to those factors that will excuse performance. The court concluded that the three cost factors cited by the builder were not grounds to excuse performance within the meaning of the contract and that the builder failed to show that it was particularly and substantially affected by the scarcity of labor.[15]

CLEAN-UP

Industry practice requires the builder to leave the completed job in a clean condition. The inclusion of cleaning in the contract makes the builder's obligation clear.

> Upon completion of the project, all of the builder's construction debris and equipment shall be removed by the builder, and the premises shall be left in neat, broom-clean condition, unless otherwise agreed upon herein.

SIGNAGE

Projects that are run in an orderly manner represent one of the best advertisements a builder can have. A sign displayed at the job can produce more work for the builder. Although common practice allows a builder to display a sign at the project, contract language to that effect will make that right clear. Please note, however, that signage (including the size, location, and number of signs) may be regulated by local ordinance.

The buyer agrees to permit the builder to display a sign on the site until the project is completed.

UNCOVERING AND CORRECTING WORK

General contract conditions may also provide for uncovering and correcting work, for example, work that (a) was covered up or enclosed before inspections occurred, (b) work that does not meet the contract specifications, or (c) work that violates some other aspect of the contract. The contract conditions can provide for acceptance of work that may not be done in accordance with contract specifications but is still acceptable to the buyer. The builder could use the following sample language for trade contractors' agreements, to protect the builder.

> **Uncovering Work.** If work is covered or enclosed in contradiction to the terms of the contract or in contradiction to any applicable laws, the builder shall uncover the work for observation or inspection and replace it without charge. However, if the home buyer or the architect requests that any work that has been completed and inspected in compliance with the contract and applicable laws be uncovered, the buyer shall sign a change order agreeing to pay for the additional work, subject to the following: If the work uncovered subsequently does not comply with the contract documents or applicable laws, then the builder shall bear the costs of the uncovering and redoing of the work, unless the home buyer, or a third party not under the builder's control, has caused the condition that needs to be corrected.
>
> **Correcting Work.** Upon written notice by the buyer, the builder shall promptly redo and recover work that does not meet contract specifications or applicable laws. The builder shall pay the costs of redoing that work and recovering that work as well as any reasonable additional expenses for necessary testing or inspections.
>
> **Acceptance of Nonconforming Work.** The buyer may choose to accept work that does not meet contract specifications so long as it conforms to the applicable laws. If the owner chooses to do so, the total contract price will be decreased accordingly to reflect any savings of material cost or labor, regardless of whether the buyer has made the final payment.

TERMINATION OF THE CONTRACT

Occasionally, unpredictable or uncontrollable events substantially change a construction project and one or both parties want to be released from the contract. The builder and the buyer can negotiate how to allocate responsibility for this possibility. Some of the terms in this clause will depend on the builder's business philosophy. For example, a well-known custom builder allows for termination at the convenience of the owner so long as the owner pays for all labor and materials furnished plus a proportional share of the overhead and profit associated with the job. This builder is confident that such an event is unlikely to occur, but he is also comfortable giving the owner the power to terminate the contract.

A more conventional clause provides for termination for cause, such as the owner's nonpayment, the builder's substantial failure to comply with the contract terms, a substantial delay caused by a government entity that interrupts the work, or a substantial cost increase resulting from the discovery of a hidden or unforeseen condition. In the absence of such a clause, and unless termination is the result of mutual agreement, a party may not terminate the contract without liability unless the other party defaults, and this default goes to the essence of the contract—often referred to as a material breach of the contract.

The termination clause should give the parties the right to cure their default. For example, the contract may include a provision that allows the buyer to cure a breach of contract within a specific time by bringing all payments and other obligations up to date. This action permits the parties to reinstate the agreement so the builder can complete the job.

Similarly, if the contract authorizes the owner to remove the builder from the job because of deficiencies in the work, the builder will include wording in the contract stating that the builder is entitled to notice of the deficiency and provided an opportunity to correct the deficiency before the termination is effective. (See also Notice and Opportunity to Cure Contract Provision in Chapter 4, Warranties and Disclaimers.) The contract should require that all termination notices be in writing (see Notices).

> **Builder's Remedies.** If the buyer materially fails to comply with the provisions of this contract or terminates the contract for any reason other than the builder's failure to perform, the builder may (a) terminate this contract and retain any downpayments and/or deposits as liquidated damages; (b) recover all unpaid costs, expenses, and fees earned up to the time of default or termination; the prorated cost of overhead expenses; and the costs, fees, and prorated overhead expenses for all change orders approved by the buyer before the termination; and (c) institute judicial proceedings for specific performance and/or any other legal and equitable remedies. (The costs specified in this section shall be based upon the costs specified in Section ___, Price, Deposit, and Payment, of this agreement.)
>
> **Buyer's Remedies.** If the builder fails to supply proper materials and skilled workers; make payments for materials, labor, and trade contractors in accordance with their respective agreements; disregards ordinances, regulations, or orders of a public authority; or materially comply with the provisions of the contract, the buyer may give the builder written notice. After ___(_____) days if the builder has failed to remedy the breach of contract, the buyer can give a second written notice. If the builder still fails to cure the breach within ____(_____) days after the second notice, the buyer

may terminate the contract. When the buyer terminates the contract for one of the reasons stated above, he/she may be entitled to seek legal and equitable remedies.

ARBITRATION, MEDIATION, AND OTHER ALTERNATIVE DISPUTE RESOLUTION

During or after of construction, a disagreement may arise between the builder and the home buyer that cannot be resolved through negotiations. Because of the expense of a lawsuit and the long wait to have a case heard in court, litigation may not be a wise or efficient method of resolving the matter. The contract can provide for an alternative method of dispute resolution through arbitration or mediation.

ARBITRATION

Binding arbitration is a process in which the parties submit their case to a neutral third person or a panel of individuals (arbitrators) for a final and binding resolution. Arbitration provides a mechanism for resolving disputes without the publicity of a lawsuit and usually at a lower cost. Arbitrators generally are professionals and therefore may be more likely than a jury composed of laymen to understand the technical aspects of a construction controversy. Arbitration may provide a speedier resolution than litigation. Additionally, the mere existence of an arbitration provision as an exclusive remedy may deter any consideration of filing a lawsuit.

Arbitration is a recognized method of dispute resolution in all fifty states. But states may vary in their willingness to enforce arbitration provisions. Because arbitration requires the waiver of the constitutionally protected right to a jury trial, mandatory arbitration clauses will be strictly construed and may not be enforced if the clause is vaguely worded or ambiguous. Many courts have taken the position that to be enforceable, an arbitration clause must be entered into knowingly. Fine print clauses, or clauses located in less prominent locations (such as on the backs of contract pages), may be stricken by a court. Some states by statute require a larger type size, specific contract locations, or even an additional signature or initialing to make a mandatory arbitration agreement valid. A local attorney should be consulted for the appropriate language, type size, location, and endorsement requirements for your jurisdiction.

If the building materials for construction come from across state lines (interstate commerce), the Federal Arbitration Act (FAA) may supercede special requirements of state law. Both the FAA and all individual state arbitration acts provide that if a contract has a valid arbitration clause, one party may compel the other into an arbitration proceeding. In the majority of states an arbitrator's decision is final and binding and neither party can appeal the decision except in the case of improprieties or fraud on the part of the arbitrator.

A formal dispute resolution organization such as the American Arbitration Association (AAA) can conduct an arbitration proceeding. The AAA follows its Construction Industry Arbitration

Rules. An AAA proceeding under these Rules can be expensive because the parties pay both the AAA and the arbitrator(s) of the dispute. Generally, the AAA assigns three arbitrators for disputes over $100,000 and only one for cases under $100,000. The AAA rules for construction industry disputes do provide for a "fast track" procedure on claims of $75,000 or less. Under fast track rules, discovery is limited, the hearing takes place within 30 days of the arbitrator's appointment, and the arbitrator's decision is announced within 60 days of the date of appointment. If your contract calls for referral to the AAA rules (or any other published rules), it is recommended that you familiarize yourself with the rules before signing the contract. Also, it is advisable to refer to the rules that are in effect on a certain date (such as the date the contract is signed). Rules can and do change. The AAA can be contacted at:

American Arbitration Association
140 West 51st Street
New York, NY 10020
(212) 484-4000
Or on the Internet at www.adr.org

Alternatively, the parties can provide tailor-made arbitration rules either in the contract or in a separate contract document and thus eliminate the need for an arbitration association. For example, the parties can agree that each party to the contract independently would select an arbitrator, and those arbitrators jointly would choose a third.

The contract also may:

- Provide for discovery and application of the rules of evidence. During formal discovery each side unearths facts and documents from the other side that may be helpful in defending or prosecuting its case. Discovery includes depositions, interrogatories (written questions and answers), and production of documents. Usually, discovery is too expensive and time-consuming.

- Set time limits for presentation of each party's case.

- Limit the maximum damages allowed in the arbitrator's decision and award.

Rather than develop their own dispute resolution procedures, the parties can agree to follow the procedures outlined in the federal Magnuson-Moss Warranty Act, 15 United States Code, sec. 2301 et seq. (see also 16 Code of Federal Regulations sec. 107).[16] If this procedure is unwanted, however, an alternative dispute resolution clause should not be set out in the body of the contract warranty provisions. If the express warranty contains such a clause, the builder may be required to use the Magnuson-Moss settlement procedures. (See Chapter 4, Warranties and Disclaimers).

> All disputes between the parties to this contract arising out of or related to any contract term(s) or any breach or alleged breach of this contract will be decided by binding arbitration, unless the parties should subsequently mutually agree otherwise in writing.

The arbitration shall be conducted by (specify the organization or named arbitrator(s) agreed upon) in accordance with [the rules adopted by the arbitration body chosen, the rules specified below, or the alternative dispute resolution proceeding specified in the federal Magnuson-Moss Warranty Act, 15 U.S.C.A., sec. 2301 et seq. (see also 16 C.F.R. sec. 107)]. The parties reference the Magnuson-Moss Act only to provide rules of arbitration in the event of a dispute, and they specifically do not incorporate the Magnuson-Moss warranties into this contract.

The parties must file a written notice of arbitration with the other party to this contract and with [the arbitration association or arbitrator(s) chosen]. The notice of arbitration may not be filed after the date that a claim based on the dispute would have been barred in a judicial proceeding by the applicable statute of limitations or repose (cessation of activity).

Either party may specifically enforce (a) a decision rendered under this agreement to arbitrate or (b) any valid agreement to arbitrate with additional persons, under applicable arbitration laws. The award rendered by the arbitrator(s) will be final and binding, and any court with jurisdiction over the decision may enter a judgment upon the arbitrator's decision.

MEDIATION

Like arbitration, mediation is a process whereby the conflicting parties meet voluntarily to negotiate a private and mutually satisfactory agreement aided by a neutral third party. A key difference between the two methods is that unlike the arbitrator, the mediator does not make a decision in favor of one party or the other. Instead, a mediator focuses on negotiation and problem solving. The mediator assists the parties in this process. Builders' mediation may follow the Construction Industry Mediation Rules of the American Arbitration Association.

If mediation has a down side, it may be that if mediation is not successful, the parties are back where they started and may have to resort to litigation or another form of alternative dispute resolution. For this reason the parties may want to include a provision in the contract making all communications during the mediation confidential to prevent their use in any subsequent proceedings.

If a dispute arises between the parties relating to or arising out of any provision of this agreement or any breach or alleged breach of this contract, either party may request mediation. Either party may invoke the dispute resolution procedure of this clause by giving written notice to the other. The notice should include a brief description of the disagreement. A mediator will be selected by mutual consent of the parties. The parties agree to participate in good faith in the mediation to its conclusion as determined by the mediator. No party will be obligated to continue in the mediation if a resolution has not been reached and put in writing within (number of days) of the first mediation session. The costs of mediation, including fees and expenses, shall be borne equally by the parties.

At this point the clause would include the sample language from the arbitration clause printed above, beginning with the phrase, "No arbitration proceeding under this provision . . ." and ending with the phrase "and any court with jurisdiction over the decision may enter a judgment upon the arbitrator's decision."

ATTORNEY'S FEES

The general rule in this country is that each party to a lawsuit pays its own attorney's fees—win or lose. Thus, the prevailing party in a lawsuit often ends up paying a considerable amount of the judgment to his/her attorney or pays a considerable sum of his/her own money to the attorney for successfully defending a suit. One way the parties can handle such an expense is to contract for the award of attorney's fees to the prevailing party in any action arising out of the project. If the contract includes such a clause, a decision to pursue a claim may be made strictly on the merits of the case. If the contract is silent on the matter of attorney's fees, the claimant must factor in the cost of the legal fees in deciding whether to pursue the claim. Also, the inclusion of such a clause may discourage frivolous suits and may force the parties to deal more forthrightly with each other. Some attorneys, however, do not favor including such a clause in the contract because of concern that it will have an opposite effect and will encourage litigation.

If either party needs to enforce provisions of this contract or to obtain redress for the violation of any provision hereof, whether by litigation, arbitration, or otherwise, the prevailing party shall be entitled to any reasonable attorney's fees, court costs, or other legal fees incurred herein in addition to any other recovery obtained in such action.

ENTIRE AGREEMENT AND SEVERABILITY

This provision emphasizes that this contract supersedes all previous agreements between the parties. It also assures that if a court determines that one provision is unenforceable, the remainder of the contract will remain in effect. The merger clause, necessary only where the builder is selling the land or lot on which the house is built, specifies that the provisions of the contract will not become void upon transfer of the deed.

The parties can agree not to assign or sell their rights and responsibilities in the contract to another party. The assignment clause restricts the buyer's right to sell the contract (and its payment obligations) to another person who may not have adequate financial resources to pay the builder. The contract can also designate the jurisdiction (state) whose laws will apply in interpretation and enforcement of the contract.

> This contract (including the documents incorporated by reference herein) constitutes the entire agreement between the parties. It supersedes all previous or contemporaneous agreements and understandings, whether written or oral. This contract may be changed only by a written document signed by all parties to this contract. The contract shall be binding upon each of the parties' respective heirs, executors, administrators, successors, and assigns. This contract shall not be assigned, however, without the written consent of all parties.

Each provision of this contract is separable from every other provision of the contract, and if any provision is unenforceable or revised the remainder of the contract will remain valid and enforceable.

This contract will be governed by the law of the jurisdiction in which the property is located.

The provisions of this contract shall survive the execution and delivery of the deed and shall not be merged therein.

SPECIFICATIONS

The general building specifications should be prepared as a separate document and referenced in the agreement along with other documents such as plans and drawings. The specifications are contained in a written document that describes the work to be performed (construction specifications) and the materials to be used and how they are to be installed (material or product specifications). The parties to the contract should initial every page of the specifications and plans to preclude a charge that a different page has been substituted or a plea of ignorance in the event of a disagreement between the builder and the owner.

The specifications should be as detailed as possible. They should reference plans and drawings where appropriate and include provisions for the items listed in Figure 2.5. This list is provided only as an example. Other necessary parts of the construction process may not be listed here, and some of the listed items may not apply to a particular project. All work should be listed and described on the specifications document. Wherever possible the material specifications should include size, color, material, quantity, construction, style, brand name, model number, and other descriptive information.

The construction specifications should be equally detailed. For example, the specifications for painting should read something like, "Painting, Exterior—One coat prime [brand name, color, and latex or oil-based, if the parties have agreed on these items]; [one or two] coats finish [brand name, color, and latex or oil-based, if the parties have agreed on these items]."

The commonly accepted format for residential specifications is the four-page Description of Materials used for application for mortgage insurance by the Federal Housing Administration, the Department of Veterans Affairs, and the Farmer's Home Administration. It appears in Figure 3.4, Items Included in Specifications.

DESCRIPTION OF WORK TO BE PERFORMED

The cost of the work and the builder's fee are based on the work described here. To avoid disputes about whether certain work is required by the contract or is outside of and entirely independent of the contract, this section and the specifications must clearly describe the work to be performed under the contract. The distinction is important because unless the contract otherwise provides,

Figure 2.5 Items Included in Specifications

- Excavation and land conditions
- Footings and foundation or slab (including moisture barrier and termite treatment)
- Chimneys
- Fireplaces
- Exterior walls
- Floor framing
- Subflooring
- Partition framing
- Ceiling framing
- Steel columns and girders
- Roof framing and sheathing (including built-up roofing and roofing materials)
- Gutters, downspouts, flashing, and other sheet metal work
- Masonry or frame exterior walls
- Insulation
- Drywall or lath and plaster
- Windows, glazing, and mirrors
- Interior doors and trim
- Entrances and exterior detail (including entrance doors and trim)
- Cabinets, countertops, backsplashes, and interior detail
- Stairs
- Special floors and wainscot
- Plumbing and plumbing fixtures
- Heating and air conditioning
- Electric wiring, lighting, and other electrical fixtures
- Decorating (painting and wallpaper)
- Finish hardware
- Special equipment (appliances)
- Porches or decks (framing, flooring, railings, pillars)
- Terraces
- Garages, garage doors, and carports
- Backfilling, grading, and drainage
- Other on-site improvements including termite treatment
- Landscaping and plants

the owner has no right to order the contractor to perform work outside the scope as defined by the contract documents, and the contractor will not normally perform it except in exchange for extra compensation.[17]

This section specifically defines the scope of the work in the following ways:

- Specifies what the builder will do and, with respect to certain items, what the builder will not do—particularly items that the builder may have reason to believe the owner or buyer is expecting

- Possibly describes the portions of the project for which each of the other parties is responsible
- Authorizes the builder to purchase materials for the project
- Identifies any unusual responsibilities that the buyer may request of the builder

The project shall consist of and the builder shall perform all of the work that is required by the contract documents as follows:

_____ (describe work) _____

_____

_____

_____

The following items are specifically excluded from the terms of this contract, and the builder shall not be responsible for the same:

A. Interior papering, finishing of doors or any other decorating

B. Installation or construction of walks, pavements, or curbing

C. Ground fill, finish grading, seeding, planting shrubs, or landscaping

D. Sewer or water permits

E. Any item on the plans marked "Not in the contract" or "NIC"

CONFORMANCE WITH PLANS AND SPECIFICATIONS

Builders must explain to their buyers that the actual construction of their homes may deviate somewhat from the plans and the specifications or from models that the buyers may have seen. Furthermore, builders may want to protect themselves from possible deviations from property lines, survey lines, and the like. These facts should be disclosed to the buyer in conversations at the beginning of the marketing and negotiation processes.

These provisions should also be included in the contract and in the certificate of acceptance that is to be signed or initialed separately by the buyer as evidence that the builder disclosed the possibility of deviations or inconsistencies to the buyer. The buyer should initial each of the provisions in the sample language below.

Construction of the House. The project shall be constructed to conform substantially with the plans and specifications that are set forth in this contract. The buyer acknowledges that in the course of construction of the house, certain changes, deviations, or omissions may be necessary because of the requirements of governmental authorities, suggestions and design changes made

_____

by the architect or buyer, or particular conditions of the job. The buyer hereby (a) recognizes that minor changes may occur in the work and (b) agrees that as long as the project is substantially the same as described in the contract documents and within accepted industry tolerance, minor deviations will be accepted.

Furnishings and Models. Furniture, wall-coverings, furnishings, and the like as shown in or about any model are for display purposes only and are not considered a part of such home for the purposes of this contract. Further, the location of wall switches, thermostats, plumbing, electrical outlets, and similar items may vary from home to home and may not be as shown in any model home. Any floor plans, sketches, or sales drawings are for display purposes only and may not be exactly duplicated.

3

CONTRACT BETWEEN REMODELER AND OWNER

AS DISCUSSED IN CHAPTER 2, a written contract records the exact terms of an agreement between parties. The agreement defines the scope and price of the product and also allocates the risks inherent in a particular transaction between the parties. The remodeler, like the new home builder, should have a written contract with the customer. This chapter should help remodelers and their attorneys write remodeling contracts that lessen the remodeler's risk.

No boilerplate contract clause is suitable for every situation. Therefore, remodelers should critically examine every transaction into which they enter to foresee contingencies or events that could lessen the transaction's benefits to them. They should make sure that each contract is written to provide them adequate protection from events that may expose them to unintended liability. Many states regulate remodeling or home improvement contractors, dictating that certain information must be included in any remodeling or home improvement contract. These regulations may dictate that individual provisions appear in a certain style and size of type. Some states may even provide a purchaser with a right of contract rescission within a stated period of time after signing a home improvement contract. Failure to comply with these laws may subject the remodeler to a fine or imprisonment. Accordingly, remodelers are advised to consult their local laws when drafting their contracts (see sample state law in Figure 3.1).

Remodeling contracts and contracts for new construction share many of the same types of provisions, such as contract price and when it will be paid, a specific description of the work, the time for performance, change orders, and warranties. Differences exist between remodeling and homebuilding, however, and a well-drafted contract will reflect those differences.

The obvious difference is that a remodeler is working with an existing structure. As a result, removal of portions of the structure that may contain potentially hazardous materials, such as mold or lead paint, may be a factor in remodeling but less of a factor in homebuilding. Accordingly, the remodeler's contract should expressly provide who (the owner or the remodeler) is responsible for the actual removal and who should bear the cost of removal for mold, lead paint, asbestos, or other hazardous substances.

Figure 3.1 State Home Improvement Contractor Law; Contract Requirements

[Any changes to] California home improvement contracts that exceed $500 must be presented in writing and include the following [items]:

- The name, address, and license number of the contractor.
- The name and registration number of any salesperson who solicited or negotiated the contract.
- The approximate dates when the work will begin and end.
- A plan and scale drawing showing the shape, size, dimensions, and construction equipment specifications.
- A description of the work to be done, descriptions of the materials to be used, a list of the equipment to be used or installed, and. . .compensation [agreed upon] for the work.
- A schedule of payments and a statement that, upon satisfactory payment for any portion of the work performed [before any further payment is made], the contractor shall. . .furnish the person contracting for the home improvement a full unconditional release from any claim or mechanic's lien for that portion of the work for which the payment has been made.
- A notice in close proximity to the signatures of the owner and contractor in at least 10-point type stating that the owner or tenant has the right to require the contractor to have a performance and payment bond.
- A statement that no extra or change order work shall be required to be performed without written authorization of the person contracting for the construction of the home improvement.
- Notice that, if the contract provides for payment of a salesperson's commission out of the contract price, that payment shall be made on a percentage basis in proportion to the schedule of payments made to the contractor by the disbursing party in accordance with the schedule of payments.
- A description of what constitutes substantial commencement of work pursuant to the contract.
- A notice that failure by the contractor without lawful excuse to substantially commence work within 20 days from the approximate date specified in the contract for work to begin is a violation of the Contractors' State Licensing Law.

A violation of this section by a contractor, his or her agent, or salesperson is a misdemeanor punishable by a fine of not less than one hundred dollars ($100) nor more than five thousand dollars ($5,000), imprisonment in the county jail not exceeding one year, or both that fine and imprisonment.

EXAMPLE

> In the event that the remodeler encounters what he reasonably believes to be existing hazardous material(s) within the home, to include but not be limited to mold, lead paint, or asbestos, the remodeler reserves the right to stop work and to remove his/her employees, equipment, and materials from the site. It shall be the sole responsibility of the homeowner to properly contain the hazardous material(s) and to properly conduct remediation by appropriate measures using qualified experts, as may be necessary. In the event that the homeowner does not properly contain the hazardous material(s) and/or conduct remediation to the satisfaction of the remodeler within a reasonable period of time (a specific number of days could be used as an alternative), then the remodeler shall have the right to cancel the contract and to receive liquidated damages, as provided in the remodeling agreement.

Matching materials is another potential source of trouble for remodelers but not new home contractors. A remodeler may have to match existing materials that are no longer produced or materials that have faded because of age. To shape the owner's expectations about matching materials, remodelers should include specific language in their contracts to alert homeowners to the limitations of matching certain materials.

Another obvious difference between remodeling and homebuilding involves customer contact. Remodelers sell a service, whereas home builders, particularly speculation builders, sell a product.

Because remodelers are likely to be working in an owner's current home or place of business, they must be concerned with such items as:

- Access to the work place

- Working while people are living on the premises

- Access to bathrooms and telephones

- Removal of debris and daily clean-up

- Protection of the owner's property

- Ownership of salvage material

This chapter explains the purpose of various clauses and provides sample language that may be used in remodeling contracts between owners and remodelers.

These suggested provisions do not address every contingency, nor do they apply to all remodeling agreements. This book also does not cover all of the provisions that a remodeler should consider for inclusion in a remodeling contract. However, if they are written correctly, these and other provisions may protect a remodeler against unnecessary liability.

Contracts are legal documents that greatly determine a remodeler's liability if a homeowner alleges that the remodeler failed to perform the contract obligations. Therefore, an attorney experienced in construction contract law should prepare (or at least review) any such documents before a remodeler signs them. To find such an attorney, the remodeler would contact the local NAHB Remodelors® Council, local home builders association, local branches of the Associated General Contractors or the Associated Builders and Contractors, or the State Bar Association. Sample language that appears in brackets presents an option for the reader. Depending on the particular transaction, the reader may choose one or the other, both, or neither of the possible wordings presented.

Warning! The National Association of Home Builders has provided this guide and sample contract language merely to point out the types of provisions of which the remodeler should be aware. These suggested provisions should not be used without review by an attorney experienced in construction law.

This chapter addresses the major sources of potential liability that a remodeler may face. The written contract may encompass three documents: the agreement, the general conditions, and the plans and specifications. Often remodelers combine the agreement and general conditions in the same document. The contract also may include other documents and clauses. (In reading the sample language that appears in the section that follows, note that the items in brackets require a decision by the remodeler.)

THE AGREEMENT

The agreement is the document that the parties sign. The plans and specifications are named in the agreement as being part of the contract.

CAPTION

The caption is the heading or introductory part of a legal document. It should include the names of all persons listed as property owners. The full legal name of each party should appear in all documents in the transaction. If the owner is a corporation or other business entity, the documents should include the full name and type of business entity. The names of the parties should be exactly the same in the contract as in all other project documents. The caption also should give a legal description of the property (such as lot, block, subdivision, and the specific property address).

> This contract specifies the terms between (owner's name), the customer, and (remodeler's name), the remodeler, to [remodel, renovate, rehabilitate, or build an addition to] the [home or other structure] on the property located at: (legal description of property).

THE CONTRACT DOCUMENTS

The agreement that the parties sign contains such items as the names of the parties and other information specific to the project. But some terms are more fully described in other documents, such as the plans and specifications. The remodeler's warranties and warranty limitations also are often drafted separately (see Chapter 4). If the written agreement specifically references these other documents, however, their requirements and limitations will constitute part of the contract (see Fig. 2.1). The agreement should specifically and accurately describe the referenced documents by date, number of pages, plan number, name, and any other appropriate information. The requirements contained in the incorporated documents should not conflict with each other nor with the terms of the agreement. Examples of contract documents appear in Figure 2.1.

The terms of this agreement include the conditions of this agreement and, by reference, the provisions in the other documents specifically listed below. The terms of this agreement prevail over any conflicting provisions in the documents incorporated by reference.

The remodeler shall perform all of the work that is required by this agreement and any documents incorporated by reference below, which are incorporated by reference and shall be considered a part of this contract.

Except for written modifications signed by both parties subsequent to the execution of this agreement, the terms of the agreement are limited to the provisions contained in this agreement and the documents described as follows:

(title of document), dated the _____ day of _____, 20____, consisting of ____ pages;

(title of document), dated the _____ day of _____, 20____, consisting of ____ pages;

(title of document), dated the _____ day of _____, 20____, consisting of ____ pages;

CASE STUDY

In an action by a homeowner against a contractor for breach of a contract to remodel a house, the evidence supported the court's conclusion that the contractor was bound by the minimum building standards required by the homeowner's lender. The primary contract, dated and signed by the parties, stated that the contractor agreed to provide all materials and to perform all the labor shown on the work drawings and described in the specifications. The contract further provided that the contract incorporated the specifications, including the proposal signed by the parties. The proposal stated in part that all material was guaranteed to be as specified and that work would be performed in accordance with drawings and specifications submitted for the work. Finally, the instructions incorporated in the description of the materials provided that "the specifications include this Description of Materials and the applicable Minimum Construction Requirements." The court's conclusion that the contractor was bound by the minimum requirements set by the lender was supported "by the fact that he signed a certification indicating that they would be followed and by the fact that their existence was recognized in the contract documents." Although some of the minimum requirements conflicted with the other specifications expressed in the contract, the contractor was the author of those terms and they were construed against him.[18]

OWNERSHIP OF PLANS AND SPECIFICATIONS

If the owner provides the plans, the remodeler should specifically impose responsibility on the owner for any defects in the plans. Remodelers who provide their own plans should expressly prohibit owners from giving or selling those plans to other potential owners or remodelers. The best way to ensure enforcement of this latter provision is to register the copyright for the plans. Sample clauses are set out below for both owners' and remodelers' plans.

> **Owners' Plans.** The remodeler agrees to perform the work in accordance with the building plans supplied by the owner (reference by title, author, and number of pages). Remodeler assumes no responsibility or liability for defects in the design or engineering of these plans. Only the owner will be liable for any damages caused by defective or negligently drawn building plans, including but not limited to additional costs caused by delay in substantial completion of the work, additional costs for materials necessitated by any changes, additional labor costs, and percentage profit on the additional work.

> **Remodelers' Plans.** The remodeler has provided the building plans to be used under this contract (reference by title, date, author, and number of pages). The owner of the property to be (remodeled, renovated, rehabilitated, or added to) has no ownership rights in the architectural plans used under this contract, and the owner will be liable to the builder in the amount of lost profits and all consequential damages for the reuse or resale of these plans.
>
> The remodeler makes no representations or warranties about the quality of these plans except those specifically provided in the limited warranty references in this contract.

TIME OF COMMENCEMENT AND SUBSTANTIAL COMPLETION

The date work begins should be no earlier than the date of execution of the contract. Instead of a specific date, a flexible starting date may be established by using a notice to proceed, for example, "The work shall commence on the date stipulated in the notice to proceed." An alternative is to tie commencement to the date the building permit was issued. Some states and local jurisdictions require that the contract give start and completion dates. The remodeler should have evidence of the owner's financing before commencing work (see General Conditions). In addition, before beginning the project, the remodeler should require evidence of a valid title and copies of a current survey, deed restrictions, and easements, if any. These items may help protect the remodeler's lien rights if a lien must be filed on the property for lack of payment, or they may identify potential problems with the site that the remodeler can avoid.

The date of substantial completion of the work may be a specific date expressed as a number of days (preferably calendar days). The contract should make clear to the owner when substantial completion will occur (e.g., the date that the certificate of occupancy is issued, actual occupancy or use by the owner, or some other identifiable point of time).

The contract should provide that the owner has a certain number of days to sign and return the contract. Additionally, the contract should include a provision for extending the time of completion, as described in Liquidated Damages and Unavoidable Delay in this chapter.

Assuming all conditions precedent are satisfied and weather permits, the work to be performed under this contract shall commence on the _____ day of _____, 20____, and be substantially completed no later than the _____ day of _____, 20____. These starting and completion dates are subject to the owner signing and returning the contract within 10 working days from receipt of the contract.

PRICE, DEPOSIT, AND PAYMENT

This section of the contract specifies and defines the remodeler's compensation for his/her work. It also instructs the parties in the manner and time of payment. To achieve these goals, this section should include the cost of the work. Some remodelers charge owners a total fixed price for the project. Others bill on a cost-plus-fee or cost-plus-percentage basis. The cost-plus contract should specify the percentage or fee required, the guaranteed maximum price (if any), what constitutes costs (see section on costs), how the fixed fee is to be adjusted for change orders, the type of fee schedule, and all anticipated costs and fees, when applicable. Whatever the type of contract, it should specify (in both words and numbers) (a) the total price of the construction or sales transaction and (b) the amount of owner's deposit to be paid to the remodeler upon execution of the contract.

Fixed-Price Contract. The owner agrees to pay and the remodeler agrees to [remodel, renovate, rehabilitate, restore, or build an addition to] the building _____ for the consideration of _____ dollars ($_____), the total price. The owner will pay _____ dollars ($____) to the remodeler as a deposit [if one is required] upon signing this contract.

Cost-Plus-Fee Contract. The owner agrees to pay and the remodeler agrees to construct the project for the consideration of the remodeler's actual costs and expenses (as defined in Section _____ of this contract, Costs to Be Reimbursed) plus ____ percent (____%) of these costs and expenses. The owners will pay _____ dollars ($____) as a deposit upon signing this contract [or on or before some date other than the date the contract is signed]. The owner will make progress payments [by the ___(_____) day of each month] based upon applications for payments submitted by the remodeler. The owner will make final payment (including all costs and expenses plus the fee specified above) to the remodeler within ___(_____) days of substantial completion. Substantial completion has occurred when the owner can use the project for its intended purpose. The owner has ___(_____) days from receipt of each bill to pay the remodeler. Payments due under the contract but not paid shall incur daily interest at the rate of _____ percent (___%) from the date payment is due.

Establish due dates for payments. The due dates should be mutually acceptable to the remodeler and the owner and should reflect specific stages of construction. The contract may include an up-front payment payable upon the signing of the contract. Thereafter the payments could be triggered by the commencement of a particular phase of the project rather than upon the completion of a phase of the project. (Some remodelers use monthly bills to show the progress of the job). Regardless of the plan, final payment should be due upon substantial completion and not upon final completion.

State how much time the owner has to make the payment after receiving the request for payment. For example, the contract might state, "The owner has ten (10) days from the statement date to pay the remodeler."

Require interest for late payments. For example, "Payments due under the contract but not paid shall incur daily interest at the rate of _____ percent (___%) from the date payment is due."

Instead of charging interest on late payments, the contract might provide for a late payment fee similar to liquidated damages. Such a late fee might be included in a cost-plus-fee contract as well as in a fixed-cost contract using this alternate language:

- The owner hereby acknowledges that late payment by the owner to the remodeler of progress payments and final payment may cause the remodeler to incur costs not contemplated elsewhere in this contract, the exact amount of which will be difficult to ascertain. Accordingly, any sum due the remodeler under this contract shall be paid within ___(_____) days of written request. If full payment is not received within ___(_____) days, the buyer shall pay ____ percent (___%) of the total amount overdue as a late charge. The parties agree that such late charge represents a fair and reasonable estimate of the costs the remodeler will incur by reason of late payment by the owner.
- Specify whether retainage is allowed. If it is allowed, specify when it will be disbursed.
- Require evidence of financing. The remodeler should be allowed to verify that the owner has satisfactory financing, including an allowance for subsequent change orders. The owner can be made to produce evidence of financing before the remodeler is obligated to start work.
- Satisfy any special state or local requirements. Some states require that the contract specifically identify certain expenses.
- Specify that work covered by change order falls within the general scope of the work contemplated by the contract, and specify a percentage of profit for additional work. Change orders for deductions from the work usually involve no reduction of profit, and this should be clearly stated.
- If the buyer requires an addition to the scope of the work, the builder shall account for the cost of these additions separately and shall be reimbursed _____ percent (____%) of the cost of the changes.

COSTS TO BE REIMBURSED

This section is applicable to cost-plus-percentage or cost-plus-fee contracts. This list of items suggests some costs that may need to be reimbursed in a remodeling project, but it may not include all costs to be reimbursed on every job. The remodeler should include all relevant items, especially every contingency negotiated with the owner. Remodelers should check this section against their general ledgers and other accounting practices to make sure all appropriate costs are included.

Many contracts also will include a section regarding costs not to be reimbursed. These provisions should be carefully reviewed because by definition they exclude some of the remodeler's actual costs. These items would be paid out of the percentage or fee added to the defined costs and, therefore, cut into a remodeler's profit.

The term cost of work means costs necessarily incurred in the remodeler's proper performance of the work contained in the contract documents, including the following items:

- Wages, benefits, costs of contributions and assessments for workers' compensation, unemployment compensation, Social Security, taxes, or any other costs incurred by the remodeler for labor during performance of this contract.

- Salaries for remodeler's personnel (including production supervisor or manager, where applicable) to the extent their time is spent on work helping to complete this contract. This payment of salaries includes (but is not limited to) work performed at shops, on the construction site, or in transporting materials or equipment.

- The remodeler's and the remodeler's agent's reasonable travel and subsistence expenses incurred toward the completion of this contract.

- Payments made by the remodeler to trade contractors for work performed pursuant to subcontracts under this agreement.

- Cost of all materials, supplies, and equipment incorporated in the work and consumed in the performance of the work; cost less salvage value of such items used, but not consumed, that remain the property of the remodeler, including all costs of installing, repairing and replacing, removing, transporting, and delivering the machinery and equipment.

- Rental charges consistent with those prevailing in the area for machinery and equipment used at the construction site, whether rented from the remodeler or others, including all costs of installing, repairing and replacing, removing, transporting, and delivering the machinery and equipment.

- Sales, use, excise, or any other taxes related to the work imposed by governmental authorities.

- Permit fees, charges, inspection costs, or any other fees related to the work imposed by governmental authorities.

- Royalties, damages for infringement of patents, costs of defending related lawsuits, and deposits lost for causes other than the remodeler's negligence.

- Expenses for telephone calls, telegrams, postage, delivery fees, stationery, and other similar petty cash items related to work.

- Costs incurred for security at the job site.

- Costs incurred because of any emergency affecting the safety of persons or property.

- All landscaping and backfilling necessary under the contract documents, including the cost of all grading, removing or planting of trees, removing snow, frost breaking, pumping water, excavating and related work, delivering the necessary materials to the site, and hauling away excess fill and material or trash and debris.

- Remodeler's risk or other insurance, soil fees and civil engineering fees, performance bonds, and labor and suppliers bonds in an amount equal to one hundred percent (100%) of the maximum costs.

- Differing site conditions, as provided for in Section _____ of this contract.

- Any other costs incurred in the work that are within the scope of the work as defined in the contract documents, or any other overhead expenses.

CASE STUDY

In an action to foreclose a lien on the owner's residential property for work done and materials furnished in remodeling and redecorating under a cost-plus contract, the court held that the contractor's charges for certain work and materials were excessive. The court's decision was based in part on a Mississippi case from which it quoted as follows:

"The rules of law controlling 'cost plus' contracts are well established. Upon reason and authority, where a person agrees to do work for another upon a cost plus basis, it is his duty to keep accurate and correct accounts of all materials used and labor performed, with the names of the material, men and laborers, so that the owner may check . . . [on] the same. He must use the same skill and ability as is used in contract work for a gross sum. If the aggregate cost upon the face of the account is so excessive and unreasonable as to suggest gross negligence or fraud, the law would impose upon the contractor the duty of establishing the bona fides of his performance of the work. The contractor does not have the right to expend any amount of money he may see fit upon the work, regardless of the propriety, necessity, or honesty of the expenditure, and then compel repayment by the other party, who has confided in his integrity, ability, and industry.

In an action upon his contract for payment, the contractor must show that the moneys which he claims to have expended were necessarily paid for materials and work upon the job and if the contractor fails to do this he should only be allowed the reasonable cost and his percentage. . . ."[19]

DRAW SCHEDULE AND APPLICATION FOR PROGRESS PAYMENT

The remodeler and the owner may negotiate any form of payment schedule that is mutually agreeable. In the absence of a payment schedule, the remodeler is not entitled to receive payment until the work is completed. Typically, if the owner is financing the project, the method of payment is through "progress payments" from the owner to the remodeler. One alternative allows the remodeler to establish a draw schedule with the homeowner and construction lender. With a draw

---

schedule a specified amount (for example, 10 percent) is sometimes paid up front, the remodeler can withdraw from the account at successive phases during construction, and the lender may hold a retainage until the structure is accepted by the owner.

A draw schedule should require the owner to make or authorize each payment to the remodeler within a specified number of days after the remodeler's application for payment. The remodeler uses the application for payment document, along with various supporting documents, to establish the remodeler's right to payment. Before requesting final payment, the remodeler should ensure that all claims have been settled and should obtain signed confirmations from the owner that, based on the final inspection, the contract requirements have been fulfilled.

Alternatively, the contract may provide for inspection by the lender or another third party at certain stages of the construction, with payment due directly from the lender upon satisfactory inspection. The parties should specify who will schedule the inspections and who will pay the inspector. In any case, the contract should specify whether the progress payments provision includes payment not only for the work in place but also for materials and equipment suitably stored at the site or at an off-site location agreed upon by the owner.[20]

Such a provision might give the owner the right to withhold progress payments otherwise due to the remodeler under certain circumstances enumerated in the contract, for example, if the remodeler fails to pay his/her trade contractors or suppliers. Similarly, this provision might provide that the remodeler can stop work until he/she is paid, and if payment is not made within a specified number of days after it is due, the remodeler also may terminate the contract.

The following sample language provides for two methods of payment.

Regular Periodic Payment. The remodeler shall prepare [weekly, biweekly, or monthly] itemized statements for the owner that specify all costs incurred by the remodeler in furtherance of performance of the terms of this contract. The owner will place adequate funds in an escrow account from which the remodeler may draw to pay for the cost of the work. Each draw will be based on an application for payment submitted to the owner by the remodeler. The owner will make funds available to the remodeler within _____ (_____) days of receipt of the statement (less ____ percent [____%] retainage) as provided for in the Notices provision of this contract.

The owner shall make final payment to the remodeler, including the entire unpaid balance of the cost of the work and all other compensation due to be paid to the remodeler, as defined in Section ____, Costs to Be Reimbursed, of this contract [at final settlement or within ___(_____) days after substantial completion of the work].

Payments Tied to Construction Activity. The remodeler shall prepare [weekly, biweekly, or monthly] itemized statements for the owner that specify all costs incurred by the remodeler in furtherance of performance of the terms of this contract.

The owner will place adequate funds in an escrow account from which payments are made for the cost of the work. Each draw will be based on beginning various phases of the work as described below. The owner will make funds available to the remodeler within ___(_____) days of receipt of the notice (less ____ percent [____%] retainage) as provided for in the Notices provision of this contract.

The remodeler agrees to furnish materials and labor in accordance with the provisions of this contract for _____ dollars ($_____) payable in the following stages:

1. $____ upon signing the contract

2. $____ upon start of _____

_____

3. $____ upon start of _____

[Depending on the job, it might have 2 to 10 stages.]

The owner shall make final payment to the remodeler, including the entire unpaid balance of the cost of the work and all other compensation due to the builder, as defined in Sections ____, Price and Deposit, and ____, Costs to Be Reimbursed, of this contract upon substantial completion of the work. This project shall be substantially complete upon the issuance of a certificate of occupancy. The owner may retain _____ dollars ($____) for ___(_____) days after substantial completion to assure:

- Final issuance of permits required of the remodeler under the contract
- Correction of defects
- System performance
- Passage of inspection

DELAYS AND EARLY COMPLETION

LIQUIDATED DAMAGES AND UNAVOIDABLE DELAY

A liquidated damages clause is a provision for the payment of predetermined money damages in the event of a breach of contract, such as inexcusable late completion of the work or inexcusable late payment of a draw. In this context the word liquidated means determined or settled and is used to indicate damages that are agreed to or settled in advance.[21]

Contracts with trade contractors and suppliers should include a provision stating that they have read and are bound by the remodeler's agreement with the owner (see Chapter 7). This statement will put the trade contractors and suppliers on notice that the remodeler may be liable to the owner in the event of a delay in construction, and if the delay is caused by a trade contractor or supplier, that firm may be liable to the remodeler for damages.

The liquidated damages clause should not impose a penalty on the party who fails to perform but it should reasonably approximate the actual losses that may occur because of the nonperformance. If the contract allows liquidated damages against the remodeler for work not completed on time, the liquidated damages clause should specify that the remodeler is not responsible for delays beyond his/her control. If the contract allows the remodeler to extend the time for performance, the remodeler should notify the owner in writing of his/her intention to do so. The remodeler should not wait until after the time for performance has passed to explain to the owner that he/she was delayed, thereby necessitating an extension of time to perform. Estimating actual losses an owner would suffer can be difficult, and if the owner cannot establish actual damages a liquidated damages clause may work against the interests of the remodeler. However, a homeowner may suggest the use of a liquidated damages clause. Therefore, the remodeler should be prepared to address this issue. In addition, a liquidated damages clause may actually benefit the remodeler by limiting the damages to the amount agreed upon if the contract specifies that the owner's liquidated damages remedy is exclusive of all other remedies.

In the event that the work to be performed under this agreement is not substantially completed by the completion date, the remodeler will compensate the owner in the amount of _____ dollars ($____) for each day of the week (including weekends) of inexcusable delay until the work is substantially completed. If the remodeler's failure to perform the terms of this contract in full does not result in any additional expenses to the owner, the remodeler's damages shall be limited to the cost of completion of performance of the terms of this contract. The owner shall not recover any compensation from the remodeler for delay caused by differing site conditions, as defined and provided for in Section ____ of this contract.

The remodeler will use his or her best efforts to complete construction of the project before the completion date. However, if reasons beyond the remodeler's control cause an unavoidable delay in the progress of construction (including, but not limited to, such factors as the unavailability of materials, inclement weather, strikes, changes in governmental regulation, acts of governmental agencies or their employees, acts of God, work changes made by the owner, or the failure of the architect or the owner to cooperate), the remodeler may, in his or her sole discretion, extend the date of completion for a period equal to the time of the delays.

This liquidated damages remedy is exclusive of all other legal and equitable remedies.

CASE STUDY

James Brink, as president of Audubon Builders, Inc., entered into a contract for the building of an addition to the home of the Hanrahans on November 21, 1987. Mrs. Hanrahan's mother was to reside in the addition. The contract was signed with an addendum in James Brink's writing, which stated: "All work to be completed by February 2, 1988 or contractor agrees to $150/day compensation." The project was ultimately completed on December 22, 1988. The Hanrahans sued Audubon and Brink alleging that certain work had not been completed in a proper and workmanlike manner, and alleging that they were entitled to compensation in the amount of $150 per day because of the delay in the completion of the contract. The trial court awarded the Hanrahans $150 a day in liquidated damages from February 15, 1988, through December 22, 1988, and Audubon and Brink appealed. The appellate court reversed the trial court opinion because that court failed to consider whether the $150-a-day liquidated damages provision was a reasonable approximation of probable damages or that actual damages would be impossible or difficult to calculate. The court concluded that the provision was agreed to by the parties as a penalty to ensure performance and was not reasonably related to the actual damages caused by the delay in performance.[22]

Bonus for Early Completion

As a corollary to the liquidated damages clause, remodelers often include a bonus provision that entitles them to a per diem sum of money for finishing early.

> If the remodeler substantially completes the work before the substantial completion date in Section _____ of this contract, the owner will pay the remodeler the sum of _____ dollars ($_____) for each day of the week, including weekends, between the date when the work is substantially completed and the substantial completion date set by the contract.

Notices and Records

The contract is written to minimize disputes about the terms of the agreement. Likewise, all notices provided for under the contract should be written. The remodeler should ideally store the records until all applicable statutes of limitations have expired. The statute of limitations is the period of time within which an owner must file a lawsuit. That period can run for many years, and under certain circumstances the courts may extend the limits. (See the section on statutes of limitations and repose in Chapter 2).

> Any notice required or permitted to be delivered under this contract shall be mailed to the respective party at the following addresses:

_____	_____
(remodeler)	(owner)
_____	_____
(street address)	(street address)
_____	_____
(city, state, zip)	(city, state, zip)

> For purposes of this contract, notice is received when sent by certified mail, postage prepaid, return receipt requested via the United States Postal Service.

Practice Pointer. Certified mail is often employed as the method of delivery because the signed return receipt is evidence of actual receipt if that issue should come under dispute. As a practical matter, certified mail is relatively expensive, particularly in instances where many notices might be required. Further, many less than scrupulous individuals have adopted the habit of never accepting (signing for) certified mail. The certified letter is returned undelivered, and the contractual notice receipt provision has failed. It may be preferable to state that for the purposes of this contract, notice is deemed to be received when sent by first class mail at the above-stated addresses. Always retain copies of all notices, and particularly for important or significant notices, it may be advisable to personally post the mailing and to obtain a post office receipt that can be attached to your record copy.

———————

Effective Date and Signatures. Ideally, all parties to a contract sign the document at the same time. If that is not possible, however, this provision assures that the remodeler is not bound by the terms of the contract until the remodeler (or an authorized representative) has signed the contract.

If any changes are made to the contract after it is printed or typed, both parties must initial each revision for it to be valid. Of course, a change order should cover any changes to the work after the contract is signed in accordance with the change order requirements of the section on changes in work. Any changes to the contract after it is signed require a written amendment according to the section on Entire Agreement and Severability.

The owner and the remodeler should sign at least two original contract documents, one for the owner and one for the remodeler. (Computer-generated hard copies are useful for this purpose.) The parties should execute the contract in their proper capacities, as individual owner or as partners, officers, or directors of a partnership or corporation that is a party to the contract. The parties should use their complete legal names on all contract documents and any subsequent change orders or contract amendments. Once both parties have signed the document, they should complete and initial the date-of-contract provision.

This contract has no force or effect and will not be binding upon the remodeler until it is accepted and executed by the owner and countersigned by the remodeler. This contract shall become effective on the date designated below or on the day it is executed by both parties, whichever is later.

We, the undersigned, have read and understand and agree to each of the provisions of this contract and hereby acknowledge receipt of a copy of this contract.

_____	_____
(owner's signature)	(name of remodeler, corporate name where applicable)
_____	By _____
	(authorized signature)
Date _____	Title _____
_____	Date _____

This contract is dated, and becomes effective:

_____	_____
(month, day, year)	
_____	_____
(buyer's initials)	(builder's initials)

CASE STUDY

When a remodeler's corporate existence did not begin until some 14 days after entering into a contract with the owners for the construction of an addition to their home, the court properly found the remodelers individually liable for breach of the contract.[23]

GENERAL CONDITIONS

Every construction contract has terms and conditions that apply to all contracts and that are not specific to a single project.

General conditions are sometimes included on the same page as the agreement. Some builders include the agreement and the general conditions in one document; others separate the two.

Obviously, the contract cannot cover every contingency. The more time the parties spend identifying their respective obligations before the project begins, however, the fewer surprises will occur later.

FINANCING AND OTHER CONTINGENCIES

If he/she has not already done so, the owner should agree to apply for a loan within a certain period after execution of the contract. If the owner does not receive a loan, the contract generally provides for cancellation. Therefore, the remodeler should not begin work under the contract until the owner has obtained the necessary financing.

An owner who does not need financing should place funds equal to the total price of the agreement in an escrow account. Similarly, if the owner needs only partial financing, the balance of the funds due should be placed in escrow.

> The owner represents that he or she has arranged sufficient financing to comply with this agreement. Before commencing work under this agreement or at any time during the progress of the work, the remodeler may request evidence in writing (acceptable to the remodeler) of financing for the work. Failure of the owner to produce the requested information within ___(_____) calendar days of the written request will constitute a breach of contract by the owner, and the remodeler may suspend the work. If the owner fails to provide the requested information within an additional ___(_____) calendar days thereafter, the remodeler may terminate this agreement. Should the remodeler suspend or terminate this agreement, he or she shall be entitled to collect payment for materials and labor expended on or for the project, along with a reasonable profit and overhead.

Any other reasonable contingencies that the parties can contemplate should be specifically identified. The contract should specify the period in which those events or requirements must occur, what will happen to the agreement if the conditions are not fulfilled, and how the deposit money will be divided.

ALLOWANCES

The total contract price shall include any allowances mentioned in the contract documents. Allowances are frequently included when an item of work is not sufficiently detailed in the contract documents to enable the remodeler to determine the final cost of the item. Their inclusion in the contract establishes that the item is within the scope of the remodeler's scope of work subject to final price adjustment.[24]

Allowance items may be of two types: (a) items that the owner still needs to select, such as wallpaper, cabinets, and the like, and (b) items of work for which the actual cost cannot be determined until actual conditions are verified or until additional information regarding the scope of the work is received. In the former situation the remodeler should closely monitor the owner's spending habits during construction and periodically notify the owners of the status of the allowance. In the latter situation the remodeler must be able to justify the original estimate because, if the actual cost greatly exceeds the allowance, the remodeler may have to deal with an angry customer. If the allowance was grossly underestimated, a court may allow the remodeler to recover only his reasonable costs.

The prudent remodeler will provide in this clause or in the separate Allowance Schedule that if costs are more or less than allowances, the contract price shall be adjusted accordingly by change order, and that the change order shall reflect the difference between actual costs and the allowance. The remodeler should make sure that the owner understands that if the actual cost exceeds the allowance, the owner is responsible for paying the difference. The remodeler shall supply items for which allowances are provided within the amounts specified. Those amounts must cover the applicable taxes as well the builder's cost for materials and equipment delivered to the site. Trade discounts will be passed on to the owner. The allowance item should clearly state whether the allowance is for material only, installation only, or material and installation.

To avoid delaying the work, the owner must promptly select all materials and equipment for which allowances are provided. So long as the remodeler has no reasonable objections to the vendors selected, the owner may specify the vendors for these items.

PERMITS, LICENSES, AND OTHER APPROVALS

The remodeler may assume responsibility for obtaining all permits, licenses, fees, and approvals associated with construction. A remodeler must be careful, however, about agreeing to obtain all permits. Permits associated with the site, as opposed to remodeling activity, should be the responsibility of the owner. The remodeler should identify in the contract the various permits, licenses, fees, and approvals for which he/she will be responsible. The contract should provide for the contingency that a permit may not be issued. If the owner's lot is located in a development that requires approval of plans and specifications, materials, and colors by an architectural review committee, the approvals should be obtained by the owner.

The remodeler shall obtain and pay for all local building and construction permits, licenses, governmental charges and inspection fees, and all other approvals necessary for work, occupancy of permanent structures, or changes in existing structures that are applicable at the time this contract is signed, excluding variances and other changes in zoning. The owner is responsible for negotiating for contested permits, licenses, and other approvals. In the event the remodeler is unable to obtain the building permit within _____(_____) days from the date of this agreement, the remodeler shall have the option to cancel the contract, thereby relieving the parties of any further obligations under this agreement.

If required, work is to be undertaken under the following permits that will be obtained and paid for by the owner or remodeler as designated below:

_____

_____

INSURANCE AND RISK MANAGEMENT

The purpose of risk management is to reduce or eliminate the risks associated with financial loss. Insurance is a key component of risk management.

Many types of insurance coverage are available to remodelers, and an agreement to buy insurance is often written into remodeling contracts. The contract will generally require both parties to buy and maintain insurance for specified injuries or risks and in specified dollar amounts. The contract should clearly state the insurable interest of each party and establish who owns or is responsible for what property, during what period of time, and the type and amount of coverage required.

The need for insurance and the exclusions to insurance policies vary according to the type of construction involved. Some common types of insurance include the following:

- Comprehensive general liability
- Builder's risk
- Workers' compensation
- Automobile liability
- Property insurance
- Professional liability
- Completed operations
- Umbrella liability
- Contractor's equipment insurance

The contract should require the owner to raise his/her coverage to include the added value of the remodeling. The contract also should require the owner to list the remodeler and his/her trade contractors as additional insurers on any existing insurance policy. The contract also should require the owner to obtain insurance against loss resulting from injury to third parties or their property. Third parties could include persons not parties to the contract or the owner's employees or invitees. Remodelers should consult a construction insurance expert to determine their insurance needs and an attorney for specific contract language.

RISK OF LOSS

Remodelers obtain insurance to cover numerous risks, but one risk that goes to the heart of the transaction is the risk of loss caused by accidental destruction of or damage to the house during remodeling. In addition to obtaining insurance to cover such a loss, the parties to a contract should discuss their respective rights and obligations if such a contingency occurs. Destruction of the building excuses the parties from further performance under the contract and entitles the remodeler to recover the value of work and materials furnished before the destructive event. Despite the general rules the parties would be wise to expressly provide who must bear the loss under the contract if the work is accidentally destroyed or damaged.

CASE STUDY

The Kaufmans engaged Gray to make certain renovations in their home for a total price of $5,000, payable one-third when work commenced, one-third when the work was half completed, and the balance upon completion. After the first two payments had been made, but before completion of the work, a fire at the house destroyed or damaged much of the work that had been done. Gray sued for the full balance remaining unpaid under the contract. The court held that Gray was not entitled to recover the balance of the contract because he had not substantially completed performance before the fire. The court held that where a contractor engaged in the repair of a building is prevented by fire on the premises from completing his contract, recovery is based on the value of work done and materials furnished by the contractor in the performance of his/her contract before the destruction of the property made full performance impossible.[25]

DIFFERING SITE CONDITIONS

Unexpected site conditions, such as rock, hidden pipes, or an unexpectedly high water table, can be expensive to work around. Generally, remodelers face two types of differing site conditions: (a) conditions that vary from conditions indicated by the contract and (b) unusual and unknown physical conditions that differ materially from those generally recognized as inherent in the work of the type covered by the contract. Accordingly, a prudent remodeler when building according to plans and specifications produced by the owner should include in the contract language that contemplates the occurrence of unexpected or concealed conditions.

Such a provision protects both remodelers and owners if such conditions are encountered. Remodelers are protected from having to absorb increased project costs arising from an unexpected hidden site condition. Without such a clause, a remodeler who agrees to construct something under a contract is not entitled to additional compensation merely because unforeseen difficulties are encountered. Remodelers who assume responsibility for differing site conditions usually increase their estimates to compensate for that possibility. A differing site condition provision benefits the owners, who may thereby receive a lower contract price and who are also protected by a cancellation option should the planned construction prove to be too expensive because of hidden conditions. [26]

The contract should include a clear definition of differing site conditions and provide for notification, work changes, or contract modification procedures upon discovery of such a problem. The definition should be broad enough to include unknown conditions in an existing structure in addition to concealed conditions below the surface of the ground.

An alternative to the cancellation provision below could require the owner to pay the extra costs incurred, plus profit at a specified percentage of the cost. These suggestions would replace the equitable adjustment language below. Under federal government contract law, the term equitable adjustment has an exact meaning. Outside this special area of law, however, the definition of equitable adjustment can vary and be confusing. Remodelers' attorneys should check the case law precedents in their states to see how the term is interpreted by the courts. The term should be used only where it has an identified meaning.

A differing site condition is a physical characteristic of the property that materially changes the construction techniques from those reasonably expected at the time of the contract. Examples of differing site conditions are subsurface or latent physical conditions at the site or within the existing structure that are materially different from those indicated in this contract, or are unknown physical conditions of an unusual nature (that are not reasonably foreseeable) located on the building site.

Before disturbing any differing site condition, the remodeler shall notify the owner of such a condition except in the case of eminent danger to persons or property. The owner shall investigate the condition within ___(_____) business days. If the owner and the remodeler agree that the differing site conditions will cause an increase in (a) the remodeler's cost of performance of any part of the work under this contract or (b) the time required for that work, the issue will be resolved as follows:

   A. If the total contract price will increase by more than _____ percent (_____%) [for example, 10 percent], the owner may terminate the contract upon paying the remodeler for all costs expended to date and for the remodeler's full profits as provided in Section _____, Price, Deposit, and Payments, of this contract; or,

   B. The remodeler and the owner shall execute a written specific cost adjustment to this contract, including any adjustments in the time for performance necessitated by the differing site conditions.

The owner's failure to investigate the condition will confer authority upon the remodeler to complete construction of the project according to the terms in Section _____, Liquidated Damages and Unavoidable Delay, of this contract and the builder shall further be entitled to [an equitable adjustment or payment of any increased costs necessitated by the differing site condition].

If the parties cannot agree on the existence or consequences of a differing site condition, the terms of this provision shall be arbitrated as provided for in Section _____, Arbitration, of this contract.

ARCHITECTS AND DESIGNERS

Before they talk to a remodeler, some owners consult an architect or designer who may participate in the project. In such a case, the contract should name the architect or designer and designate whether or not he/she is the owner's agent.

Warning! A remodeler should not rely on the directives of an architect or designer unless that person has written authorization to act on behalf of the owner. If the contract provides such authorization, it also should specifically provide that the remodeler will not be held liable for any actions made in reliance on the recommendations of the architect or the designer.

An architect or designer typically is responsible for:

- Inspection or observation
- Processing change orders
- Overseeing the payment process
- Interpreting plans and specifications with regard to aesthetic considerations

Of course, the architect or designer cannot change the obligations of the parties as spelled out in the contract. Sometimes the architect and designer have roles in disputes. For instance, the parties could agree that before a dispute can be submitted for arbitration or litigation, for instance, they must submit it to the architect (or designer) for consideration as a mediator.

This contract specifies the terms between (*owner's name*), the owner, and (*remodeler's name*), the remodeler, to [remodel, renovate, rehabilitate, or build an addition to] a home on the property located at: (legal description of property).

[*Name of architect and/or designer*] is the owner's agent, and the remodeler may rely on representations, statements, revisions, and approvals made by [architect and/or designer] related to the performance of the terms of this contract. The remodeler will not be held liable for any actions made in reliance on recommendations of [*architect and/or designer*].

CHANGES IN WORK AND CHANGE ORDERS

The owner does not have the automatic right to order changes in the work unless the contract confers that right. However, most contracts include a change order clause to give the owner that right. This section concerns the procedure for writing change orders and explains how the additional cost will be determined, including overhead and profit considerations. The actual change order form is a separate document (Figure 2.3).

Often, after the contract is signed and work commences, an owner will request changes in the design or materials used. Before beginning any new work created by an owner's request for a change, the remodeler should require that the owner sign a written change order authorizing the work and agreeing to additional payment as may result from the change. A change order is an agreement that should specify (a) revisions in the work and the price, (b) a revised payment schedule as may be necessary, and (c) a new date for substantial completion, again if necessary.

If the parties cannot agree on the price of the change order work, the contract could include a provision for the remodeler to be paid on a cost-plus basis for the additional work. If the contract includes more than one owner, getting both owners to sign a change order may be time-consuming. To expedite the work, the contract could then provide that either owner may sign a change order as the agent for the other and that the signature of one owner is binding on the other owner.

A change order should address all changes from any cause or source that affect the scope of the work, the contract price, or the time for performance and not just changes in the work requested by the owner. Thus, additional work to be performed under a differing site or concealed conditions clause should be handled by a change order. Similarly, any increase in the scope of the work that may be required by a building or planning department (that is not directed to cure a remodeler's omission or defect) should be handled by a change order. The contract should expressly provide that such an increase will be treated as extra work and that the extra work will be executed upon written change order signed by the owner. Generally, the contract will call for payment on change orders to be made (a) when the work is performed, or (b) upon completion of the change order, or (c) before the next draw. A remodeler who performs work without obtaining written change orders and who then presents the owner with a large bill for that work upon completion of the project is asking for trouble.

The owner may request changes in the work within reason. Upon written directive by the owner, the remodeler will make changes, additions, or alterations. If the owner and the remodeler agree on the cost of the modifications, they shall execute a written change order describing the changes to be made and any changes to the contract price or completion date (Fig. 2.3).

Change orders shall be signed by all parties and become part of this contract, and the owner agrees to pay the remodeler for changes [upon completion of the work performed under the change order or by the next draw]. The buyers agree that either of them may sign the change order and that the signature of one is binding on the other.

If the parties cannot agree on a fixed cost of the change, the remodeler will make the changes and will receive from the owner an equitable adjustment to include the costs of labor, materials, equipment, and supervision plus _____ percent (____%) of such costs. The owner agrees to make requests concerning any changes, additions, or alterations in the work in writing directly to the remodeler named in this contract and not to the workers, including trade contractors and trade contractors' workers on the job.

CASE STUDY

A remodeler was frequently asked to perform additional work by his customer. The remodeler presented written change orders but did not receive signatures on them all. The remodeler did the additional work anyway, but at the completion of the contract the owner refused to pay for the unsigned change orders. The remodeler sued to recover the balance due. The court ruled that since the contract did contemplate changes in the scope of the work, and since the contract did not require the written change orders to be signed, and since the customers accepted the additional work without complaint, the remodeler was entitled to a judgment award for the additional amount due for work performed pursuant to the unsigned change orders.[27]

MECHANIC'S LIENS

Mechanic's lien laws (construction lien laws in some states) ensure that participants in the construction process get paid for their work by granting them a specific interest in real property that has been improved by their labor or materials. All 50 states, the District of Columbia, and Puerto Rico have such laws. The requirements of these laws vary considerably from state to state. To benefit from or comply with a lien law, a remodeler, trade contractor, or supplier must strictly follow the procedures and requirements of the law.[28]

The claimant (the person claiming the lien) must provide one or more forms of notice before the lien can be effective. This process is often referred to as "perfecting" the lien (language that is commonly used in the mechanic's lien statute). To perfect the lien, often the claimant must file a formal Claim of Lien. Such a filing must usually be made within a fixed period of time after completion of the contract or the last furnishing of services or materials. When the lien has been perfected, it may be enforced in a lawsuit to compel the sale of the property. The time for enforcing the mechanic's lien varies from state to state but seldom exceeds one year after the date on which the lien was filed.

Some states allow a remodeler to waive his/her lien rights by signing a lien waiver before beginning work for the owner. The lien waiver clause typically provides that the remodeler will not file any liens against the property for labor, material, or equipment furnished under the contract. A lien waiver clause offers little, if any, benefit to a remodeler. Homeowners find such a provision attractive because it ensures that the property will remain unencumbered by liens.

Obviously, remodelers should be wary of signing any form that has the effect of waiving their lien rights before receipt of payment, and they should be on the lookout for such wording because the owner or the owner's attorney may suggest adding it.

> The remodeler unconditionally waives, releases, and relinquishes all right to file or maintain any mechanic's lien or other claim in the nature of a lien against the real property improved under this contract for (a) labor, material, or equipment that is furnished or that may be furnished by the remodeler under this contract or (b) any claim for extras, change order work, or increased costs.

INSPECTION, ACCEPTANCE, AND POSSESSION

Inspections allow owners to identify and give remodelers the opportunity to correct defects in materials or workmanship. Because the owner or the owner's agent makes periodic inspections, the remodeler can document an owner's satisfaction with the completed work. The remodeler should keep a record of each inspection for at least the duration of any statute of limitations or repose.

Statutes of repose and statutes of limitation limit the time within which an injured party may sue the person who caused the injury. The statutes differ with regard to when the "clock begins to tick." A statute of repose begins to run at an arbitrary point in time, such as when the contract has been substantially completed. It is not keyed from the occurrence of a loss or damage. Conversely, the time allowed by the statute of limitations begins to run when the injured party's cause of action arises, that is, when he/she discovers or reasonably could have discovered the loss or damage. From the remodeler's perspective, the difference between the two is that without a statute of repose the remodeler could potentially be liable for an indefinite period of time, perhaps even the life of the structure.

The contract should define what steps must be taken before the owner may commence or resume use of the area involved in the remodeling project. For example, remodelers frequently include provisions for inspection, formal acceptance, and final payment as a condition of use.

From time to time, and upon substantial completion, the owner or the owner's designated representative shall inspect the house in the remodeler's or remodeler's representative's presence. At the time of the final inspection for substantial completion, the owner will give to the remodeler a signed punchlist that identifies any alleged deficiencies in workmanship or materials. The remodeler shall correct any items on the owner's punchlist that are, in the good faith judgment of the remodeler, deficient in workmanship and/or materials in accordance with the contract specifications. Unless otherwise specified in the contract, the remodeler shall meet the standards of construction relevant to the community in which the project is located. The remodeler shall correct any defects within a reasonable period of time and shall be responsible for the costs of correction. The owner shall not use or resume use of the area designated as the "construction zone," as defined in the contract, before conducting final inspection, signing the certificate of acceptance, and making final payment to the remodeler.

ACCESS

Sometimes disagreements over minor matters, such as access to the site and use of a home telephone, can ruin a congenial relationship between a remodeler and a client. To guard against potential misunderstandings and a resulting loss of goodwill, and subsequent referrals, some remodelers include these terms in their contracts.

Access. Owner shall grant free access to work areas for workers and vehicles. Driveways shall be kept clear and available for movement of vehicles during scheduled working hours, which will be ____ a.m. to ____ p.m. The remodeler and the remodeler's workers shall undertake reasonable efforts to protect driveways, lawns, shrubs and other vegetation, and landscaping fixtures that may be encountered in the course of access to the property. However, the remodeler and his workers shall not be responsible for damage to any of the items referenced above, except in instances of gross negligence.

Inconvenience. The owner understands and accepts that during the course of the project, inconveniences may occur from time to time, and the remodeler agrees to keep such inconveniences to a reasonable minimum.

Removal of Personal Property. The owner shall be solely responsible for removing or protecting personal property, inside and outside. The remodeler shall not be held responsible for any damages or loss to personal property that is not removed from areas designated as "construction zones."

Removal of Material. Any materials or items removed from the building during the course of the work shall be disposed of by the remodeler, except those materials or items that may be designated by the owner in writing before work commences.

Clean-Up. The remodeler will leave the work site in an orderly condition at the end of each day. Upon completion of the project, all construction debris and the remodeler's equipment shall be removed by the remodeler. The premises shall be left in a neat, broom-clean condition, unless otherwise agreed upon herein.

Sign. The buyer agrees to permit the builder to display a sign on the site until the project is completed. [The parties might even agree upon the location of the sign.] (NOTE: Some localities may regulate the placement and size of signs.)

Telephone. (The increased usage of cellular phones makes this clause less crucial. However, such a clause may be necessary if cell phone service is unavailable.) The owner shall permit the remodeler and the remodeler's workers access to a telephone for local calls. No long-distance calls will be made from the owner's home. [Some remodelers install their own telephones for large jobs.]

Toilet. The owner shall permit the remodeler and the remodeler's workers access to specified on-site toilet facilities. In the alternative, the owner could agree to compensate the remodeler for the cost of a rented portable toilet unit.

Electricity and Water. Use of these should be included in the contract as well. Otherwise, the additional expense of increased utility usage could come as a jolt to the owner. Prolonged use of heavy power tools, or the filling of an in-ground pool as part of a project, could result in a hefty and unexpected utility bill.

Photographs. (Some owners welcome photographs of the premises, others may be extremely concerned about privacy and would object to photographs. It would be prudent to ask the owner if he/she will permit photographs before tendering a contract with this clause.) Owner agrees to permit the remodeler to take interior and exterior photographs of the residence for remodeler's use in marketing, for display, promotion, and advertising:

- At reasonable times

- Upon giving the owner reasonable notice

- Without compensation to the owner

Work Performed by Owner and Other Contractors

Some owners reserve the right to perform some of the work or they reserve the right to subcontract part of the work. Some remodelers feel very strongly that the owner should not perform any of the work. They discourage this practice and sometimes include such a warning in the contract.

If the owner reserves the right to perform some of the work or to award separate contracts in connection with portions of the work, the contract should clearly describe the work to be performed by the owner or his/her trade contractor and the time within which that work is to be performed. Usually, if the owner enters into multiple contracts with different contractors for work on one project, the owner is under an obligation to coordinate and control the operations of all contractors to avoid unreasonable disruption of, or interference with, the operations of the other contractors. If that coordination fails, then the delayed performance may be compensable. Finally, if the owner performs certain work or has other contractors perform that work, the remodeler should expressly provide that he/she is not warranting such work.

MANDATORY CLAUSES

Remodelers must take particular care to include any mandatory terms or language in their home improvement contracts. At least 13 states currently have statutes that require mandatory language or mandatory provisions in all or in certain home improvement contracts (often dependent on the amount of the contract price; as an example, mandatory provisions may apply to any home improvement contract with a contract price over $500). Many additional states have mandatory contract language and provisions for home solicitation contracts (door-to-door sales) and for home improvement financing contracts, both of which could involve some remodeling contracts.

Typically, the home improvement contract legislation requires at a minimum that the contract be in writing, be legible, include the name and address of the consumer and of the property to be improved, the name, address, and telephone number of the remodeler (some require a business license number), the date of the contract, a detailed description of the improvement, the starting and completion dates, and the contract price. These requirements can vary from state to state. Remodelers should consult with their local attorneys to determine what, if any, contract provisions must be included in their contracts.

Other mandatory requirements may include language concerning:

- Cancellation or rescission rights
- A mechanic's lien notice
- Inspection and right to cure notice
- A performance or construction bond notice
- A warning against signing a contract with blank spaces
- A consumer rights notice
- A warranty rights notice

Frequently, required language and notices must be set out in ten-point (bold) type and must be located prominently just above the contract's signature spaces. Depending on the jurisdiction, the failure to include mandatory terms and conditions can result in the invalidation of the contract and/or civil fines, and even criminal fines and imprisonment.

WARRANTIES UNDER THE MAGNUSON-MOSS WARRANTY ACT

If a remodeler gives a warranty and the warranty covers consumer products, the Magnuson-Moss Warranty Act applies. The Act does not require a remodeler to give a warranty. However, it does regulate the form of whatever consumer product warranty a remodeler may voluntarily decide to give (see Chapter 4).

RIGHT OF CANCELLATION

Under a federal law regulating door-to-door sales, a consumer entering into a remodeling contract may be entitled to cancel the contract if (a) the remodeler personally solicits the sale and (b) the contract is made in the consumer's home or a location other than the remodeler's place of business. This law gives consumers a three-day cancellation right. Compliance with this law requires including a notice of cancellation clause in the contract and following a few simple rules (Fig. 3.2).[29]

RIGHT OF RESCISSION

A federal consumer protection regulation applies to credit transactions for which a security interest is or will be retained or acquired in a consumer's principal dwelling. Under the regulation, the consumer has the right to rescind the contract through midnight of the third business day following the signing of the contract (or delivery of the right of rescission notice or delivery of the Truth in Lending disclosures, whichever comes last). If this type of contract is used, the remodeler must deliver two copies of the notice of the right to rescind to each consumer entitled to rescind. Unlike the notice of cancellation, the notice of rescission must be on a separate document (Fig. 3.3).[30]

ESCALATION CLAUSE

If a party agrees to perform work for a fixed price, that party bears the risk of an increase in the cost of compliance because of an increase in the cost of labor or materials during the project. In other words, a party will not be excused from completing the work to be performed under the contract just because it turns out to be more difficult or burdensome to perform than expected. The current saga of increases in lumber prices is evidence that the cost of materials can rise significantly during a project.

Remodelers can avoid this pitfall by providing in the contract that if there is any price increase in labor or materials before or during construction, or if there is a cost increase as a result of additional work required by the building department or other governmental agency (not involving correction of omissions or defects), the owner will pay the remodeler the increased amount upon proof thereof. As an alternative, the parties might agree that in the event there is a price increase amounting to more than a certain percentage of the project cost, the owner has the option of paying the increase or terminating the contract after reimbursing the remodeler for all work completed to date.

Figure 3.2 Sample Notice of Cancellation

Notice of Right to Cancel Contract Secured by Your Home

Your Right to Cancel

You are entering into a transaction that will result in a lien and/or security interest on [or] in your home. You have a legal right under federal law to cancel this transaction, without cost, within 3 business days from whichever of the following events occurs later:

(1) The date of the transaction, which is _____; or

(2) The date you received this notice of your right to cancel.

If you cancel the transaction, the lien and/or security interest is also canceled. Within 20 calendar days after we receive your notice, we must take the steps necessary to reflect the fact that the lien and/or security interest on [or] in your home has been canceled, and we must return to you any money or property you have given to us or to anyone else in connection with this transaction.

You may keep any money or property we have given you until we have done the things mentioned above, but you must then offer to return the money or property. If [returning the property]. . .is impractical or unfair to you, [you] must offer its reasonable value. You may offer to return the property at your home or at the location of the property. Money must be returned to the address below. If we do not take possession of the money or property within 20 calendar days of your offer, you may keep it without further obligation.

If you cancel any property traded in, any payments made by you under the contract of sale and any negotiable instrument executed by you will be returned within 10 business days following receipt by the seller of your cancellation notice, and any security interest arising out of the transaction will be canceled.

How to Cancel

If you decide to cancel this transaction, you may do so by notifying us in writing at

_____

(remodeler's name)

_____

(street or Post Office business address)

_____

(city, state, zip)

You may use any written statement that is signed and dated by you. . .[that] states your intention to cancel, or you may use this notice by dating and signing below. Keep one copy of this notice because it contains important information about your rights.

If you cancel by mail or telegram, you must send the notice no later than midnight of (date) (or midnight of the third business day following the later of the two events listed above). If you send or deliver your written notice to cancel some other way, it must be delivered to the. . .address [listed above] not later than that time.

I WISH TO CANCEL

_____

(consumer's signature)

_____

(date)

Source: Contract for Repairs or Alterations (Louisville, Ky. Home Builders Association of Louisville, 1988), p. 2

Figure 3.3 Sample Notice of Rescission

Notice of Cancellation for Contract Solicited at Your Home Under Federal and Kentucky Law
Date_____

You may cancel this transaction, without any penalty or obligation, within 3 business days from the. . . date [listed above]. If you cancel, any property traded in, any payments made by you under the contract or sale, and any negotiable instrument executed by you will be returned within 10 business days following receipt by the seller of your cancellation notice, and any security interest arising out of the transaction will be canceled.

If you cancel, you must make available to the seller at your residence, in substantially as good [a] condition as when it was received, any goods delivered to you under this contract or sale; or you may, if you wish, comply with the instructions of the seller regarding the return shipment of the goods at the seller's expense and risk.

If you do make the goods available to the seller and the seller does not pick them up within 20 days of the date of your notice of cancellation, you may retain or dispose of the goods without any further obligation. If you fail to make the goods available to the seller, or if you agree to return the goods to the seller and fail to do so, then you remain liable for performance of all obligations under the contract.

To cancel this transaction, mail or deliver a signed and dated copy of this cancellation notice or any other written notice, or send a telegram, to—

_____ at _____
(remodeler's name)   (street)
_____ not later than midnight of _____
(city, state, zip)   (date)
I hereby cancel this transaction

_____
(owner's signature)

Source: Contract for Repairs or Alterations (Louisville, Ky: Home Builders Association of Louisville, 1988), p. 2

CASE STUDY

The Einhorns entered into a contract with Ceran Corporation, a large residential builder, for the purchase of a townhouse to be constructed by Ceran. The contract, provided by Ceran, included a "price escalator" clause that gave Ceran the option of canceling the contract if the cost of labor or materials increased. The Einhorns had the option of paying any increased costs of labor and materials by providing notice within 10 calendar days after notice of any increase in cost. Subsequently, Ceran notified the Einhorns it was exercising its right to increase the cost of the contract, but despite repeated requests by the Einhorns, Ceran refused to supply any information substantiating the need for the price increase. A closing took place by order of the court.

At that time the Einhorns paid the contract price to Ceran and paid the price increase to the clerk of the court, subject to a decision by the court. Finding for the Einhorns, the court held that the since the contract gave the Einhorns the option of paying the increase, Ceran had to furnish the buyers facts sufficient to enable them to determine whether the demand reflected real cost rises. The court observed that "Without some other verifiable or calculable standard, the buyer can be charged only the builder's actual cost increases and he must be prepared to demonstrate them sufficiently for the buyer to ascertain whether they are real."[31]

UNCOVERING AND CORRECTING WORK

General contract conditions include uncovering and correcting work, for example, work that (a) was covered up or enclosed before inspections occurred, (b) work that does not meet the contract standards, or (c) work that violates some other aspect of the contract. The contract conditions can provide for acceptance of work that may not be done in accordance with contract specifications but is still acceptable to the client. The following sample language could also be adapted by the remodeler for use in trade contractors' agreements to protect the remodeler.

Uncovering Work. If work is covered or enclosed in contradiction to the terms of the contract or in contradiction to any applicable laws, the remodeler shall uncover the work for observation or inspection and replace it without charge. However, if the homeowner or architect requests that any work that has been completed and inspected in compliance with the contract and local laws be uncovered, the homeowner shall sign a change order agreeing to pay for the additional work, subject to the following: If the work uncovered subsequently does not comply with the contract documents or applicable laws, the remodeler shall bear the costs of uncovering and redoing the work, unless the homeowner or a third party not under the remodeler's control has caused the condition that needs to be corrected.

Correcting Work. Upon written notice by the owner, the remodeler shall promptly redo and recover the work that does not meet contract specifications or applicable laws. The remodeler shall pay the costs of redoing that work and recovering that work, as well as any additional expenses for necessary testing or inspections.

Acceptance of Nonconforming Work. The owner may choose to accept work that does not meet contract specifications so long as it conforms to the applicable laws. If the owner chooses to do so, the total contract price will be decreased accordingly to reflect any savings of material or labor costs, regardless of whether the owner has made the final payment.

TERMINATION OF THE CONTRACT

Occasionally, unpredictable or uncontrollable events substantially change a construction project and one or both parties want to be released from the contract. The remodeler and the owner can negotiate how to allocate responsibility for this possibility. Often, contracts permit termination for cause, such as the owner's nonpayment, the remodeler's failure to perform by a certain date, a substantial delay caused by a government entity (stop work order), or a substantial cost increase resulting from the discovery of a hidden or unforeseen condition. In the absence of such a clause, a party may not unilaterally terminate the contract without incurring liability. The parties can mutually agree to terminate, but absent that and without a termination clause the only legal excuses for nonperformance involve impossibility (not impracticality) or a material breach by the other party that defeats the purpose of the contract. The sample language at the end of this section illustrates only one solution. The parties may agree to any of the following solutions if the owner terminates the contract without cause:

- The remodeler keeps any money earned up to the date of termination.

- The remodeler is entitled to a specified percentage of the remodeler's total anticipated profits.

- The owner must pay the remodeler for all work performed together with a sum of money equal to the amount of anticipated profits, or a reasonable profit on the entire agreement price.

- An owner must pay the remodeler a sum of money greater than the amount of anticipated profits. This provision should not call the additional fee a penalty because a court will invalidate a punitive damages clause in a contract. However, a sum designed to compensate the remodeler for downtime while arranging for a new job may be justified.

The remodeler also may include a provision that allows the owner to cure a breach of contract within a specific time period by bringing all payments and other obligations up to date. This action permits the parties to reinstate the agreement so the remodeler can complete the job. Similarly, if the contract authorizes the owner to remove the remodeler from the job because of deficiencies in the work, the remodeler should include wording in the contract stating that the remodeler is entitled to notice of the deficiency and an opportunity to cure the deficiency before the termination is effective.

If the remodeler fails to substantially fulfill the contract terms, the termination provision may permit the owner to complete the work. In such a case the contract price would be reduced by the cost to the owner of completing the project. Additionally, if the cost of completing the project exceeds the contract price, the remodeler may be responsible for the additional amount. The parties also should allocate attorney's fees incurred in connection with termination of the contract. Another provision should address the event of bankruptcy of either party.

The contract should require that all termination notices be in writing (see Notices).

Remodeler's Remedies. If the owner (a) materially fails to comply with the provisions of this contract, (b) terminates the contract for any reason other than the remodeler's failure to perform, or (c) orders the remodeler or the remodeler's agents, employees, or trade contractors to stop work performed under this contract, the remodeler may:
- Terminate this contract and retain any downpayments and deposits as liquidated damages
- Recover all unpaid costs, expenses, and fees earned to the time of default or termination; the prorated cost of overhead expenses; and the costs, fees, and prorated overhead expenses for all change orders approved by the owner before termination

---

- Institute judicial proceedings for specific performance and/or any other legal and equitable remedies

(The costs specified in this section shall be based upon the costs specified in Section _____, Price, Deposit, and Payment, of this agreement.)

Owner's Remedies. If the remodeler fails to supply proper materials and skilled workers; fails to make payments for materials, labor, and trade contractors in accordance with their respective agreements; disregards ordinances, regulations, or orders of a public authority; or fails to materially comply with the provisions of the contract, the owner must give the remodeler written notice. After ____(_____) days if the remodeler has failed to remedy the breach of contract, the owner must give a second written notice. If the remodeler still fails to cure the breach within ____(_____) days after the second notice, the owner may terminate the contract. In such a case the remodeler shall reduce the contract price by the cost to the owner of finishing the work.

Remodeler's Remedies. If the owner materially fails to comply with the provisions of this contract, to include but not be limited to nonpayment of invoices and statements due and payable under the contract, or terminates this contract without cause, the remodeler may (a) terminate the contract and retain any down payments and/or deposits as liquidated damages; (b) recover all unpaid costs, expenses, and fees earned up to the time of default or termination, including all costs of change orders and the prorated cost of overhead expenses; and (c) institute judicial proceedings for specific performance and any and all other legal and equitable remedies. Examples of material breaches may include:

- Nonpayment under the contract
- Refusal to permit access to site
- Persistent deviation from plans and specifications
- Persistent disregard for applicable law
- Repeated failure to maintain the schedule agreed upon

ARBITRATION, MEDIATION, AND OTHER ALTERNATIVE DISPUTE RESOLUTION

During the course of construction, a disagreement between the parties to the contract may arise that they cannot personally resolve through negotiations. Because of the expense of a lawsuit and the long wait to have a case heard in court, litigation may not be a wise or efficient method of resolving the matter. Accordingly, the contract should address how disputes will be settled. Arbitration and mediation are popular alternative dispute resolution (ADR) methods. For flexibility, remodelers should consider including a clause in their contracts that allows them to choose arbitration or mediation. Otherwise, if the contract does not contain such a clause and there is no subsequent agreement between the parties to use ADR, dispute resolution will have to be conducted through litigation (lawsuit).

ARBITRATION

Binding arbitration is a process in which the parties submit their case to a neutral third person or a panel of individuals (arbitrators) for a final and binding resolution. Arbitration provides a mechanism for resolving disputes without the publicity of a lawsuit and usually at a lower cost. Arbitrators generally are professionals and therefore may be more likely than a jury composed of laymen to understand the technical aspects of a construction controversy. Arbitration may provide a speedier resolution than litigation. Additionally, the mere existence of an arbitration provision as an exclusive remedy may deter any consideration of filing a lawsuit.

Arbitration is a recognized method of dispute resolution in all fifty states. However, state courts can vary in their willingness to enforce arbitration provisions. Because arbitration involves the waiver of the right to a jury trial (a constitutionally protected right that can be waived if it is done knowingly and voluntarily), mandatory arbitration clauses will be strictly construed and may not be enforced if the clause is vaguely worded or ambiguous. A fine print clause or a clause located in a less prominent location in the contract (such as on the backs of pages) may be stricken by a court on the grounds that the clause is hidden and therefore not knowingly entered into. Some states by statute require arbitration clauses to have a larger type size than other contract provisions, require a specific contract location, or may even require that the clause be separately signed or initialed. Remodelers should consult with a local attorney to determine the appropriate language, type size, contract location, and endorsement requirements for their jurisdiction.

If the building materials for the remodeling project come from across state lines (interstate commerce), the Federal Arbitration Act (FAA) may supercede any special requirements of state law. Both the federal act and individual state arbitration acts provide that valid arbitration agreements will be enforced and that one party may compel the other into an arbitration proceedings. In the majority of states, the decision of the arbitrator(s) is final and binding. Neither party can appeal that decision, except in the case of improprieties or fraud on the part of the arbitrator(s).

A formal dispute resolution organization, such as the American Arbitration Association (AAA), can conduct an arbitration proceeding. The AAA follows its Construction Industry Arbitration Rules. An AAA proceeding under these rules can be expensive because the parties pay both the AAA and the arbitrator(s) of the dispute. Generally, the AAA assigns three arbitrators for disputes over $100,000 and only one for cases under $100,000. The AAA rules for construction industry disputes do provide for a "fast track" arbitration process for claims of $75,000 or less that may be appropriate for most remodeling contracts. Under fast track rules, pre-hearing discovery is limited, the arbitration hearing takes place within a period of 30 days from the time the arbitrator is appointed, and the decision is announced within 60 days from that appointment date. If your arbitration clause refers to the AAA rules (or any other published rules), it is recommended that you familiarize yourself with these rules before signing the contract. Also, it is advisable to refer to the rules that are in effect as of a date certain (such as the date that the contract is signed). The rules can, and from time to time do, change. You can contact the American Arbitration Association at:

American Arbitration Association
140 West 51st Street
New York, NY 10020
(212) 484-4000
Or online at www.adr.org

Alternatively, the parties can provide tailor-made arbitration rules either in the contract or in a separate contract document and thus eliminate the need for an arbitration association. For example, the parties could agree that each party to the contract independently will select an arbitrator and those arbitrators jointly will choose a third.

The contract also may:

- Provide for discovery and application of the rules of evidence. During formal discovery, each side unearths facts and documents from the other side that may be helpful in defending or prosecuting its case. Discovery includes depositions, interrogatories (written questions and answers), and production of documents. Usually, discovery is too expensive and time-consuming for use in matters involving smaller claims.

- Set time limits for the presentation of each party's case.

- Limit the maximum damages allowed in the arbitrator's decision and award.

Rather than develop their own dispute resolution procedures, the parties can agree to follow the procedures outlined in the federal Magnuson-Moss Warranty Act, 15 United States Code sec. 2301 et seq. (see also 16 Code of Federal Regulations sec. 107). If this procedure is unwanted, however, an alternative dispute provision clause should not be set out in the body of the contract warranty provisions because if the express warranty contains such a clause, the remodeler may be required to use the Magnuson-Moss settlement procedures. (See Chapter 4, Warranties and Disclaimers.)

> All disputes between the parties to this contract arising out of or related to any contract term(s), or any breach or alleged breach of this contract, will be decided by arbitration unless the parties mutually agree otherwise in writing.

The arbitration shall be conducted by (specify the organization or named arbitrator[s] agreed upon) in accordance with [the rules adopted by the arbitration body chosen, the rules specified below, or the alternative dispute resolution proceeding specified in the federal Magnuson-Moss Warranty Act, 15 U.S.C. §2301 et seq. (see also 16 C.F.R. §107)]. The parties reference the Magnuson-Moss Act only to provide rules of arbitration in the event of a dispute, and they specifically do not incorporate the Magnuson-Moss warranties into this contract.

The parties must file a written notice of arbitration with the other party to this contract and with (the arbitration association or arbitrator[s] chosen). The notice of arbitration may not be filed after the date that a claim based on the dispute would have been barred in a judicial proceeding by the applicable statute of limitations or repose (cessation of activity).

Either party may specifically enforce (a) a decision made under this agreement to arbitrate or (b) any valid agreement to arbitrate with additional persons, under applicable arbitration laws. The decision made by the arbitrator(s) will be final and binding, and any court with jurisdiction over the decision may enter a judgment upon the arbitrator's decision.

MEDIATION

Mediation, like arbitration, is a process whereby the conflicting parties meet voluntarily to negotiate a private and mutually satisfactory agreement aided by a neutral third party. A key difference between the two methods is that unlike an arbitrator, the mediator does not make a decision in favor of one party or the other. Instead, the mediator focuses on negotiation and problem solving. The mediator assists the parties in this process. Remodelers' mediation may follow the Construction Industry Mediation Rules of the American Arbitration Association.

If mediation has a down side, it may be that if mediation is not successful, the parties are back where they started, and they may have to resort to litigation or another form of alternative dispute resolution. For this reason the parties may want to include a provision in the contract that makes all communications during the mediation confidential to prevent their use in subsequent proceedings.

If a dispute arises between the parties relating to or arising out of any provision of this agreement or any breach or alleged breach of this contract, either party may request mediation. Either party may invoke the dispute resolution procedure of this clause by giving written notice to the other. The notice should include a brief description of the disagreement. A mediator will be selected by mutual consent of the parties. The parties agree to participate in good faith in the mediation to its conclusion as determined by the mediator. No party will be obligated to continue in the mediation if a solution has not been reached and put in writing within [number of days] of the first mediation session. The costs of mediation, including fees and expenses, shall be borne equally by the parties.

At this point, the clause might include the language from the sample arbitration clause printed above, excluding the first paragraph, and beginning with the phrase, "The arbitration shall be conducted by . . . ."

ATTORNEY'S FEES

In the United States, each party to a lawsuit generally pays their own attorney's fees, regardless of whether they win or lose their case. Thus the prevailing party in a lawsuit often ends up paying a considerable portion of their judgment award to their attorney. And, if they are defending a claim, the attorney fees and court costs will come out of their own pocket, even if they are successful in the defense. One way that remodelers can avoid paying legal expenses for valid claims and defenses is to contract for an award of attorney's fees to be paid to the prevailing party in any action arising out of the remodeling project. If the contract includes such a clause, a potential litigant will be required to factor in the cost of the other party's legal expenses if they are unsuccessful in their claim. This will place greater focus on the merits of the case and discourage "nuisance" litigation. On the other hand, some attorneys do not favor including such a clause in the contract because they fear that it will have the opposite effect and that the prospect of recovering attorneys fees will actually encourage litigation.

> If either party needs to enforce provisions of this contract or obtain redress for the violation of any provision hereof, whether by litigation, arbitration, or otherwise, the prevailing party shall be entitled to any reasonable attorney's fees, court costs, or other legal fees incurred herein in addition to any other recovery obtained in such action.

ENTIRE AGREEMENT, SEVERABILITY, JURISDICTION

This provision emphasizes that this contract supersedes all previous agreements between the parties. It also assures that if a court determines that one provision is unenforceable, the remainder of the contract will remain in effect. The sample language in this clause also designates the jurisdiction (state) whose laws will apply in the interpretation and enforcement of the contract.

> This contract (including the documents incorporated by reference) constitutes the entire agreement between the parties. It supersedes all previous or current agreements and understandings whether written or oral. This contract may be changed only by a written contract amendment signed by all parties to this contract. The contract shall be binding upon each of the parties' respective heirs, executors, administrators, successors, and assigns. However, this contract shall not be assigned without the written consent of all parties.

Each provision of this contract is separable from every other provision of the contract, and if any provision is unenforceable or revised, the remainder of the contract will remain valid and enforceable.

This contract will be governed by the law of the jurisdiction in which the property is located.

The provisions of this contract shall survive the execution and delivery of the deed and shall not be merged therein.

SPECIFICATIONS

The general specifications should be prepared as a separate document and referenced in the contract along with other documents, such as architectural plans and blueprints. Specifications describe the work to be performed (construction specifications) and the materials to be used and the manner of installation (material and product specifications). The parties to the contract should initial every page of the specifications and plans to preclude an assertion that a different page may have been substituted or to preclude a plea of ignorance in the event of a subsequent disagreement between the owner and the remodeler.

The specifications should state that they cover labor and materials for construction of an addition or alteration to a specific building, and they should include a legal description of the property as it appears in the contract (see Caption earlier in the chapter). Generally, the specifications would include the following statement: "Unless otherwise specified in the contract, the specifications are as listed" (Fig. 3.4). The list in Figure 3.4 is provided only as an example. Other necessary parts of the construction process may not be listed there, and some of the listed items may not apply to a particular project. All work should be listed and described in the specifications document. Whenever possible, the material specifications should include size, color, material, quantity, brand name, model number, and other descriptive information.

DESCRIPTION OF WORK TO BE PERFORMED

The cost of the project and the remodeler's fee will be based on the description of the work to be performed. To avoid a dispute over whether certain work may be required under the contract or may be outside of the contract and considered additional work, this clause and the contract specifications must clearly describe the work to be performed under the contract. This distinction is important because a remodeler will normally not perform additional work (and the owner cannot insist that additional work be performed) without further compensation.

The sample clause below defines the scope of the work as follows:

- Specifies what the remodeler will do and what he/she will not do
- Possibly describes the portions of the project for which each of the other parties is responsible

Figure 3.4 Items Usually Included in Specifications

- Permits and inspections
- Excavating
- Footings and foundation
- Termite treatment
- Rough framing
- Roofing
- Gutters and downspouts
- Windows
- Doors
- Plumbing
- Electrical
- Heating, ventilation, and air conditioning
- Drywall
- Ceramic tile
- Closet finish
- Interior trim
- Paneling
- Ceilings
- Painting and staining
- Finish floors
- Finish hardware
- Landscaping
- Venting
- Carpet
- Walks and driveways
- Bath fixtures
- Kitchen cabinets
- Countertops
- Kitchen appliances

- Spells out how the work is to be performed and describes the remodeler's responsibility for trade contractors

- Specifies the kind or brand of materials to be used

- Specifically identifies any unusual responsibilities that the owner may request of the remodeler and limits the remodeler's responsibilities, to wit: The remodeler's scope of work shall not include any of the following:

  - Detection, treatment, encapsulation, or removal of asbestos, lead paint, mold, or other potentially hazardous material (for a more complete discussion, see Chapter 5)

  - Correction of damage caused by termites, dry rot, or similar cause

  - Changes to existing wiring in areas undisturbed by alterations

---

CASE STUDY

In this case, Spotswood I. Quinby, Inc., promised to construct and sell to Denice a house with a finished recreation room in the basement in a fashionable section of Montgomery County, Maryland, While visiting the premises, Denice inspected the work in the recreation room and noticed that the ceiling was low. Later through his attorney, Denice wrote the builder to complain that the height of the recreation room was only six feet nine inches and that the BOCA Code (which by ordinance was the Montgomery County building code) required not less than 7 ½ feet.

The contract was silent as to the height of the recreation room. The parties were unable to resolve the problem, and Denice sued the builder, alleging in part that the finished recreation room did not conform to the county building code.

Finding for Denice, the court relied on the general rule that unless a contract provides otherwise, the applicable law is read into and becomes a part of the contract. The court concluded that compliance with the building code was an implied condition of the contract and that the builder's failure to comply with the code justified Denice's refusal to complete the deal. The court noted, however, that only a substantial noncompliance with the provisions of the building code would excuse performance.[32]

CONFORMANCE WITH PLANS AND SPECIFICATIONS; CHANGES IN WORK, PROPERTY LINES, OR MATCHING MATERIALS

Remodelers should explain in the language of the contract that their actual work may deviate somewhat (nonmaterially) from the plans and the specifications. For example, the remodeling contract should state that there is no guarantee that new materials, textures, colors, and planes will exactly duplicate the existing ones. Furthermore, remodelers may want to protect themselves from possible deviations from property lines, survey lines, and the like. These circumstances should be disclosed to the owner in conversations at the beginning of the marketing and in the negotiation process. These provisions should be included in the contract and in the certificate of acceptance, which should be signed or initialed separately by the owner, as evidence that the remodeler disclosed the possibility of deviations or inconsistencies to the owner.

EXAMPLE

Remodeling Work. The remodeling work shall be constructed to conform substantially with the plans and specifications that are set forth in the attached Exhibit(s) (include numbers and names of exhibits), the terms of which are incorporated in this contract by reference. The owner acknowledges that during the course of the work certain changes, deviations, or omissions may

---

be necessary because of (a) the requirements of governmental authorities having jurisdiction of the property, (b) suggestions and design changes made by the architect, or (c) particular conditions of the job. The owner hereby authorizes the remodeler to undertake, without the need for specific authorization, any changes, deviations, or omissions required by governmental authorities or authorized by the architect. Changes in the particular conditions of the job shall be handled in accordance with Section _____, Changes in Work and Change Orders, of this contract.

Property Lines. Owner shall locate and point out the property lines to the remodeler. When necessary, owner shall furnish, at owner's expense, all necessary surveys. Owner assumes all responsibility for the accuracy of all boundary markers.[33]

Matching Materials. The remodeler calls attention of the owner to the limitations of plaster and stucco. While the remodeler shall make every effort to blend existing textures, colors, and planes, exact duplication is not guaranteed. Roofing materials and/or the color of the roofing material may not match existing roofing because of manufacturer's discontinuance of color or product, shading difference of product, age, or changes in the product or the product's manufacturing process.[34]

4

WARRANTIES AND DISCLAIMERS

EXPRESS AND IMPLIED WARRANTIES

To a large extent, builders' and remodelers' liabilities for correcting problems after the work is completed depend on the warranties that they give to their customers. Every time builders or remodelers, their agents, and their employees make a promise to a buyer or an owner, they may be extending a warranty. This fact also applies to any representations made in advertisements, brochures, and correspondence. However, warranties do not have to be in writing; they may also be spoken or implied. An "express warranty"—a warranty in words, whether spoken or written— is treated by the courts like any other agreement. Therefore, if a builder or remodeler breaches such a warranty, that act is like breaching a contract.

In addition to express warranties, courts have found "implied warranties" in contracts to construct new homes or to remodel existing ones. Even if builders or remodelers make no specific written or oral promises about the condition of the houses or their residential remodeling projects, many courts read into the contract a promise to provide a house that is reasonably free from defects in workmanship or materials and, in the case of a new home, that is habitable. In some states, home improvement contracts may be covered by an implied warranty or a statutory express warranty. For example, the Indiana Home Improvement Warranty Act allows a remodeler to disclaim implied warranties in a home improvement contract only if the remodeler offers the owner the express warranties defined in the Act (Ind. Code §32-27-1-13). These implied warranties are dangerous because the courts—not the parties to the contract—determine what is covered by the warranties.

The warranty of habitability or fitness requires that the new home be fit for its intended use— habitation. What constitutes habitability is a difficult question to answer. At a minimum, however, a new home must:

- Substantially comply with all building and housing codes
- Keep out the elements and provide its inhabitants with a reasonably safe place to live, without fear of injury to person, health, safety, or property
- Be structurally sound, and it should include sufficient heat, ventilation, and light, adequate plumbing and sanitation (including potable water), and proper security

Under the implied warranty of workmanship, the builder warrants that the home meets the standards of quality prevailing at the time and place of construction. The builder is not required to build a perfect home. However, the courts have upheld implied warranty claims for an assortment of defects, including but not limited to shrinkage of exterior siding, cracking foundations, wet basements, leaky roofs, sagging roofs and floors, defective air conditioning and heating systems, defective tank and drain field systems, and unusable water supplies.

Numerous states now extend the implied warranties to second, third, or later owners of homes, although those warranties are limited to latent defects (not discoverable on reasonable inspection) that manifest themselves within a reasonable period of time after construction of the house. The length of time the original or subsequent buyer has to enforce the warranty varies from state to state, but a number of courts have established a standard of reasonableness. The age of the home, its maintenance, and the use to which it has been put are a few of the factors that a court considers. What is reasonable depends on the component part of the home involved. For example, a roof may be expected to have a longer useful life than a termite treatment.

Implied warranties add to the provisions of an express warranty. Thus, a builder who offers an express warranty also may be bound by the implied warranties unless the builder has properly disclaimed the implied warranties.

CASE STUDY

Ferrell built a single-family residence in 1980 and sold the residence to a private party who subsequently resold the house in 1981 to the Bridges. The original sales contract provided for a "one-year Builder's Warranty," and it was transferred to the Bridges upon resale. Shortly after the Bridges took possession, they experienced structural problems with the house and they sued Ferrell for breach of implied warranty of habitability, recovering $9,000.

Ferrell appealed on the grounds that the court erroneously instructed the jury that the implied warranty of habitability controlled over an express warranty agreed on by the parties. The Oklahoma Court of Appeals concluded that Ferrell was asking the court to instruct the jury that a written warranty agreed to by the parties for 1 year controlled over an implied warranty for a reasonable period of time. The Appeals Court rejected Ferrell's requested instruction as an incorrect statement of the law. The court held that, in the absence of an agreement to the contrary, the mere existence of an express warranty does not displace the obligations arising by operation of law under an implied warranty of habitability.[35]

In theory, because a warranty is like any other promise in a contract, a builder or remodeler should be able to write a contract disclaiming or limiting any warranties, even implied warranties. In an increasing number of states the courts have enforced contract provisions in which the parties agree to waive implied warranties. In other states, however, courts have held that (a) consumers need special protection when purchasing or remodeling their homes, which often are their most expensive investments, and (b) they must not be allowed to waive the implied warranties.

Before attempting to disclaim all implied warranties, builders and remodelers need to consider the following issues:

- The trend in the courts is toward including more items within the reach of the Magnuson-Moss Warranty Act, and if builders and remodelers offer a full express warranty they cannot limit implied warranties under the Act (see the Magnuson-Moss Act described below).

- Some courts will not uphold a contract provision that is deemed unscrupulous or unfair to the consumer.

- From a marketing perspective, some builders and remodelers have found that providing a warranty that restricts the duration of the implied warranties to the period of time covered by the express warranties makes better business sense than to eliminate all implied warranties. For example, the builder might offer the owner a 1-year builder-backed warranty and a 1-year implied warranty.

The warranty should conform to certain standards because the buyers' or owners' personal standards may differ from industry standards. If the parties do not spell out the construction standards, they run the risk of having an arbitrator or court decide for them. One source of industry standards is "Residential Construction Performance Guidelines for Professional Builders and Remodelers."[36] Alternately a builder or remodeler could develop his or her own standards.

CASE STUDY

The purchasers of a new home brought an action against the builder for breach of implied warranty of habitability. The builder argued that the purchasers waived their right to sue for breach of implied warranty of habitability by signing and initialing the agreement that provided for a homeowners' warranty in lieu of the implied warranty of habitability. The agreement provided that (a) the seller expressly disclaimed the implied warranty of habitability and (b) as a result of that disclaimer by the seller, the seller's sole warranty given to the purchaser was the homeowners' warranty. Finding for the builder, the court held that the evidence showed that the disclaimer language was brought to the purchasers' attention, that the consequences of the agreement were made known to them, and that they knowingly waived their rights to pursue an action against the builder for breach of the implied warranty of habitability.[37]

THE MAGNUSON-MOSS WARRANTY ACT

The Federal Trade Commission (FTC), a government agency, regulates warranties on consumer products under the Magnuson-Moss Warranty Act.[38] The act does not require a builder or remodeler to give a warranty. It merely regulates the form of whatever warranty a builder may voluntarily decide to give. The act applies to builder- and remodeler-backed warranties and insured warranty programs. The act states that these warranties must meet certain disclosure requirements if they are to be valid. These requirements do not apply to new or remodeled houses themselves but only to the following items that are installed or included in new or remodeled houses: appliances, manufactured equipment, and anything else defined as a consumer product under the Act.

Builders' and remodelers' warranty provisions that cover consumer products must be written according to FTC regulations.

Builders and remodelers face three choices when considering their responsibilities under the Magnuson-Moss Act:

- Give no written warranty at all, which may not be practical in many markets.

- Exclude consumer products entirely from their warranty and thereby avoid triggering the Magnuson-Moss requirements. However, builders and remodelers should keep in mind that they will be excluding an enormous variety of appliances and pieces of equipment.

- Conform their warranties to comply with Magnuson-Moss guidelines.

Because the Act applies only if a warranty covers consumer products, a warranty that excludes all consumer products from coverage is not affected by the Act. Following are examples of language that a builder or remodeler might use to exclude consumer products from his or her written warranty:

> 1. "This warranty does not cover any appliance, piece of equipment, or other item that is a consumer product for purposes of the Magnuson-Moss Warranty Act (15 U.S.C. Sec. 2301 through 2312)."
>
> 2. "This warranty does not cover any appliance, piece of equipment, or other item in the home that is a 'consumer product' for the purposes of the Magnuson-Moss Warranty Act (15 U.S.C. §2301 through 2312). The following are examples of 'consumer products,' but . . . other items in the home . . . also [may be] consumer products: (List the items from the FTC list)."

(See the discussion of limited warranty agreements excluding items covered by the Magnuson-Moss Act later in this chapter.)

The second example above offers more protection legally but may be awkward to include in a brief warranty document.[39]

Excluding appliances and pieces of equipment from a builder's or remodeler's written warranty will prevent it from being subject to the FTC's requirements regarding its form and language. However, if the warranty exclusions leave nothing covered, the FTC could consider the warranty a sham under Section 5 of the Federal Trade Commission Act, which covers "unfair and deceptive acts and practices."[40]

Because the act pertains primarily to the form of a warranty rather than to a builder's or a remodeler's obligations, the easiest solution might be to write "the entire warranty in the form required by the act, even though doing so goes beyond what the law technically requires . . . [Thus, the builder or remodeler can] provide a warranty on any appliances and pieces of equipment . . . [without deciding] precisely which are consumer products . . . something no one has been able to explain adequately in any type of language."[41]

If any part of a builder's or a remodeler's warranty is covered by Magnuson-Moss and the builder provides for alternative dispute resolution of claims, the warranty must follow the settlement procedures outlined in the Act. The Act authorizes the FTC to regulate devices under which warranty disputes between a builder and purchaser are submitted to a third party for mediation or arbitration (see Arbitration and Mediation in Chapter 2 for builders and in Chapter 3 for remodelers).

These informal devices are referred to in the Act as "informal dispute settlement mechanisms." A builder is not required to provide such a mechanism. If he or she voluntarily provides for one in his or her warranty document, however, it must meet FTC standards. These rules are complicated, and builders and remodelers are advised to review their warranty documents with their attorneys to assure that the warranty documents do not run afoul of the Act.

The Magnuson-Moss Act does not allow builders or remodelers to disclaim implied warranties on consumer products if they give a full, written warranty (see Limited Warranties later in this chapter). If builders and remodelers follow the Magnuson-Moss Act guidelines for limited warranties, they are permitted to restrict the duration of the implied warranties (unless state law does not permit the restriction). The fairly simple requirements are designed merely to make warranties more understandable to consumers. Some courts are more likely to enforce a limited warranty if it is simple, clear, and easy for a homebuyer or homeowner to understand even if the Magnuson-Moss Act does not specifically apply.

Under the FTC regulations, consumers must have access to consumer product warranties before a sale. Sellers can display the warranty near the warranted product or make it available on request. Sellers who choose to make warranties available on request must post signs to that effect, and the warranty document must include the information in Figure 4.1.

Figure 4.1 Federal Trade Regulation Requirements for Warranty Documents

- The name of the person who is receiving the warranty and whether it is transferable to subsequent purchasers.
- Precisely what the warranty covers and what is excluded.
- What the builder or the remodeler will do if a warranted defect or problem occurs and how much the consumer will be charged.
- The duration of the warranty and when it begins.
- The procedures a buyer or homeowner must follow to have a problem corrected.
- Limitations on consequential or secondary results must stand out from the rest of the document, and they must be followed by these exact words: "Some states do not allow the exclusion or limitation of incidental or consequential damages, so the above limitation or exclusion may not apply to you."
- Any limitations on the duration of implied warranty rights also must appear conspicuously in the document, along with the statement: "Some states do not allow limitations on how long an implied warranty lasts, so this limitation may not apply to you."
- A provision stating: "This warranty gives you specific legal rights, and you may also have other rights which vary from state to state."

FULL AND LIMITED WARRANTY

The language of any written warranty that a builder provides to a buyer or that a remodeler provides to a homeowner may determine the extent of the builder's or remodeler's liability. Although the language is simple, it has legal effect.

The Magnuson-Moss Act distinguishes between full and limited warranties. A full warranty must do the following:

- Provide for remedies within a reasonable time (at no charge) for consumer products with defects, malfunctions, or for failure to conform to the warranty

- Avoid imposing any limitation on the duration of implied warranties

- Conspicuously state on the document itself whether consequential damages are limited or excluded

- Permit the consumer to elect either a refund for or a free replacement of an item with a defect that cannot be repaired after a reasonable number of attempts

Any warranty that does not meet the minimum standards of a full warranty as outlined above is considered a limited warranty. A full warranty provides for replacement of the product warranted, so the consumer would receive a new one if anything goes wrong with the original product during the warranty period. Replacement of an entire house if something goes wrong with one part is preposterous, so warranties on houses are always limited warranties—providing for repair of specified items or redoing work rather than replacement.

As explained in the opening of this chapter, builders and remodelers should use a limited express warranty that restricts the duration of implied warranties. After evaluating the risks previously outlined in this chapter, builders and remodelers should consider totally disclaiming all implied warranties in those states that permit it.

The remainder of this chapter includes the following items:

- An alternative limited warranty agreement excluding items covered by the Magnuson-Moss Act (Figure 4.2 for builders and Figure 4.3 for remodelers)

- A limited warranty agreement conforming to the Magnuson-Moss Act (Figure 4.4 for either)

- A statement of nonwarrantable conditions (Figure 4.5)

Figure 4.2 Builder's Sample Limited Warranty Agreement That Excludes Items Covered by the Magnuson-Moss Act

This limited warranty agreement is extended by (builder's name), (the builder), whose address is (builder's address), to (buyer's name), (the buyer), who is the original buyer of the property at the following address:[1]

_____

_____

_____

_____

This limited warranty excludes consequential damages, limits the duration of implied warranties, and provides for liquidated damages.

1. What is Covered by the Warranty?

The builder warrants that all construction related to the house substantially conforms with the plans and specifications and change orders for this job. The builder warrants that during the first 30 days after the buyer moves in, the builder will adjust or correct minor defects, omissions, or malfunctions, such as missing equipment or hardware; sticking doors, drawers, and windows; dripping faucets; and other minor malfunctions reported by the buyer upon inspection of the property.

Within one (1) year from the date of closing or occupancy by the buyer, whichever is first, the builder will repair or replace, at the builder's option, any latent defects in material or workmanship by the standards of construction relevant in (city, state). A latent defect is defined as one which was not apparent or ascertainable at the time of occupancy. The buyer agrees to accept a reasonable match in any repair or replacement in the event the original item is no longer available.

2. What is Not Covered?

This limited warranty does not cover the following items:
  A. Damage resulting from fires, floods, storms, electrical malfunctions, accidents, or acts of God
  B. Damage from alterations, misuse, or abuse of the covered items by any person
  C. Damage resulting from the buyer's failure to observe any operating instructions furnished by the builder at the time of installation

Figure 4.2 Builder's Sample Limited Warranty Agreement That Excludes Items Covered by the Magnuson-Moss Act (Continued)

D. Damage resulting from a malfunction of equipment or lines of the telephone, gas, power, or water companies

E. Any items listed as Nonwarrantable Conditions on the list that is incorporated in this contract; the buyer acknowledges receipt of the list of Nonwarrantable Conditions _____

(buyer's initials)

F. Any item furnished or installed by the buyer

G. Any appliance, piece of equipment, or other item that is a consumer product for the purposes of the Magnuson-Moss Warranty Act, 15 United States Code §2301 et seq., installed or included in the buyer's property

The only warranties on items listed below are those that the manufacturer provides to the buyer:[2]

Appliances

Clothes dryer	Clothes washer
Dishwasher	Freezer
Garbage disposal	Ice maker
Kitchen center [a type of food processor]	Microwave
Oven and oven hood	Refrigerator
Range, stove, or cooktop	Trash compactor

Heating and Ventilation

Air conditioning	Boiler	Electronic air cleaner
Exhaust fan	Furnace	Heat pump
Humidifier	Space heater	Thermostat

Mechanical and/or Electrical

Burglar alarm	Central vacuum system	Chimes
Electric meter	Fire alarm	Fire extinguisher
Garage door opener	Gas meter	Gas or electric barbecue grill
Intercom	Smoke detector	Water meter
Water pump		

Plumbing

Garbage disposal	Sump pump	Water heater
Water softener	Whirlpool bath	

The following items are not consumer products under the Magnuson-Moss Warranty Act when sold as part of a new home:

Heating and Ventilation

Duct	Register	Radiator

Mechanical and/or Electrical

Circuit breaker	Electrical switch and outlet	Electrical panel box
Fuse	Garage door	Light fixture
Wiring		

Figure 4.2 Builder's Sample Limited Warranty Agreement That Excludes Items Covered by the Magnuson-Moss Act (Continued)

Plumbing

Bidet	Bathtub
Laundry tray	Medicine cabinet
Sink	Shower stall
Sprinkler head	Plumbing fittings (showerhead, faucet, trap, and drain)
Toilet	Vanity

Miscellaneous Items

Cabinet	Ceiling
Chimney and fireplace	Door
Fencing	Floor covering (includes carpeting, linoleum, tile, parquet)
Gutter	Shelving
Shingles	Wall or wall covering
Window	

The following separate items of equipment are not consumer products under the Magnuson-Moss Act when sold as part of a condominium, cooperative, or similar multiple-family dwelling . . . [because] they are not normally used for "personal, family, or household purposes" within the meaning of the act:

Elevator	Emergency back-up generator
Institutional trash compactor	Fusible fire door closer
Master TV antenna	TV security monitor

[If the item has a function separate and apart from the house, it is likely to be considered a consumer product (such as a water heater, stove, or refrigerator), whereas other items (such as floorboards and trusses) are not.]

(1) The builder has made any such warranties available to the buyer for the buyer's inspection and the buyer acknowledges receipt of copies of any warranties requested. _____
(buyer's initials)

(2) The builder hereby assigns (to the extent that they are assignable) and conveys to the buyer all warranties provided to the builder on any manufactured items that have been installed or included in the buyer's property. The buyer accepts this assignment and acknowledges that the builder's only responsibility relating to such items is to lend assistance to the buyer in settling any claim resulting from the installation of these products. _____ _____
(buyer's initials) (builder's initials)

3. Remedies and Limitations

   A. The buyer understands that the sole remedies under this limited warranty agreement are repair and replacement as set forth here. _____
(buyer's initials)

   B. With respect to any claim whatsoever asserted by the buyer against the builder, the buyer understands that the buyer will have no right to recover or request compensation for, and the builder shall not be liable for:
(1) Incidental, consequential, secondary, or punitive damages
(2) Damages for aggravation, mental anguish, emotional distress, or pain and suffering
(3) Attorney's fees or costs _____
(buyer's initials)

_____

Figure 4.2 Builder's Sample Limited Warranty Agreement That Excludes Items Covered by the Magnuson-Moss Act (Continued)

C. The builder hereby limits the duration of all implied warranties, including the implied warranties of habitability, and workmanlike construction to one (1) year from the date of sale or the date of occupancy, whichever comes first. _____
(buyer's initials)

D. These limitations shall be enforceable to the extent permitted by law. [Some states do not allow the exclusion or limitation of incidental or consequential damages or the limitation of implied warranties, so the limitations or exclusions listed above may not apply in a particular location.]

[Alternative to 3C]

C. The buyer understands that no implied warranties whatsoever apply to the structure of the house and items that are functionally part of the house. The builder disclaims any implied warranties, including (but not limited to) warranties of habitability, workmanship, and materials to the extent allowed by law, and any implied warranty that exists despite this disclaimer is limited to a period of one (1) year. These limitations shall be enforceable to the extent permitted by the law. Some states do not allow limitations on how long an implied warranty lasts, so this limitation may not apply. _____
(buyer's initials)

   [The buyer acknowledges acceptance of these limitations on the warranties offered by the builder in consideration for the limited warranty and the other provisions of the construction contract.]

D. Notwithstanding the provisions of this limited warranty agreement, if any liability arises on the part of the builder, the builder will pay the amount of actual provable damages arising from such liability, but the amount shall not exceed $_____. This amount, fixed as liquidated damages and not as a penalty, shall be the builder's complete and exclusive amount of liability. The provisions of this paragraph apply if loss or damage results directly or indirectly to persons or property from the performance of, or failure to perform, obligations imposed by the construction contract or from negligence, active or otherwise, of the builder, the builder's agents, or employees.

   The buyer (a) understands that this provision limits the damages for which the builder will be liable and (b) acknowledges acceptance of this liquidated damages provision in consideration for the limited warranties provided by the builder and the other provisions of the construction contract. Therefore the buyer agrees to this liquidated damages clause if, notwithstanding the provisions of this limited warranty, liability should arise on the part of the builder.

E. This warranty is personal to the original buyer and does not run with the property or the items contained in the house. The original buyer may not assign, transfer, or convey this warranty without the prior written consent of the builder. _____
(buyer's initials)

4. How to Obtain Service

If a problem develops during the warranty period, the buyer should notify the builder in writing at the address given above of the specific problem. The written statement of the problem should include the buyer's name, address, telephone number, and a description of the nature of the problem. The builder will begin performing the obligations under this warranty within a reasonable time of the builder's receipt of such a request and will diligently pursue these obligations.

_____

Figure 4.2 Builder's Sample Limited Warranty Agreement That Excludes Items Covered by the Magnuson-Moss Act (Continued)

Repair work will be done during the builder's normal working hours except where delay will cause additional damage. The buyer agrees to provide the builder or builder's representative access to the house. The buyer also agrees to provide the presence (during the work) of a responsible adult with the authority to approve the repair and sign an acceptance of repair ticket upon completion of the repair.

5. Specific Legal Rights
This limited warranty gives the buyer specific legal rights, and the buyer may also have other rights that vary from state to state.

6. Where to Get Help
If the buyer wants help or information concerning this warranty, the buyer should contact the builder.

7. The Only Warranty Given by the Builder
The buyer acknowledges (a) that [he or she] has thoroughly examined the property to be conveyed, (b) the buyer has read and understands the limited warranty, and (c) the builder has made no guarantees, warranties, understandings, nor representations (nor have any been made by any representatives of the builder) that are not set forth in this document.

I acknowledge having read, understood, and received a copy of this limited warranty agreement.

_____   _____
(buyer)   (builder)
Date _____   By _____
                                        Title _____
                                        Date _____

1. This form is designed for a single buyer. If more than one buyer is involved, the form should be adapted to accommodate the initials and signature of each of the buyers.
2. Warning—This list is not exclusive.

Figure 4.3 Remodeler's Sample Limited Warranty Agreement That Excludes Items Covered by the Magnuson-Moss Act

This limited warranty agreement is extended by (remodeler's name) (the remodeler), whose address is (remodeler's address), to (owner's name) (the owner) of the property at the following address (house):[1]

_____

_____

_____

_____

This limited warranty excludes consequential damages, limits the duration of implied warranties, and provides for liquidated damages.

Figure 4.3 Remodeler's Sample Limited Warranty Agreement That Excludes Items Covered by the Magnuson-Moss Act (Continued)

1. What is Covered by the Warranty?

The remodeler warrants that all construction related to the [remodeling, renovation, rehabilitation, restoration, or addition] substantially conforms with the plans and specifications and change orders for this job. The remodeler warrants that during the first thirty (30) days after the owner occupies the remodeled space, the remodeler will adjust or correct minor defects, omissions, or malfunctions, such as missing equipment or hardware; sticking doors, drawers, and windows; dripping faucets; and other minor malfunctions reported by the owner upon inspection of the [remodeled, renovated, rehabilitated, restored, or added] space.

Within one (1) year from the date of substantial completion or use of the [remodeled, renovated, rehabilitated, restored, or added] space by the owner, whichever is first, the remodeler will repair or replace, at the remodeler's option, any latent defects in material or workmanship by the standards of construction relevant in (city, state). A latent defect is defined as one which was not apparent or ascertainable at the time of occupancy. The owner agrees to accept a reasonable match in any repair or replacement in the event the original item is no longer available.

2. What is Not Covered

This limited warranty does not cover the following items:

    A. Damage resulting from fires, floods, storms, electrical malfunctions, accidents, or acts of God

    B. Damage from alterations, misuse, or abuse of the covered items by any person

    C. Damage resulting from the owner's failure to observe any operating instructions furnished by the remodeler at the time of installation

    D. Damage resulting from a malfunction of equipment or lines of the telephone, gas, power, or water companies

    E. Any items listed as nonwarrantable conditions on the list that is incorporated into this contract (The owner acknowledges receipt of the list of nonwarrantable conditions.) _____

                                (owner's initials)

    F. Any item furnished or installed by the owner

    G. Any appliance, piece of equipment, or other item that is a consumer product for the purposes of the Magnuson-Moss Warranty Act, 15 United States Code §2301 et seq., installed or included in the owner's property

The only warranties of items listed below are those that the manufacturer provides to the owner:[3]

Appliances

Clothes dryer	Clothes washer
Dishwasher	Freezer
Garbage disposal	Ice maker
Kitchen center (a type of food processor)	Microwave
Oven and oven hood	Refrigerator
Range, stove, or cooktop	Trash compactor

Heating and Ventilation

Air conditioning	Boiler	Electronic air cleaner
Exhaust fan	Furnace	Heat pump
Humidifier	Space heater	Thermostat

Figure 4.3 Remodeler's Sample Limited Warranty Agreement That Excludes Items Covered by the Magnuson-Moss Act (Continued)

Mechanical and/or Electrical

Burglar alarm	Central vacuum system	Chimes
Electric meter	Fire alarm	Fire extinguisher
Garage door opener	Gas meter	Gas or electric barbecue grill
Intercom	Smoke detector	Water meter
Water pump		

Plumbing

Garbage disposal	Sump pump	Water heater
Water softener	Whirlpool bath[2]	

The following items are not consumer products under the Magnuson-Moss Warranty Act when sold as part of a new home:

Heating and Ventilation

Duct	Register	Radiator

Mechanical and/or Electrical

Circuit breaker	Electrical switch and outlet	Electrical panel box
Fuse	Garage door	Light fixture
Wiring		

Plumbing

Bidet	Bathtub
Medicine cabinet	Sink
Shower stall	Sprinkler head
Plumbing fittings (showerhead, faucet, trap, escutcheon [flange around a pipe or fitting], and drain)	Toilet
	Vanity

Miscellaneous Items

Cabinet	Ceiling
Chimney and fireplace	Door
Fencing	Floor covering (includes carpeting, linoleum, tile, parquet)
Gutter	Shelving
Shingles	Wall or wall covering
Window	

The following separate items of equipment are not consumer products under the Magnuson-Moss Act when sold as part of a condominium, cooperative, or similar multiple-family dwelling. . .[because] they are not normally used for "personal, family, or household purposes" within the meaning of the act:

Elevator	Emergency back-up generator	Institutional trash compactor
Fusible fire door closer	Master TV antenna	TV security monitor

  (1) The remodeler has made any such warranties available to the owner for the owner's inspection and the owner acknowledges receipt of copies of any warranties requested. _____

(owner's initials)

Figure 4.3 Remodeler's Sample Limited Warranty Agreement That Excludes Items Covered by the Magnuson-Moss Act (Continued)

(2) The remodeler hereby assigns (to the extent that they are assignable) and conveys to the owner all warranties provided to the remodeler on any manufactured items that have been installed or included in the owner's property. The owner accepts this assignment and acknowledges that the remodeler's only responsibility relating to such items is to lend assistance to the owner in settling any claim resulting from the installation of these products. _____ _____

(owner's initials) (remodeler's initials)

3. Remedies and Limitations

   A. The owner understands that the sole remedies under this limited warranty agreement are repair and replacement as set forth here. _____

(owner's initials)

   B. With respect to any claim whatsoever asserted by the owner against the remodeler, the owner understands that the owner will have no right to recover or request compensation for, and the remodeler shall not be liable for, any of the following items:

   (1) Incidental, consequential, secondary, or punitive damages

   (2) Damages for aggravation, mental anguish, emotional distress, or pain and suffering

   (3) Attorney's fees or costs _____

(owner's initials)

   C. The remodeler hereby limits the duration of all implied warranties, including the warranties of workmanship and materials to one (1) year from the date of sale or the date of substantial completion, whichever comes first. _____

(owner's initials)

   D. These limitations shall be enforceable to the extent permitted by law. Some states do not allow the exclusion or limitation of incidental or consequential damages or the limitation of implied warranties, so the limitations or exclusions listed above may not apply.

[Alternative to 3C]

   C. The owner understands that no implied warranties whatsoever apply to the structure of the [remodeling, renovation, rehabilitation, or restoration of or addition to] house and items that are functionally part of the [remodeling, renovation, rehabilitation, or restoration of or addition to] house. The remodeler disclaims any implied warranties, including (but not limited to) warranties of workmanship and materials to the extent allowed by law, and any implied warranty that exists despite this disclaimer is limited to a period of one (1) year. These limitations shall be enforceable to the extent permitted by the law. Some states do not allow limitations on how long an implied warranty lasts, so this limitation may not apply. _____

(owner's initials)

   [The owner acknowledges acceptance of these limitations on the warranties offered by the remodeler in consideration for this limited warranty and the other provisions of the construction contract. Therefore the owner agrees to these limitations if, notwithstanding the provisions of the limited warranty, liability should arise on the part of the remodeler.

Figure 4.3 Remodeler's Sample Limited Warranty Agreement That Excludes Items Covered by the Magnuson-Moss Act (Continued)

D. Notwithstanding the provisions of this limited warranty agreement, if any liability arises on the part of the remodeler, the remodeler will pay the amount of actual provable damages arising from such liability, but the amount shall not exceed $_____. This amount, fixed as liquidated damages and not as a penalty, shall be the remodeler's complete and exclusive amount of liability. The provisions of this paragraph apply if loss or damage results directly or indirectly to persons or property from the meeting or failing to meet the obligations imposed by the construction contract or from negligence, active or otherwise, of the remodeler, the remodeler's agents, or employees

    The owner (a) understands that this provision limits the damages for which the remodeler will be liable and (b) acknowledges acceptance of this liquidated damages provision in consideration for the limited warranties provided by the remodeler and the other provisions of the construction contract. Therefore the owner agrees to this liquidated damages clause if, notwithstanding the provisions of this limited warranty, liability should arise on the part of the remodeler.

_____
(owner's initials)

E. This warranty is personal to the original owner of the [remodeling, renovation, rehabilitation, or restoration of or addition to] house and does not run with the property, the [remodeling, renovation, or rehabilitation of or addition to] house, or with the items contained in the house. The original owner may not assign, transfer, or convey this warranty without the prior written consent of the remodeler.

4. How to Obtain Service

If a problem develops during the warranty period, the owner should notify the remodeler in writing at the address given above of the specific problem. The written statement of the problem should include the owner's name, address, telephone number, and a description of the nature of the problem. The remodeler will begin performing the obligations under this warranty within a reasonable time of the remodeler's receipt of such a request and will diligently pursue these obligations.

    Repair work will be done during the remodeler's normal working hours except where delay will cause additional damage. The owner agrees to provide the remodeler or remodeler's representative access to the house and to make available during the work a responsible adult with the authority to approve the repair and sign an acceptance of repair ticket upon completion of the repair.

5. Specific Legal Rights

This limited warranty gives the owner specific legal rights, and the owner may also have other rights that vary from state to state.

6. Where to Get Help

If the owner wants help or information concerning this warranty, the owner should contact the remodeler.

7. The Only Warranty Given by the Remodeler

The owner acknowledges (a) that the owner has thoroughly examined the [remodeling, renovation, rehabilitation, or restoration of or addition to] house that is to be conveyed, (b) the buyer has read and understands the limited warranty, and (c) the remodeler has made no guarantees, warranties, understandings, or representations (nor have any been made by any representatives of the remodeler) that are not set forth in this document.

Figure 4.3 Remodeler's Sample Limited Warranty Agreement That Excludes Items Covered by the Magnuson-Moss Act (Continued)

I acknowledge having read, understood, and received a copy of this limited warranty agreement.

_____	_____
(owner)	(remodeler)
Date _____	By _____
	Title _____
	Date _____

1. This form is designed for a single owner. If more than one owner is involved, it should be adapted to accommodate the initials and signature of each of the owners.
2. Remodelers should exclude from this list any items that are not applicable to the job for which the warranty is being provided. For instance, if the job did not involve any kitchen appliances, the remodeler need not include them in the list.
3. Warning—This list is not exclusive.

Figure 4.4 Sample Limited Warranty Agreement Conforming to the Magnuson-Moss Act for Builders or Remodelers

Warning—This warranty form must be adapted to conform to applicable state law. This form is only one possible form of warranty conforming to the Magnuson-Moss Act. Builders and remodelers should consult their attorneys for a more complete discussion of a builder's and a remodeler's duties under the act and alternative language. Other language may provide more complete protection for a builder and a remodeler than is included here.

1. Consequential and Incidental Damages
Consequential and incidental damages are excluded, and the implied warranties are limited in duration.

2. Term
The terms of the various coverages of this warranty begin on—
   [For Builders—The date of final settlement or the date when the buyer first occupies the home, whichever comes first]
   [For Remodelers—The date of substantial completion (which is the date when the [remodeling, renovation, rehabilitation, or restoration of or addition to] renders the house usable for the purpose(s) for which the work was intended)]

3. Coverage
The [builder or remodeler] warrants that by the standards of construction relevant in (city, state) for a period of one (1) year—
   A. The floors, ceilings, walls, and other internal structural components of the [home or remodeling, renovation, rehabilitation, or restoration of or addition to the home] that are not covered by other portions of this limited warranty will be free of defects in materials or workmanship.
   B. The plumbing, heating, and electric wiring systems, and the septic tank (if the [builder or remodeler] installed it), will be free of defects in materials or workmanship.

Figure 4.4 Sample Limited Warranty Agreement Conforming to the Magnuson-Moss Act for Builders or Remodelers (Continued)

C. The roof will be free of leaks caused by defects in materials or workmanship.

The [builder or remodeler] warrants that by the standards of construction relevant in (city, state) for a period of 60 days that the following items will be free of defects in materials or workmanship: doors (including hardware); windows; jalousies; electric switches, receptacles, and fixtures; caulking around exterior openings; plumbing figures; and cabinet work.

4. Manufacturers' Warranties

The [builder or remodeler] assigns and passes through to the [buyer or owner] (to the extent they are assignable) the manufacturers' warranties on all appliances and equipment. The following items are examples of such appliances and equipment, although not every [house or remodeling, renovation, rehabilitation, or restoration of or addition to a house] includes all of these items and some [homes or remodelings, renovations, rehabilitations, or restorations of or additions to] may include appliances or equipment not in this list: refrigerator, range, furnace or heat pump, washing machine, dishwasher, garbage disposal, ventilating fan, air conditioner.

5. Exclusions from Coverage

The [builder or remodeler] does not assume responsibility for any of the following, all of which are excluded from the coverage of this limited warranty:

A. Consequential or incidental damages (Some states do not allow the exclusion or limitation of incidental or consequential damages, so the limitation or exclusion may not apply to you.)

B. Defects in appliances and equipment that are covered by manufacturers' warranties (The [builder or remodeler] has assigned these manufacturers' warranties to the [buyer or owner] to the extent they are assignable. If defects appear in these items, the [buyer or owner] should follow the procedures in these warranties.)

C. Damage resulting from ordinary wear and tear, abusive use, or lack of proper maintenance of the [house or the remodeling, renovation, rehabilitation, or restoration of or additions to the house]

D. Defects that result from characteristics common to the materials used, such as (but not limited to) warping and deflection of wood; fading, chalking, and checking of paint from exposure to sunlight; cracks that occurred in the drying and curing of concrete, stucco, plaster, bricks, and masonry; drying, shrinking, and cracking of caulking and weather stripping

E. Defects in items installed by the [buyer or owner] or anyone other than the [builder or remodeler] or, if requested by the [builder or remodeler], by the [builder's or remodeler's] subcontractors

F. Work done by the [buyer or owner] or anyone other than the [builder or remodeler] or, if requested by the [builder or remodeler], by the [builder's or remodeler's] subcontractors

G. Loss or injury attributable to the elements

H. Conditions resulting from condensation on, expansion of, or contraction of materials

I. Paint applied over newly plastered interior walls

6. No Other Warranties

This limited warranty is the only express warranty the remodeler gives. Implied warranties, including (but not limited to) warranties of merchantability, fitness for a particular purpose, habitability, and good workmanship are limited to the warranty period (term) set forth above. Some states do not allow limitations on how long an implied warranty lasts, so this limitation may not apply to you. This limited warranty gives you specific legal rights, and you may have other rights that vary from state to state.[3]

Figure 4.4 Sample Limited Warranty Agreement Conforming to the Magnuson-Moss Act for Builders or Remodelers (Continued)

7. Claims Procedure

If a defect appears that the [buyer or owner] thinks is covered by this limited warranty, the [buyer or owner] must write a letter describing it to the [builder or remodeler] and send it to the [builder or remodeler] at the [builder's or remodeler's] office address given below:

Customer Service Representative _____

Company _____

Street _____

City, state, zip _____

Emergency phone number (_____)_____

The [buyer or owner] must tell the [builder or remodeler] in writing what times during the day that the [buyer or owner] will be at home, so that the [builder or remodeler] can schedule service calls appropriately. If a delay will cause extra damage (for instance, a pipe has burst), the [buyer or owner] should telephone the builder. Only emergency reports will be taken by phone. Failure to notify the [builder or remodeler] of defects covered under this limited warranty or any implied warranties relieves the [builder or remodeler] of all liability for replacement, repair, and all other damages.

8. Repairs

Upon receipt of the [buyer's or owner's] written report of a defect, if the defective item is covered by this warranty, the [builder or remodeler] will repair or replace it at no charge to the [buyer or owner] within sixty (60) days (longer if weather conditions, labor problems, or material shortages cause delays). The work will be done by the [builder or remodeler] or subcontractors chosen by the [builder or remodeler]. The [builder or remodeler] has sole discretion to choose between repair or replacement.[4]

9. Not Transferable

[For Builders—This limited warranty is extended to the buyer only if the buyer is the first purchaser of the home. When the first purchaser sells the home or moves out of it, this limited warranty automatically terminates. It is not transferable to subsequent purchasers of the home nor to the first purchaser's tenants.

[For Remodelers—This limited warranty is extended to the owner only if the owner continues to own and live in this house after it is [remodeled, renovated, rehabilitated, restored, or added to] by (remodeler's name). When the owner sells the home or moves out of it, this limited warranty automatically terminates. It is not transferable to subsequent purchasers of the home nor to the owner's tenants. _____   _____

               (buyer or owner)   (builder or remodeler)

Date _____   By _____

                                          Title _____

                                          Date _____

1. This form is designed for a single buyer or owner. If more than one buyer or owner is involved, the form should be adapted to accommodate the initials and signature of each of the buyers or owners.
2. Builders and remodelers should consult Section 6C, Statement of Nonwarrantable Conditions, for further exclusions to be included here.

Figure 4.4 Sample Limited Warranty Agreement Conforming to the Magnuson-Moss Act for Builders or Remodelers (Continued)

3. This limitation of implied warranties applies to only implied warranties on consumer products. If it is allowed by state law, builders or remodelers can still exclude or disclaim all implied warranties on the house itself; on the remodeling, renovation, rehabilitation, or restoration of or addition to the house; and on any other items not considered consumer products under the act.
4. Although builders and remodelers should have a written policy for dealing with emergencies, they probably do not want to include it in their contracts or warranties if they do not define emergencies and response time in a brief statement related to matters affecting health and safety. However, buyers will interpret it to suit themselves.

Figure 4.5 Sample Statement of Nonwarrantable Conditions

This statement of conditions that are not subject to the [builder's or remodeler's] warranties explains some of the changes and need for maintenance that may occur in a [new house or a house that is remodeled, renovated, rehabilitated, or restored or added to] over the first year or so of occupancy. A house requires more maintenance and care than most products because it is made of many different components, each with its own special characteristics.

The [buyer or owner][1] understands that like other products made by humans, a [house or a house that is remodeled, renovated, rehabilitated, restored, or added to] is not perfect. It will show some minor flaws and unforeseeable defects and may require some adjustments and touching up.

As described in the limited warranty provided to the [buyer or owner] of which this statement of Nonwarrantable Conditions is made a part, the [builder or remodeler] will correct certain defects that arise during defined time periods after construction is completed. Other items that are not covered by the [builder's or remodeler's] warranty may be covered by manufacturers' warranties.

Some conditions, including (but not limited to) those listed in this statement of nonwarrantable conditions, are not covered under the [builder's or remodeler's] warranties. The [buyer or owner] should read these carefully and understand that the [buyer or owner] has not contracted for the [builder or remodeler] to correct certain types of problems that may occur in [the buyer's house or the owner's remodeled, renovated, rehabilitated, restored, or added space]. These guidelines will alert the [buyer or owner] to certain types of maintenance (a) that are the responsibility of the [buyer or owner] and (b) that could lead to problems if they are neglected.

The following list outlines some of the conditions that are not warranted by the [builder or remodeler]. The [buyer or owner] should be sure to understand this list. If the [buyer or owner] has any questions, [he or she] should ask the [builder or remodeler] and feel free to consult an attorney before signing the acknowledgment.

[Of the items listed and discussed below, remodelers might want to include only those that pertain to a particular job in the warranty for that job because many of the items would not apply to every job.]

1. Concrete
Concrete foundations, steps, walks, drives, and patios can develop cracks that do not affect the structural integrity of the building. These cracks are caused by characteristics of the concrete itself. No reasonable method of eliminating these cracks exists. This condition does not affect the strength of the building.

Figure 4.5 Sample Statement of Nonwarrantable Conditions (Continued)

2. Masonry and Mortar

Masonry and mortar can develop cracks from shrinkage of either the mortar or the brick. This condition is normal and should not be considered a defect.

3. Wood

Wood will sometimes check or crack, or the fibers will spread apart because of the drying-out process. This condition is most often caused by the heat inside the house or by exposure to the sun on the outside of the house. This condition is considered normal, and the homeowner is responsible for any maintenance or repairs resulting from it.

4. Sheetrock and Drywall

Sheetrock or drywall will sometimes develop nail pops or settlement cracks, which are a normal part of the drying-out process. These items can easily be handled by the homeowner with spackling during normal redecorating. If the homeowner wishes, however, the [builder or remodeler] will send a worker at the end of one (1) year to make the necessary repairs. The [builder's or remodeler's] repairs will not include repainting.

5. Floor Squeaks

After extensive research and writing on the subject, technical experts have concluded that much has been tried but that little can be done about floor squeaks. Generally floor squeaks will appear and disappear over time with changes in the weather and other phenomena.

6. Floors

Floors are not warranted for damage caused by neglect or the incidents of use. Wood, tile, and carpet all require maintenance. Floor casters are recommended to prevent scratching or chipping of wood or tile, and stains should be cleaned from carpets, wood, or tile immediately to prevent discoloration. Carpet has a tendency to loosen in damp weather and will stretch tight again in dryer weather.

7. Caulking

Exterior caulking and interior caulking in bathtubs, shower stalls, and ceramic tile surfaces will crack or bleed somewhat in the months after installation. These conditions are normal and should not be considered a problem. Any maintenance or repairs resulting from them are the homeowner's responsibility.

8. Bricks Discoloration

Bricks may discolor because of the elements, rain run-off, weathering, or bleaching. Efflorescence— the formation of salts on the surface of brick walls—may occur because of the passage of moisture through the wall. Efflorescence is a common occurrence, and the homeowner can clean these areas as the phenomenon occurs.

9. Broken Glass

Any broken glass or mirrors that are not noted by the [buyer or owner] on the final inspection form are the responsibility of the [buyer or owner].

10. Frozen Pipes

The [buyer or owner] must take precautions to prevent freezing of pipes and sillcocks during cold weather, such as removing outside hoses from sillcocks, leaving faucets with a slight drip, and turning off the water system if the house is to be left for extended periods during cold weather.

Figure 4.5 Sample Statement of Nonwarrantable Conditions (Continued)

11. Stained Wood

All items that are stained will normally have a variation of colors because of the different textures of the woods. Because of changes in weather, doors that have panels sometimes dry out and leave a small space of bare wood, which the homeowner can easily touch up. These normal conditions should not be considered defects.

12. Paint

Good-quality paint has been used internally and externally on this home. Nevertheless, exterior paint can sometimes crack or check. The source of this defect is most often something other than the paint. To avoid problems with the paint, [buyers or owners] should avoid allowing lawn sprinklers to hit painted areas, washing down painted areas, and so on. [Buyers or owners] should also not scrub latex-painted inside walls and should be careful of newly painted walls as they move furniture. The best paint will be stained or chipped if it is not cared for properly. Any defects in painting that are not noted at final inspection are the [buyer's or owner's] responsibility.

13. Cosmetic Items

The [buyer or owner] has not contracted with the [builder or remodeler] to cover ordinary wear and tear or other occurrences subsequent to construction that affect the condition of features in the home. Chips, scratches, or mars in tile, woodwork, walls, porcelain, brick, mirrors, plumbing fixtures, marble and Formica tops, lighting fixtures, kitchen and other appliances, doors, paneling, siding, screens, windows, carpet, vinyl floors, cabinets, and the like that are not recognized and noted by the [buyer or owner] at the final inspection are nonwarrantable conditions, and the upkeep of any cosmetic aspect of the [house or the remodeled, renovated, rehabilitated, restored, or added space] is the [buyer's or owner's] responsibility.

14. Plumbing

Dripping faucets, toilet adjustments, and toilet seats are covered by the [builder's or remodeler's] warranty for a _____-day (_____) period only. After that, they are the [buyer's or owner's] responsibility. If the plumbing is stopped up during the warranty period and the person servicing the plumbing finds foreign materials in the line, the [buyer or owner] will be billed for the call.

15. Alterations to Grading

The [buyer's or owner's] lot has been graded to ensure proper drainage away from [the home or the remodeled, renovated, rehabilitated, restored, or added space]. Should the [buyer or owner] want to change the drainage pattern because of landscaping, installation of patio or service walks, or other reasons, the [buyer or owner] should be sure to retain a proper drainage slope. The [builder or remodeler] assumes no responsibility for the grading or subsequent flooding or stagnant pool formation if the established pattern is altered.

16. Lawn and Shrubs

The [builder or remodeler] accepts no responsibility for the growth of grass or shrubs. Once the [builder or remodeler] grades, seeds and/or sods, and fertilizes the yard, the [buyer or owner] must water the plants and grass sufficiently, and plant ground cover where necessary to prevent erosion. The builder will not regrade a yard, nor remove or replace any shrubs or trees, except for those that are noted as diseased at final inspection.

Figure 4.5 Sample Statement of Nonwarrantable Conditions (Continued)

17. Roof

During the first year the warranty on the [buyer's roof or the roof of an owner's addition] is for workmanship and materials. After that the warranty on the roof is for materials only and is prorated over the period of the lifetime use of the roof. Warranty claims for any defects in materials will be handled with the manufacturer with the builder's or remodeler's assistance. The builder or remodeler will not be responsible for any damages caused by walking on the roof or by installing a television antenna or other item on the roof.

18. Heating and Air Conditioning

The [buyer's or owner's] source of heating and air conditioning is covered by a manufacturer's warranty. The buyer is responsible for making sure the filters are kept clean and changed every thirty (30) days. Failure to do so may void the warranty. Having the equipment serviced or checked at least yearly is a good idea.

19. Indoor Air Quality

[An appropriate disclaimer and warning regarding possible indoor air quality problems, including radon, should be inserted here by the builder or remodeler (see Chapter 5).]

    I acknowledge having read and understood and received a copy of the outline above of nonwarrantable items. I understand and agree that these are conditions for which we have not contracted and for which I will not hold the builder liable.

_____   _____

(buyer or owner)   (builder or remodeler)

Date _____   By _____

                                   Title _____

                                   Date _____

   1. This form is designed for a single buyer or owner. If more than one buyer or owner is involved, the form should be adapted to accommodate the initials and signature of each of the buyers or owners.

    For additional information, to write better warranties, and to better understand your obligations under express, limited, and implied warranties, builders and remodelers are invited to consult the two warranty and disclaimer handbooks by David S. Jaffe (_Warranties and Disclaimers for Remodelers_[42] and _Warranties and Disclaimers for Builders_[43]).

NOTICE AND OPPORTUNITY TO CURE

Builders and remodelers provide express warranties because they stand behind their work. They want the customer to be satisfied, and in the event that there should be any problems with workmanship or materials, the warranty provides a means for resolution through replacement or repair. But what about the homeowner who decides that he or she wants another contractor to make repairs at the expense of the original builder or remodeler? And what about the homeowner who never even informs the original contractor that there is a problem? The only notice that the original contractor may receive is a letter (or lawsuit) from an attorney demanding money damages. These problems do arise. In response to these inequitable circumstances, and with the aim providing for the resolution of warranty claims short of litigation (thereby avoiding considerable legal expense and increased insurance rates), several states have enacted (15 to date[44]) and a number more have proposed legislation to require notice to the contractor and an opportunity to repair construction defects. The specifics of the legislation can vary from state to state, but the majority of the laws generally require a homeowner to give the original contractor notice of the problem and then give the builder or remodeler the right to cure the defect within a certain time frame before litigation can be filed. Please note: Some of these acts apply only to new home construction and may not be applicable to remodeling.

In those states that have not enacted applicable notice and opportunity to repair legislation, the builder or remodeler may wish to include language in the contract or warranty that provides rights and responsibilities similar to the legislative protections. An example of a notice and opportunity to repair contract provision can be found in Figure 4.6.

Builders and remodelers should not use the warranty provisions in this book without consulting an attorney experienced in building industry warranties and revising them to fit the facts of each situation. Builders and remodelers should study the preceding portion of this chapter to better understand the significance of the language contained in these limited warranties. They also should coordinate the warranties they use with specific sections of their contracts to avoid conflicting terms and provisions.

Builders and remodelers who participate in insured warranty programs should redraft the sample language presented in this chapter or disregard it to avoid conflict with their insured warranty programs.

Figure 4.6 Notice and Opportunity to Repair Contract Provision

---

The parties agree to be bound by the following procedure in the resolution of any construction defect claim for which the owner contends the contractor should be liable or responsible under any express warranty provision, under any statutory warranty requirement, under any implied warranty, including an implied warranty of habitability or an implied warranty of workmanlike construction, under any allegation of negligence, misrepresentation or fraud, or under any other asserted grounds.

1. The owner shall serve the contractor with a written notice of any asserted construction defect and shall specify the nature of the asserted defect. Any additions or modifications to the description of the asserted defect(s) shall require the service of an additional written notice, as provided herein.

Figure 4.6 Notice and Opportunity to Repair Contract Provision (Continued)

2. Upon service of the written notice, the owner shall provide the contractor with reasonable and timely access to the premises for inspection of the asserted defect(s). Inspection shall be undertaken not more than ___(___) days from the date of service. The contractor shall respond to the owner in writing not more than ___(___) days from the date of inspection. The contractor's written response shall include either an offer to remedy or repair the asserted defect, and/or an offer to settle the claim by monetary payment, or a denial of liability or responsibility for the asserted claim. The failure of the contractor to inspect and/or respond as provided herein, or the denial by the contractor of liability or responsibility, shall permit the owner to take immediate action to arbitrate any asserted construction defect claim set forth in the written notice, or in the absence of a mandatory arbitration agreement, to litigate the aforesaid claim.

3. The owner agrees to accept any reasonable offer made by the contractor to remedy, repair, and/or to pay such monetary damages as may be proximately caused by the construction defect. If any consequential damages are excluded under the provisions of an express limited warranty provided under this contract, then the "monetary damages," described above, shall not include payment of those excluded consequential damages. The failure of the owner to accept a reasonable offer made by the contractor shall limit any recovery by the owner to the express terms of the contractor's reasonable offer. Upon acceptance by the owner, the contractor shall have ___(___) days to comply with the terms of the accepted offer.

4. The owner agrees to take no action to initiate arbitration and/or agrees not to file suit in any court of law against the contractor pertaining to any construction defect claim unless and until the above-stated procedures have been followed and the prescribed time periods have expired without resolution as provided herein. Failure to adhere to these procedures and the prescribed time periods shall serve as grounds for summary dismissal, without prejudice, of any arbitration proceeding or lawsuit filed by the owner against the contractor pertaining to any construction defect claim.

5. Any applicable statute of limitations shall be tolled for the period of time necessary to comply with the procedures and prescribed time periods set forth above. The remainder of the applicable statute of limitations period, if any, shall resume its run upon completion of the repairs in question. The parties specifically agree that these repairs shall not serve to start an entirely new statute of limitations or warranty period; only the remainder of the original statute of limitations or warranty period will be in effect upon completion of repairs. It is specifically agreed that any and all efforts by the contractor to remedy or repair any asserted construction defect shall not operate to extend (except as provided herein) any applicable statute of limitations, shall not cause a new statute of limitations period to commence from the date of any repair, and shall not cause a new statute of limitations to commence or be created on account of any remedy or repair effort. It is specifically agreed that any and all efforts by the contractor to remedy or repair any asserted construction defect shall not operate to extend (except as provided herein) any existing warranty period, and shall not operate to create a new period of warranty.

6. It shall be a sufficient service of any written notice or response required herein if the same is made by first class mail at the following respective addresses:

   (a) Contractor _____

   (b) Owner _____

ENVIRONMENTAL CLAUSES AND LIABILITY ISSUES

SPECULATIVE BUILDERS, CUSTOM BUILDERS, and remodelers face several kinds of potential liability for environmental conditions. These liabilities include hazards to the general public, to employees, and to individual buyers or occupants. This chapter discusses these liability issues and the contract provisions designed to reduce environmental liability exposure. The hazardous substance laws of the federal and state governments cover a wide range of chemicals and pollutants. Failure to comply with the applicable laws can result in severe penalties. The major environmental liability issues of concern to builders and remodelers currently include exposure to mold, radon, asbestos, lead, and arsenic, but there are many other toxic substances that can adversely affect health and safety.

HAZARDOUS WASTE LIABILITY

BUILDERS AND DEVELOPERS BUYING PROPERTY

The Comprehensive Environmental Response, Compensation, and Liability Act (CERCLA). Commonly referred to as Superfund, this Act authorizes the federal government to require any "potentially responsible party" (PRP) (this includes the current owner or operator of a contaminated site; any person who operated a facility on site or who owned the site at a time when the toxic substance was deposited or was present; any person who created the toxic substance or who deposited the toxic substance on the site; and any person who selected the site for the deposit, treatment, or disposal of the toxic substance) to pay for the entire clean-up cost resulting from the release or threatened release of hazardous substances into the environment. Any one of the parties listed may be held liable regardless of their lack of knowledge, their degree of negligence, their contribution to the total contamination, and their compliance with laws in effect at the time of disposal.

CERCLA does have some exclusions and defenses. Persons who acquire property through inheritance or bequest are exempt from liability. Petroleum, including crude oil and natural gas, is exempt but can be a source of liability under other statutes. Naturally occurring substances are exempt, but if released by "unnatural" processes it may fall outside of the exclusion. There are defenses for acts of God, acts of war, a contiguous property defense, and a defense based on the unauthorized acts of third parties. There is also an innocent purchaser or landowner defense that may apply if the property was acquired without knowledge of the hazardous substance, but only if prior to acquisition the landowner made all appropriate inquiries concerning prior ownership and uses of the property and only if the landowner has taken reasonable steps to stop releases, prevent future releases, and prevent or limit exposure to the hazardous substance.

There is a new CERCLA defense created by the Small Business Liability Relief and Brownfields Revitalization Act signed into law in January of 2002. The defense applies to bona fide prospective purchasers who are to acquire ownership after all the hazardous substance has been disposed of or deposited on-site, have made all appropriate inquiries into previous ownership and uses, have provided all required notices regarding the discovery or release of the hazardous substance, have exercised appropriate care to stop any continuing releases and to prevent future releases and exposure, have cooperated with those involved with the Superfund response actions, have complied with all land use restrictions imposed by the Superfund response actions, have complied with all EPA information requests, and are not otherwise a PRP or related by family or business ties to a PRP.

Be sure to also acquaint yourself with applicable state and local environmental laws. Many states have enacted Superfund-like statutes that impose liability on landowners for the clean-up of hazardous waste. These laws may contain additional requirements or have differing provisions from the federal legislation.

Hazardous waste liability is not limited to those properties associated with current or former industrial sites. Rural and suburban properties (and the groundwater in these parcels) can be contaminated by such events as pesticide runoff, seepage from underground storage tanks, or improper disposal (illegal dumping) of chemicals used in remote industrial, commercial, or agricultural activities. Depending on the size of the lot or project, the prudent builder or developer may want to hire a consultant to conduct an environmental assessment or audit of the site.

Title insurance generally does not protect real estate purchasers against hazardous waste liability. Buyers should review land records at both the U.S. District Court (federal) and the state court of record for the jurisdiction in which the property is located to find out if the property is encumbered by any federal or state hazardous waste liens. Federal liens are not necessarily recorded in the local (county or city) recorder's office, so it is necessary to check in both venues.

A buyer of real estate should seek indemnification provisions from the seller to hold the seller liable for any costs related to unforeseen hazardous waste problems on the property. The government can and will sue any of the listed PRPs for clean-up costs. However, an indemnification clause can establish the right of the buyer to recover any clean-up costs that the buyer may incur from the seller. The indemnification clause should provide for the inclusion of all out-of-pocket costs, including attorney's fees, and should not place a dollar cap or a time limit on indemnification. Buyers should pay careful attention to the seller's financial ability to back the indemnification provisions and may even want to consider requiring the seller to post a bond (or reserve a portion of the purchase price) in situations wherein the land to be purchased has a potential for incurring clean-up costs.

Taking the steps listed in Figure 5.1 will help to minimize the risk of purchasing contaminated property, and will help to limit a builder's liability in the event a prospective site should turn out to be contaminated by hazardous substances.

Figure 5.1 Steps for Recognizing a Contaminated Site

- Inspect the property and surrounding area.
- Note any discolored or defoliated soils or vegetation, odors, chemical drums and other containers, corroded drains, stained pavement, or discolored surface water.
- Look for storage tanks; industrial, mechanical, and electrical equipment; manhole covers; loading docks; fill pipes; and vent pipes.
- Investigate the historical use of the property:
  — Has the property been the site of commercial, industrial, agricultural, or residential use?
  — Identify potential hazardous or toxic materials associated with the past or present use of the land.
  — If the land is vacant, determine whether it has ever been used as a landfill or storage area.
- Are hazardous waste problems common to the area?
- Review any easements on the property to determine whether easement holders may have used hazardous or toxic materials. Look for railroad easements, pipeline easements, or mineral rights granted to mining or oil companies.
- Determine and evaluate all occupants of the property. Do not limit the inquiry to previous record owners of the property.
- Consult with local, state, and federal environmental agencies to determine if the site is on a list of properties suspected of contamination or awaiting clean-up.
- Check for the following government permits issued to current or previous owners that could indicate the use of toxic chemicals:
  — Underground storage tank permits
  — Above-ground storage tank permits
  — Hazardous waste permits
  — Solid waste facility permits
  — Well abandonment permits
  — Well appropriation permits
- Review records in both the U.S. District Court and state courts for the jurisdiction in which the property is located to find out if the property is encumbered by any existing state or federal liens.

INSPECTION PROVISIONS AND OPTION TO TERMINATE CONTRACT

A real estate purchase agreement should allow sufficient time for the buyer to inspect the land for hazardous waste and to conduct an environmental audit. The audit generally reviews past practices, business records, and government documents. A buyer may decide to conduct an environmental audit after either a physical inspection of the property or a review of the chain of title provides indications that former owners could have used or stored or disposed of toxins or chemicals on site. The audit should be conducted to verify or discount this suspicion and should include both soil and water testing. The purchase agreement should give the buyer the option of terminating the contract upon discovery of a potential hazardous waste problem. Three options are provided in the sample language below.

Option 1. [At any time prior to the closing of title or for ___(_____) days following the execution of this contract] the buyer may enter upon the premises for the purposes of investigating the property or conducting an environmental audit to determine whether hazardous waste or toxic substances are present on the site. The terms hazardous waste or toxic substances in this agreement have the same meaning that they have in these state and federal laws: [List the laws.] If the inspection discloses the presence of hazardous waste or toxic substances and the seller is unwilling to correct the problem to the satisfaction of the buyer, the buyer or seller may cancel this contract, and all rights of both parties under the contract shall cease. The canceling party must serve a written notice of cancellation upon the other party or the other party's attorneys either in person or by registered mail.

The seller shall return to the buyer _____ percent (_____%) of the deposit [with interest at percent (%) per annum)]. Costs and damages shall be allocated as follows: [List costs and damages and how they are to be allocated.]

Option 2. The seller hereby grants to the buyer and the buyer's agents and employees the right to enter the property or any portion thereof [at any time prior to the closing of the title or for ___ (_____) days following the execution of this contract] for the purpose of conducting at the buyer's own cost any soil, geologic, engineering, or environmental investigations that the buyer may desire.

If any of these investigations disclose the presence of hazardous waste or toxic substances and the seller is unwilling to correct the problem to the satisfaction of the buyer, the buyer or the seller may cancel this contract and all rights of both parties under the contract shall cease. The canceling party must serve a written notice of cancellation upon the other party or the other party's attorney either in person or by registered mail.

The buyer agrees to indemnify and hold the seller harmless from any costs or liability incurred by any investigations conducted pursuant to this provision. If this contract is voided for any reason not caused by the seller, the buyer, at the written request of the seller, shall repair any damages caused to the property by these investigations and restore the property to the condition it was in before the investigation began.

Option 3. The buyer shall promptly cause (designate testing facility), the testing facility, to inspect and, if necessary, test the soil, subsoil, water, and air conditions of the property to ascertain whether the property contains hazardous waste or toxic substances as defined under state or federal law. The testing facility shall determine the number and quality of tests required to ascertain the presence or absence of hazardous waste or toxic substances. The buyer agrees to furnish a copy of the report of the testing facility to the seller on or before (date). If the report indicates that, in the judgment of the testing facility, the property contains hazardous waste or toxic substances, the buyer shall have the option to terminate this agreement. The buyer shall deliver written notice of the option to terminate to the seller within _____ (_____) days of receipt of the report of the testing facility. Costs and damages will be allocated as follows: [List costs and damages and how they will be allocated.]

COOPERATION FROM SELLER

The buyer may want to include in the contract a provision obligating the seller to cooperate in an investigation of the property, such as provided in the clause below.

The seller agrees to sign and execute any and all documents that may be required by any person, firm, partnership, company, or local, state, or federal agency as a part of conducting an environmental audit of the property to determine the presence or absence of hazardous waste or toxic substances.

SELLER WARRANTY AND INDEMNIFICATION

The seller can warrant that no hazardous substances are on the property. Should such substances be discovered, the warranty makes the seller liable for clean-up costs. The indemnification clause allows the buyer to recover any additional costs or expenses incurred thereby. The contract should specify that the warranty in the contract and indemnification clause will survive the closing.

The seller warrants that the use, maintenance, operation, or condition of the property complies with all regulations, statutes, rules, and codes of all local, state, and federal governmental agencies having jurisdiction over the property.

The seller further warrants that the property does not contain any hazardous waste or toxic substances that may create liability for the purchaser or its agents, heirs, or assigns under local, state, or federal laws.

In the event that it is determined that hazardous waste or toxic substances are present on said property as of the date of this contract, then the seller agrees to indemnify and hold the buyer harmless from any costs or liability incurred by the buyer or the buyer's agents, heirs, or assigns for damages paid to any individual or entity for property damage, personal injury, loss of use, mental anguish, or wrongful death related to the presence of hazardous waste or toxic substances, and to any local, state, or federal agency or other government or other entity, public or private, for fines, assessments, penalties, or punitive awards, and for all costs of identifying, locating, and cleaning up hazardous waste or toxic substances. Damages shall include the actual clean-up costs incurred, costs for testing, costs incurred for expert consultants associated with clean-up, and any legal or litigation costs and attorneys' fees related to matters involving the presence of hazardous waste or toxic substances and to the clean-up thereof.

The provisions of this contract of sale will survive the real estate closing and shall not be merged with the deed.

CONTRACT PROVISIONS THAT MAY INCREASE EXPOSURE OR EXPENSES

Builders hired to construct new homes on others' lots and remodelers hired to remodel or renovate existing structures must be alert to contract provisions that could expose them to unexpected liability resulting from the presence of hazardous waste or toxic substances on the property. For example, when a new home or major addition is under construction, a common environmental concern is the discovery of an underground storage tank or some form of contaminated ground soil. If the builder's or remodeler's contract does not anticipate such a situation, the builder or remodeler may find himself/herself responsible for one or more of the following actions:

- Notifying the appropriate agencies of the environmental problem
- Obtaining specialized permits
- Removing the storage tank or hazardous material at his/her own expense or arranging for a third party to do so, also at the builder's expense

Several contract provisions may expose the builder or remodeler to increased liability or may serve to reduce the profitability of the project. For example, a construction contract or remodeling contract might require the builder or remodeler to comply with all federal, state, and local laws and regulations. Such a clause might read: "The project will be completed in compliance with all laws, ordinances, rules, and regulations of the applicable governmental authorities." Builders and remodelers should delete the clause where possible or they should limit their obligation to comply with laws and regulations to those that govern the means, method, and manner in which they perform their work and not the compliance with laws associated with the conditions at the site.

Another problem area involves concealed site conditions. Normally, one might view a concealed site condition as involving subsurface rock or a high water table, but an unexpected, concealed condition could also involve hazardous substances. Contract language contemplating the effect of unforeseen or concealed conditions should include a provision for concealed hazardous waste or toxic material. The clause should provide for notification, work changes, or contract modification procedures upon discovery of such a problem. The contract could require the owner to pay the extra costs incurred plus profit at a specified percentage of the cost or it could provide the builder or remodeler with the option of canceling the contract. (See Differing Site Conditions in Chapter 2.)

The process of removal or abatement of hazardous substances can be very complicated and very expensive. A builder or remodeler may not be properly licensed or otherwise trained or equipped to remove a specific hazardous substance, and the builder or remodeler certainly does not want to assume responsibility for the costs involved. Therefore, the contract should specifically provide that the property owner is responsible for any abatement and is further responsible for all associated costs. Should the owner elect not to abate or if the process of abatement results in excessive delays, the contract should provide the builder or remodeler with the option to cancel the contract and to receive liquidated damages in that event.

MOLD

Mold is a type of fungus that occurs naturally in the environment and is necessary for the normal decomposition of plant and other organic material. It spreads by means of microscopic spores borne on the wind and is found everywhere that life can be supported. Contractors should avoid installing any materials containing a visible mold growth. However, residential home construction is not designed to exclude the invisible microscopic mold spores. To grow into a visible mold colony, mold spores require three things: First, an organic food source that might be supplied by items found within the home, such as fabric, carpet or wallpaper, or by the building materials, such as drywall, wood, and insulation, to name a few. Second, mold growth requires a temperate climate. The best growth occurs at temperatures between 40° F and 100° F. And finally, mold growth requires moisture. Moisture in the home can have many causes. Spills, leaks, overflows, condensation, and high humidity are common sources. Good construction practices and good housekeeping and home maintenance practices are essential in the effort to prevent or eliminate moisture within the home. If moisture is allowed to remain on the growth medium, mold can develop within 24 to 48 hours. Of the three growth requirements, moisture is the only one that can be controlled in a residential setting.

Mold is not necessarily harmful, but certain strains of mold have been shown to cause adverse health effects in susceptible persons (much like pollen affects those susceptible to hay fever). The most common effects are allergic reactions, including skin irritation, watery eyes, runny nose, coughing, sneezing, congestion, sore throat, and headache. Individuals with suppressed immune systems may risk infections. Experts disagree, however, about the level of mold exposure that may cause these health problems. Some individuals contend that certain "toxic" mold species cause more serious symptoms and diseases or may even be life threatening. These opinions have not been supported by recognized scientific or medical evidence, and the Centers for Disease Control and Prevention's National Center for Environmental Health specifically states that a causal link between the presence of so called "toxic" mold species and serious health conditions has not been shown. (See www.cdc.gov/nceh/airpollution/mold/stachy.htm.)[45]

Nonetheless, homeowners are concerned about the presence of mold and the possibility of health consequences. In addition to employing good construction practices that are keyed to preventing both moisture intrusion and moisture retention within the home (such as a proper installation of flashing and an avoidance of barrier systems that hold and retain moisture against building materials), builders and remodelers should consider providing homeowners with factual information concerning mold to allay unwarranted fears and reactions should mold growth occur. (For example, *Get the Facts on Mold.[46]*) Builders and remodelers should also consider providing homeowners with information about recommended home maintenance practices designed to reduce or prevent the growth of mold in their residences (see Form A below). Remodelers should consider including a clause concerning mold as a hidden site condition (see Form B below), and builders and remodelers may wish to consider disclaiming liability for the consequences of mold (see Form C below).

FORM A

What the Homeowner can do to prevent mold.

The homeowner can take positive steps to reduce or eliminate the occurrence of mold growth in the home and thereby minimize any possible adverse effects that may be caused by mold. These steps include the following:

1. Before bringing items into the home, check for signs of mold. Potted plants (roots and soil), furnishings, or stored clothing and bedding material, as well as many other household goods, could already contain mold growth.

2. Regular vacuuming and cleaning will help reduce mold levels. Mild bleach solutions and most tile cleaners are effective in eliminating or preventing mold growth.

3. Keep the humidity in the home low. Vent clothes dryers to the outdoors. Ventilate kitchens and bathrooms by opening the windows, by using exhaust fans, or by running the air conditioning to remove excess moisture in the air and to facilitate evaporation of water from wet surfaces. Consider the installation of a dehumidifier in basements or other areas of the home that may have elevated levels of humidity.

4. Promptly clean up spills, condensation, and other sources of moisture. Thoroughly dry any wet surfaces or material. Do not let water pool or stand in your home. Promptly replace any materials that cannot be thoroughly dried, such as drywall or insulation.

5. Inspect for leaks on a regular basis. Look for discolorations or wet spots. Repair any leaks promptly. Inspect condensation pans (refrigerators and air conditioners) for mold growth. Take notice of musty odors and any visible signs of mold.

6. Should mold develop, thoroughly clean the affected area with a mild solution of bleach. First, test to see if the affected material or surface is color safe. Porous materials such as fabric, upholstery, or carpet should be discarded. Should the mold growth be severe, call on the services of a qualified professional cleaner.

FORM B

Existing Mold—Concealed Site Conditions

The homeowner is advised that mold can grow and be present in concealed areas of the home, such as the interior of walls, beneath flooring, or behind ceilings. The remodeler has made no analysis or verification of existing mold growth and assumes no responsibility for such a determination. The remodeler shall not be responsible for the detection, containment, or remediation of any existing mold.

Remodeling may involve both deconstruction and reconstruction. The homeowner is advised that if existing mold is present in the home, the deconstruction process potentially could result in the release and dissemination of mold and mold spores to other areas of the house. The remodeler shall not be liable for any effects or possible damage caused by the release of existing mold. The homeowner waives all claims against the remodeler based, in whole or in part, on the release or spread of existing mold during the remodeling process and will indemnify and hold the remodeler harmless from third-party claims in that regard.

In the event that the remodeler encounters what he reasonably believes to be existing mold within the home, the remodeler reserves the right to stop work and to remove his employees, equipment, and materials from the site. It shall be the sole responsibility of the homeowner to properly contain existing mold contamination and to properly conduct remediation of the existing mold by appropriate measures using qualified experts, as necessary. In the event that the homeowner does not properly contain and/or conduct remediation of the existing mold to the satisfaction of the remodeler within a reasonable period of time (a reasonable period of time is determined to be _____), then the remodeler shall have the option to cancel the contract and to receive liquidated damages, as provided in the remodeling agreement.

Warning! The sample language in this disclaimer is provided for educational purposes and may not necessarily be compatible with the laws of each state. Some states may require disclaimers to contain specific language, may require a specific type size, and/or may require a specific location in the contract document. Some states may not consider disclaimers for new home sales to be valid under any circumstances. Builders and remodelers should consult with their local attorney concerning the validity of disclaimers in their jurisdiction and concerning the appropriate language and form of disclaimer instruments.

RADON LIABILITY

All parties to a real estate transaction or to a remodeling project should be concerned about the problem of radioactive radon. Radon is a naturally occurring gas that is caused by the radioactive decay of the element radium. No one can be blamed for its existence, but claims arising out of high

---

FORM C

Disclaimer

The homebuilder (remodeler) has furnished you, the home purchaser (homeowner), with a written warranty that provides for the replacement or repair of defects in construction or materials as stated in that warranty instrument. However, the occurrence of mold growth in your home depends primarily on how you, the resident, manage, inspect, and maintain your household. Our responsibility under the warranty must be limited to things that the homebuilder (remodeler) can control. Therefore, the home-builder (remodeler) will not be responsible for any damages caused by mold, including those that are alleged to be associated with defects in our construction or materials, to include, but not be limited to, property damage, loss of use, loss of value, loss of income, emotional distress, personal injury, or any adverse health effects, death, or any other effects, damages, expenses, or losses. Any implied warranties, including an implied warranty of workmanlike construction, an implied warranty of habitability, or an implied warranty of fitness for a particular use, are hereby waived and disclaimed.

This notice, disclosure, and disclaimer agreement is hereby appended to and made a part of the con-tract of sale (home improvement agreement). The consideration for this agreement shall be the same consideration as stated in the aforesaid contract. Should any term or provision of this agreement be ruled invalid or unenforceable by a court of competent jurisdiction, the remainder of this agreement shall nonetheless stand in full force and effect.

I acknowledge receipt of the notice, disclosure, and disclaimer agreement. I have carefully read and reviewed its terms, and I agree to its provisions.

_____	_____	_____	_____
Buyer	Date	(Builder/Remodeler)	Date

---

radon levels found in homes can be brought against builders and remodelers under many differ-ent legal theories, including breach of express and implied warranties, negligence, strict liability, and fraud. The only known health consequence of radon is an increased risk of developing lung cancer. Because lung cancer can be attributed to a number of causes, such as smoking cigarettes, a plaintiff may have difficulty proving in court that the radon in a particular home was the actual cause of his/her disease. However, a court could accept a damage theory based on an increased risk to health posed by radon, even if the home occupant exhibits no actual signs of lung cancer. In some states, homeowners can recover damages for mental anguish and emotional distress caused by the fear of getting cancer. The cost of correcting a radon problem in most homes averages be-tween $800 and $2,500 and is small in comparison with the expense of a lawsuit.

REDUCING THE LEGAL RISKS

Providing in the building or remodeling contract a specific notice or warning concerning the hazards of radon can reduce the potential for liability on the asserted grounds that the builder or remodeler failed in their duty to warn the homeowner about an unsafe condition (see Example below). Further steps that builders and remodelers can take to reduce the risk of liability from radon are listed in Figure 5.2.

Figure 5.2 Steps for Reducing Radon Liability Risks

- Builders and remodelers should use construction methods recommended by the EPA (Environmental Protection Agency) and by state environmental agency technical experts designed to help prevent radon from entering homes. All parties should understand, however, that no construction technique is foolproof. Most techniques are relatively inexpensive, but some could add significant cost to the price of a home or a remodeling project. Most of the techniques require periodic homeowner maintenance to retain effectiveness. The homeowner must be informed of recommended maintenance.

- Builders and remodelers can contact the Tool Base Hotline of the NAHB Research Center (800-898-2842) or contact the EPA or your state environmental agency to obtain guidance on the latest construction techniques for radon reduction.

- Builders, remodelers, and developers should include a specific notice regarding radon in their contracts. An effective notice should (a) eliminate potential fraud and misrepresentation claims and (b) prevent potential negligence suits based on a failure to warn. A contract should not make the sale contingent only on short-term (3 to 7 days) radon test results. Radon levels can fluctuate, and short-term tests are not always reliable. If there must be a contingency, require retesting before the contract can be avoided and provide the option for repairs to reduce radon levels.

- Builders and remodelers should not give any warranties that cover radon. No builder, remodeler, or seller of real estate can guarantee that a certain home will be safe from naturally occurring radon because the actual level of radon in a specific home depends on many factors that have nothing to do with the construction methods used, such as the occupants' living habits and weather conditions.

- Builders and remodelers should disclaim or waive all warranties, expressed or implied, that are not specifically enumerated in the builder's or remodeler's limited express warranty. Consult with local counsel concerning whether disclaimers involving new home construction will be enforced in your jurisdiction, and, if so, what language and format may be necessary for an effective disclaimer.

- An important point with all warranty provisions is for builders and remodelers to be up front with potential buyers or owners, to let them know exactly what is warranted and what is not. The warranty language should be precise and not leave any room for alternative interpretations by either party to the contract or by a judge or a jury called on to adjudicate its meaning.

- Builders and remodelers should include an indemnification (hold harmless) clause in their subcontracts with foundation and ventilation trade contractors and also in their contracts with design professionals to protect against incurring costs, and/or possibly a civil judgment, as the result of the negligence or defective work performed by trade contractors or designers.

EXAMPLE

RADON NOTICE. "Radon is a radioactive, colorless, and odorless gas that has been found in homes throughout the United States and has been determined to be the second leading cause of lung cancer (next to smoking). The gas is naturally occurring in soil and may enter a home through cracks or holes in the foundation, or through water supplied by wells. If you are building or buying a new home or planning any major structural renovation, such as converting an unfinished basement area into living space, it is important to test the lower levels of the home for radon. If your test results indicate a radon problem, radon-resistant techniques can be inexpensively included as part of the construction or the renovation process. Because major renovations can change the level of radon in any home, always test again after the renovation work is completed."

In addition to the radon notice, builders and remodelers should consider supplying their clients with pamphlets published by the Environmental Protection Agency (EPA) (available on the Internet for downloading), such as "A Citizen's Guide to Radon: The Guide to Protecting Yourself and Your Family".[47]

RADON CONTRACT PROVISIONS

Builders and remodelers should not use these sample contract provisions without consulting an attorney who is experienced in drafting and interpreting construction contracts. Laws may and do differ from state to state, and the specific requirements of a particular builder or remodeler's business transactions necessitate that local counsel be consulted.

Option 1. Radon Notice and Disclaimer—The U.S. Environmental Protection Agency, the U.S. Department of Health and Human Services, the U.S. Public Health Service, and the (name the state department of health or environmental protection agency) have expressed concern over the presence of radon gas in homes. The Surgeon General warns that prolonged exposure to high levels of indoor radon may be a cause of lung cancer. The [builder or remodeler] has made no investigation to determine whether radon gas is present in your home, and the [builder or remodeler] makes no representation or warranty as to the presence or lack of radon. The buyers agree that this contract is not contingent on any radon testing results or on the presence or lack of radon in the home and further agree that the [builder or remodeler] shall have no responsibility for mitigating any elevated levels of radon gas that may be found. The buyers further agree that they shall not extend the closing date or withhold from the builder any payment or any portion thereof of the contract price for any reason related to awaiting results from radon tests or because of the presence of radon in the home. The [builder or remodeler] disclaims, and the [buyer or owner] waives all implied warranties, including but not limited to the implied warranties of workmanlike construction, habitability, and fitness of purpose, or any other warranties that could be construed to cover the presence or effects of radon in the home. The only warranties the [builder or remodeler] provides to the buyer are those contained in the express limited warranty document. The owner acknowledges receiving from (the builder or remodeler a copy of the EPA's public information pamphlet on radon, "A Citizen's Guide to Radon: The Guide to Protecting Yourself and Your Family."

_____

(buyer's signature or initials)

_____

Option 2. Radon Notice—Radon is a naturally occurring gas that is caused by the radioactive decay of uranium found in soil and rock. Radon can be found almost everywhere in varying concentrations. The Surgeon General states that prolonged indoor exposure to high levels of radon gas may cause lung cancer.

This notice serves to advise the [buyer or owner] that above-average levels of radon gas may accumulate in any home, regardless of the type of home or who builds it. Specific radon levels depend on an array of factors, including:

- Site-specific variables, such as soil type, wind, climate conditions, geology, and groundwater
- Building-specific variables, such as construction materials and techniques used; the age of the structure; the type of heating, ventilating, and air conditioning systems; and the occupants' upkeep and living habits

Indoor radon levels can fluctuate on a yearly, seasonal, or even on a daily basis

The EPA has issued protocols that homeowners should follow when testing homes for radon. There are two general ways to test: short-term testing for 2 to 90 days and long-term testing of more than 90 days. The tests are easy and inexpensive. According to the EPA, if a short-term test detects an elevated level (four picocuries per liter of air [4 pCi/L], or higher), the [home buyer or the homeowner] may wish to then conduct a second short-term test or to conduct a long-term test. If the average of the two tests remains 4 pCi/L or higher, the homeowner or buyer should consider taking steps to reduce the level of radon in home. The cost of such repairs can vary but generally range between $800 and $2,500.

Builders can add the disclaimers set out in Option 1. Remodelers can add the following sample language:

The EPA advises testing for radon before renovation begins and after the renovation work is completed. The owner hereby releases the remodeler from all claims, losses, or demands (including personal or bodily injuries) and from all of the consequences thereof, regardless if currently unknown, that may arise from the presence of radon in any structure on the property. The buyers further agree that they shall not withhold from the remodeler any payment or any portion thereof of the contract price for any reason related to awaiting radon test results or because of the presence of radon in the home.

The remodeler disclaims and owner waives any implied warranties, including an implied warranty of workmanlike construction, habitability, and fitness of purpose, or any other warranty that could be construed to cover the presence or effects of radon in the home. The only warranties the remodeler provides to the owner are those contained in the express limited warranty document.

The owner acknowledges receiving from (the builder or remodeler a copy of the EPA's public information pamphlet on radon, "A Citizen's Guide to Radon: The Guide to Protecting Yourself and Your Family."

_____

(buyer's signature or initials)

_____

Option 3. The builder or remodeler may wish to offer to test the home for radon at the buyer's expense, by stating:

At closing [upon completion of the renovation], the builder [remodeler] shall deliver to the homeowner a certificate from a firm that participates in the EPA's Radon Measurement Proficiency Program indicating the level of radon gas, if any, that was present in the home at the time of the screening. The owner acknowledges that the builder [remodeler] has not independently gathered any of the information that is contained in the certificate and that the builder [remodeler] is merely providing the owner with that information provided by the independent firm. The owner further acknowledges that the builder [remodeler] is not warranting the accuracy of the screening or the information contained in the certificate. Any re-screening of the residence, any update of the radon test certificate, or any radon reduction and mitigation undertakings shall be the sole responsibility of the owner and shall be performed at the owner's sole expense.

The owner understands that the builder [remodeler] does not claim or possess any special expertise in the measurement or reduction of radon and further acknowledges that the builder [remodeler] did not provide any advice to the owner as to acceptable levels or possible health hazards of radon gas. The buyers or owners agree that they shall not withhold from the builder or remodeler any payment or any portion of the contract price for any reason related to the radon test results or the presence of radon in the home.

Option 4. If the builder or the remodeler employs construction techniques specifically designed to prevent or reduce the intrusion of radon gas, the contract may state:

Relying on the expertise and the recommendations of the government agencies that have studied the radon issue, the builder [remodeler] has constructed [renovated] the home using the following radon mitigation methods and techniques, as recommended in the EPA's "Model Standards and Techniques for Control of Radon in New Residential Buildings" and/or EPA's "Consumer Guide to Radon Reduction, revised February 2003."[48] (Describe techniques used, such as sub-slab ventilation, extra caulking, and so on.)

No construction method is known to absolutely prevent the occurrence of radon gas. The builder [remodeler] makes no warranty and assumes no responsibility for the operation, maintenance, or effectiveness of the above-described construction methods and techniques that have been used with the intention of reducing the level of radon gas.

ASBESTOS

Remodelers face the greater risk of encountering asbestos in the course of renovation. The risk is much less in the case of new home construction because today fewer building materials contain asbestos. Asbestos is the name for a group of fibrous minerals found in rocks and soil. Because its

Figure 5.3 Asbestos Warning Signs

- Vinyl floor tiles
- Vinyl floor sheeting
- Vinyl-asbestos ceiling tiles
- Vinyl wallpaper
- Asbestos shingles and siding
- Pipe wrap used to insulate pipes, ducts, and furnaces
- Insulation sprayed behind walls and into ceilings for fire-proofing, insulation, and sound-proofing
- Heating and ventilation equipment
- Putty used at elbow and T-fittings and for flexible joints on heating equipment
- Drywall compound

fibers are heat-resistant and durable, asbestos-containing building materials were commonly used in older construction, especially for fire-proofing and insulation purposes (see Figure 5.3). Asbestos use peaked in 1973. About that time it was determined that serious diseases are caused by detached asbestos fibers that become suspended in the air and are inhaled into the lungs or are ingested. These diseases include asbestosis (scarring of the lungs), mesothelioma (a cancer), and lung, esophagus, stomach, colon, and rectal cancer. Older buildings in particular may contain materials that when disturbed in the course of renovation or demolition can release detached asbestos fibers into the air.

Asbestos and asbestos-containing materials (ACMs) generally fall into two broad categories—friable (easily crumbled) and nonfriable (stable, secure). Friable ACMs are dry, and hand pressure can crumble, pulverize, or reduce them to powder, causing them to emit asbestos fibers into the atmosphere. ACMs are nonfriable so long as the material surface is undamaged, and well-sealed against the release of fibers. However, building materials that would ordinarily be considered nonfriable can release asbestos fibers (become friable) if the materials are subjected to sawing, sanding, drilling, grinding, or other similar treatment during renovation. Nonfriable asbestos products can include such materials as vinyl floor and wall coverings and asbestos roofing shingles.

A remodeler who works in older homes or in public or commercial buildings may encounter asbestos-containing materials. Disturbing these materials can pose a serious health threat to the remodelers, their workers, and to the residents of and visitors to the house or building. ACMs should not be damaged and should not be removed unless the remodeler is properly trained to do so. Depending on the jurisdictional requirements, this may involve certification training and licensing.

Federal, State, and Local Requirements and Regulations

Every construction contractor must comply with the applicable regulations of federal, state, and local authorities. A failure to observe these laws may expose contractors to considerable financial risk as well as civil or criminal penalties. Remodelers need to be sure that they are familiar with all applicable laws before they begin a renovation project that could involve ACMs.

Four federal agencies regulate the use and handling of asbestos and ACMs: the EPA; the U.S. Department of Labor through the Occupational Safety and Health Administration (OSHA); the U.S. Department of Transportation (DOT); and the Consumer Product Safety Commission (CPSC).

EPA regulations (National Emissions Standards for Hazardous Air Pollutants [NESHAP]) apply to all structures, installations, and buildings but exclude residential buildings having four or fewer dwelling units (unless they are part of a larger housing complex installation).[49] Before any regulated structure can be demolished or renovated, it must be inspected for the presence of asbestos. For renovations and demolitions, NESHAP work practice regulations must be followed if the amount of asbestos-containing materials exceed certain minimums (260 linear feet of ACMs on pipes, 160 square feet on other components, or 35 cubic feet of components where the amount could not be measured before stripping). The appropriate agency (in almost every instance, the primary responsibility for implementing NESHAP regulations has been delegated to the individual states) must be notified of the intended demolition of any qualifying facility, even if no asbestos is present.

OSHA regulations apply to the construction, alteration, repair, maintenance, renovation, or demolition of any structure that has asbestos-containing materials (excluding only cements, mastics, or asphalt roof coatings that may contain asbestos). Every employer involved in these activities is responsible for monitoring, exposure control, warning signs, labeling, record keeping, and, when required (depending on exposure levels), furnishing protective clothing, respirators, hygienic facilities, and medical examinations (29 C.F.R. s. 1926.1101).[50] Some states have implemented stricter regulations than those imposed by OSHA. Be familiar with the controlling regulations of your jurisdiction.

Transportation of asbestos-containing products and asbestos-containing debris is regulated by the federal Department of Transportation because asbestos is classified as a hazardous material (HAZMAT) (49 C.F.R. s. 173.216).[51] The federal Consumer Product Safety Commission (CPSC) provides warnings and educational material to the public regarding ACMs. It also bans certain hazardous consumer products such as consumer patching compounds that contain asbestos (40 C.F.R. s. 1304).[52]

CONTRACTUAL ISSUES

Remodelers must be careful that their contract does not unwittingly bind them to remove or arrange for the removal of any asbestos-containing materials. If a site investigation clause, inspection clause, or other provision is drafted too broadly, it could expose the remodeler to unanticipated liability. Such a clause might read: "By executing the contract, the remodeler confirms that he has visited the site and familiarized himself with the work and the conditions under which the work is to be performed." Based on this broad language, and in the absence of any caveat or disclaimer, remodelers might find that under the terms of their contract they have assumed responsibility for removing or stabilizing any ACMs (or other hazardous substances) that are subsequently discovered.

The remodeler can substantially reduce such a risk by including language in the contract that expressly excludes removing or stabilizing asbestos from the scope of the work. For example, remodelers may modify the language that appears above as follows:

> However, the remodeler has not analyzed or verified the extent of environmental hazards or other health hazards, if any, that may affect the residents of the premises. Therefore, the remodeler shall not be responsible for the detection, treatment, encapsulation, enclosure, or removal of asbestos, or any other hazardous or toxic material.

Statutes may require that such disclaimers be set in a larger size than the type size of other contract language to make the disclaimer conspicuous to the homeowner. For example, a statute may specifically require disclaimers to be set out in 10-point bold type or the computer equivalent of that size and density. **This sentence is set in 10-point bold type.** Statutes may also require disclaimer clauses to be located in certain prominent areas, such as on the first page of a contract or immediately above the signature blocks. Statutes, or the courts of that jurisdiction, may require specific language (magic words) to be included in disclaimers to be effective. Some statutes may even require disclaimers to be additionally signed or initialed by the homeowner. Courts will not enforce disclaimers that do not strictly conform to the requirements of such statutes, so always check to determine if your state (the state where the construction is taking place) has a statute (or a court decision) regulating the form and content of disclaimers.

Should ACMs be discovered, there will undoubtedly be delays in the renovation associated with engaging a certified asbestos removal contractor and remediating the job site. Should the length of the delay be unacceptable to the remodeler, it may be advisable to include a clause providing the option to cancel the contract and to receive liquidated damages to compensate the remodeler for his/her time and expenses. Or the contract could remain in effect and (a) address the costs likely to result from delayed completion of the project while the asbestos is being removed and (b) specifically provide for reimbursement for any additional costs incurred by the remodeler due to the discovery and abatement of the ACMs. The contract could also require the owner to indemnify the remodeler for any costs that might be imposed against the remodeler by a regulatory agency as a result of any environmental contamination that may accidentally occur.

The remodeler has made no analysis or verification of the extent of any environmental or health hazard that may affect residents on the premises. The remodeler shall not be responsible for the detection, treatment, encapsulation, enclosure, or removal of any asbestos or other hazardous material determined to be present at the site. The owner will be responsible for any treatment, encapsulation, enclosure, and removal of all hazardous materials, including all associated expenses. Should the remodeler encounter materials on the site reasonably believed to be asbestos (or other hazardous waste), the remodeler shall have the right to stop work and remove its employees from the project until the nature of the substances has been determined and, if necessary, the substances have been removed or made harmless. The remodeler shall not be required to return to the site until the owner provides him or her with evidence that the asbestos has been removed or made harmless by a licensed asbestos abatement contractor. In the event that the homeowner does not properly contain and/or conduct asbestos removal within a reasonable period of time (a reasonable period of time is determined to be _____), then the remodeler shall have the option to cancel the contract and to receive liquidated damages, as provided in the remodeling agreement.

In the event that the contract is not canceled but the work is suspended while asbestos is removed or stabilized, the remodeler shall be reimbursed for any additional cost resulting from the discovery of the asbestos and the resulting delay. Reimbursable costs shall include, but not be limited to, increased labor or material costs, increased finance costs, additional overhead costs, and start-up costs. To the fullest extent permitted by law, the owner shall indemnify and hold the remodeler harmless from and against all claims, costs, losses, damages, fines, penalties, and expenses, including attorney's fees, arising from or involving asbestos or any other hazardous materials that may be encountered on site.

The remodeler disclaims and owner waives all warranties that could be construed to cover the presence of asbestos or other environmental pollutants. Should the owner elect not to proceed with this project because of asbestos or some other environmental health hazard, the remodeler shall be entitled to terminate the contract and shall be entitled to receive money for all unpaid costs, fees, and expenses, including the prorated cost of overhead expenses, earned to the time of termination, as well as a prorated percentage of the remodeler's total anticipated profits.

Inclusion of a clause like the immediately preceding one may require modification of other contract provisions. For example, if the contract contains a no-damages-for-delay clause, arguably that provision would conflict with language in the preceding clause that requires the owner to reimburse the remodeler for any additional cost caused by the discovery of the asbestos and the resulting delay. This problem can be avoided by providing that the remodeler will not be entitled to damages for delay, except where the delay results from the discovery of asbestos or other hazardous material.

Builders and remodelers normally do not want to include a no-damages-for delay clause in their contracts. But often home buyers, homeowners, or their attorneys do want to include such a clause in their contracts, so be aware of potentially conflicting clauses.

LEAD

Remodelers are likely to encounter lead paint in older homes. Prior to 1978, lead was commonly used as a pigment and drying agent in oil-based paint. It is estimated that two thirds of the homes built before 1940 and one half of the homes built between 1940 and 1960 have interior and exterior surfaces containing lead paint. Lead paint is a hazard, particularly for young children, but adults can be adversely affected as well. Ingestion of paint chips and respiration of dust from old, deteriorating painted surfaces can result in lead poisoning with associated brain damage and developmental problems in children. In adults, lead poisoning can cause muscle and nerve damage.

The EPA under the authority of the Residential Lead-Based Paint Hazard Reduction Act of 1972 has promulgated rules that apply to compensated renovations in all homes built before 1978 involving any activity that will disrupt more than two (2) square feet of paint. Prior to renovation (but not more than 60 days in advance), every such remodeler must provide to the owner of the residential unit (and also to the occupying tenant, if the owner is not in residence) a specific EPA pamphlet, entitled *Protect Your Family From Lead In Your Home*.[53] The pamphlet can be obtained by calling 1-800-424-LEAD or you can order the pamphlet on-line through the National Service Center for Environmental Publications at http://yosemite.epa.gov/ncepihom. The pamphlet is in the public domain, which means that you are free to make your own copies for distribution. After the pamphlet has been delivered, the remodeler is required to obtain a signed written acknowledgment form from the owner and, if applicable, the occupying tenant (or complete other forms if the owner and/or tenant is not available or refuses to sign) (see Figure 5.4). The remodeler is then required to retain these forms in his/her records for a period of three years.

OSHA INTERIM FINAL LEAD IN CONSTRUCTION STANDARD

Remodelers also need to be concerned about lead exposure limits for their employees. If any lead is present in the workplace, OSHA requires the employer to make an initial assessment of whether any employee's exposure to lead without a respirator will exceed an action level of thirty (30) micrograms of lead per cubic meter of air ($30 \ \mu g/m^3$) averaged over an 8-hour day. If there is a reasonable possibility that this exposure level will exist, the employer must then set up an air-monitoring program. If the employee's tasks are likely to result in lead exposure exceeding fifty (50) micrograms of lead per cubic meter of air ($50 \ \mu g/m^3$), which is the permissible exposure limit (PEL) for lead, the employee must then be provided with respiratory protection, protective clothing and equipment, change areas, hand washing facilities, biological monitoring, and training.

Figure 5.4 Lead Information Pamphlet—Acknowledgment and Certification Forms

Item A. Sample Acknowledgment

I have received a copy of the pamphlet "Protect Your Family From Lead In Your Home," providing me with information concerning the potential risk of lead hazard exposure from remodeling or renovation activities to be performed in my home. I certify that I received this pamphlet before any work began.

_____

Printed Name and Signature

_____

Date

_____

Address of residence or unit to be renovated or remodeled

Item B. Certification—Occupant Unavailable To Sign

I certify that I have made a good faith effort to deliver the pamphlet "Protect Your Family From Lead In Your Home" to the residence or unit listed below on the dates and times so indicated and that the occupant was unavailable to sign the acknowledgement. I further certify that I have left a copy of the pamphlet at the unit as specified.

_____

Printed name and signature of the remodeler

_____

Printed name of occupant (if known)

_____

Date(s) and time(s) of attempted delivery

_____

Location in the residence or unit where pamphlet was left

_____

Address of residence or unit to be remodeled

Item C. Certification—Refusal To Sign Acknowledgment

I certify that I have made a good faith effort to deliver the pamphlet "Protect Your Family From Lead In Your Home" to the residence or unit listed below on the date and time so indicated and that the occupant refused to sign the acknowledgment. I further certify that I have left a copy of the pamphlet at the unit with the occupant.

_____

Printed name and signature of the remodeler

_____

Printed name of occupant (if known)

_____

Date and time of delivery

_____

Address of residence or unit to be remodeled

This must continue until such time as a new exposure assessment is conducted that demonstrates that lead exposure is below the PEL. See 29 C.F.R. 1926.62 App B.[54]

LEAD ABATEMENT

Effective March 1, 2000, any lead-based activity described as an inspection, lead-hazard screen, risk assessment, or lead abatement must be conducted by lead abatement professionals in accordance with federal work practice standards. See 40 C.F.R. s. 745.227.[55] These professionals must be trained and certified to do such work in accordance with EPA certification requirements and be licensed by the individual states. Lead-based activities that require specialized certification and licensing do not, however, include ordinary renovation that has a primary intent of repairing, restoring, or remodeling a dwelling (as opposed to a primary intent of conducting specified lead-based activities, such as the permanent abatement of lead) even though the ordinary renovation activities may incidentally result in the reduction of lead-based paint.

LEAD LIABILITY

Remodelers risk liability for exposing their workers, their clients, and their clients' children to lead. This is especially true in the case of children under 6 years of age because they are particularly susceptible to the effects of lead poisoning. Young children should not remain in a home built before 1978 during a renovation because they may be exposed to lead dust and lead chips during this activity. If a potential client has children under 6 years of age and an older house with visible dust and/or peeling paint, the remodeler should be cautious about accepting the job. The children could already be unknowingly poisoned by lead and the remodeler could unfairly end up being blamed for causing the child's condition after the job has been completed. A wise procedure is to ask the client before accepting such a job whether the children of the household have had blood tests for lead. If not, request that the children be tested before accepting the job. This will establish a standard of reference for the children's lead exposure. If the job is accepted, it is especially important to thoroughly clean the work area and surroundings before young children are returned to the house to eliminate any lead-containing dust or debris that may have been generated during renovation.

To minimize liability, remodelers should take precautions to reduce the amount of lead dust and contain dust while working and then thoroughly clean after the job is complete. After completion, remodelers may also want to test the floor for lead dust with a lead test kit in the presence of the client and then have the client sign a statement that he/she witnessed the test. For maximum protection, the remodeler can hire a testing company to take dust samples before and after the job for analysis in a laboratory to provide better evidence that remodeling did not increase normal dust levels. (Refer to Figure 5.5, reducing lead risks from remodeling.)

Remodelers can help protect themselves against possible lawsuits by employees who may claim they became lead-poisoned in the course of their employment by requiring all new employees to

Figure 5.5 Steps for Reducing a Remodeler's Lead Liability Risks

- Provide owners with the required Environmental Protection Agency (EPA) pamphlet "Protect You Family From Lead In Your Home" advising them of health hazards associated with lead and warning them of possible hazards of lead dust generated during remodeling
- Have the owner sign the acknowledgment indicating receipt of the EPA pamphlet
- Do not undertake lead abatement work without training and certification
- Use wet sanding methods wherever feasible to keep dust at a minimum
- Isolate any work areas with plastic sheeting where significant dust is expected, including floors, furniture, heating registers, and cold air returns
- Use vacuum attachments on saws and sanders wherever possible
- Wash and vacuum floors exposed to dust during remodeling. Be sure washing will not damage them. Use only high-efficiency (HEPA) filters.
- Vacuum floors before installing new carpeting. Use only high-efficiency (HEPA) filters.

have a blood test to determine their lead exposure level before beginning to work for the remodeler. Remodelers should keep the results on file even after an employee leaves.

ARSENIC

Arsenic is a naturally occurring mineral that is found in soil and water. People are exposed to arsenic on a daily basis, and at the low exposure levels that are commonly experienced, arsenic has no discernible adverse health effects. Arsenic at higher levels of exposure, usually through ingestion but sometimes through skin absorption, causes a number of health conditions that include problems with skin, circulation, the lungs, and the nervous system. A high level of exposure to arsenic can also lead to an increased risk of several types of cancer. At very high levels of exposure, arsenic is a deadly poison. (See EPA fact sheet—"Hazard Summary—Arsenic Compounds" at www.epa.gov/ttn/atw/hlthef/arsenic.html.[56]) Even though there is no evidence that outside of acute industrial exposure or deliberate acts of poisoning, individuals are becoming ill from arsenic, there is a heightened public awareness of and concern about arsenic. Builders and remodelers need to be alert to these public health concerns because if ignored, concerns have the potential to become claims based on an assertion that there was a failure of a duty to warn.

ARSENIC IN DRINKING WATER

Under the federal Safe Drinking Water Act, the EPA regulates the amount of arsenic that can be found in public or community water systems. The EPA does not regulate the amount of arsenic found in private wells. The current permissible level of arsenic in public or community water supplies is 50 parts per billion, but in accordance with a new EPA standard, beginning January 23, 2006, the amount of arsenic in public or community supplied drinking water must be reduced to not more than 10 parts per billion.

Most builders are not directly affected by this change. Large developers who construct community water systems for their subdivisions will undoubtedly employ the technical experts and install the equipment necessary to respond to this new standard. But an individual builder may sell a house with a private well on-site or may arrange for the drilling of a well as part of the construction contract. Although the EPA does not regulate the amount of arsenic in private wells, an individual homeowner may look to the EPA standard as the "safe" level and have expectations that his/her private well is supposed to be within the EPA limit.

Arsenic in well water can be quite high in some areas of the country, sometimes bordering on levels that are known to cause illness in humans. Local health departments do not normally test for arsenic, their primary concern being bacterial contamination. One method of avoiding possible liability for a homeowner's exposure to arsenic in well water is to exclude the well drilling process from the construction contract; make it entirely the responsibility of the owner or purchaser. If that is not possible, you may wish to have the well water tested for arsenic, particularly if the property is located in an area known for high arsenic levels. Or you should at a minimum provide to the homeowner information about arsenic in drinking water, to include a recommendation that the homeowner consider having a water test conducted for arsenic. See the Example below. The departments of health in states where there are elevated levels of arsenic in the ground water often have pamphlets on the subject of arsenic in well water that can be provided to the home purchaser. (See, for example, Minnesota Department of Health's *Arsenic in Minnesota's Well Water* or Michigan Department of Community Health's *Arsenic in Well Water*. The EPA also has publications, such as *Drinking Water from Household Wells*, January 2002.[57])

EXAMPLE

Disclosure—Disclaimer: Arsenic in Well Water

Arsenic is a naturally occurring substance that may be found in ground water. At low levels, arsenic has no known health risks. High exposure to arsenic can cause illnesses, including cancer. Your property is furnished with a well that has been tested for and found free of bacterial contamination, as certified by the local health department. The builder has not conducted any tests for other substances, such as arsenic, in your well water and has no knowledge concerning the possible presence of other substances. The builder has provided you with the following publication concerning arsenic in well water, _____(name of publication)_____, and recommended that you may wish to have your well water tested for arsenic. The builder is unable to provide any warranty concerning the quantity or quality of the well water on your property and does hereby disclaim all implied warranties in that regard, specifically including an implied warranty of habitability.

Pressure Treated Lumber—CCAs

Pressure treated lumber is chemically treated wood designed to inhibit decay from mold and fungus and to prevent damage from wood-boring insects. The predominant chemical compound used in pressure-treated lumber since 1938 has been CCA (chromated copper arsenate). Pressure-treated lumber is frequently used in residential construction. Plywood, structural supports, beams, shakes, and siding may be comprised of pressure-treated lumber. Certain structures, such as decks and components using garden timbers, are commonly made with pressure-treated lumber. This treated wood has a greenish tinge that turns gray with age.

In recent years, concerns have been expressed about playground equipment in which CCA-treated lumber has been used. Although no adverse health affects have ever been noted, arsenic concentrations in the soil at the base of such playground equipment have been found to be elevated. Arsenic and chromium (components of CCA) when absorbed in excessive amounts are poisonous and carcinogenic. Lesser amounts are deemed harmless. Arsenic, chromium, and copper are naturally occurring elements that are found in our food and drinking water. Some believe, however, that exposure to these substances should be limited as a precaution, whether the exposure might come from playground equipment or from residential uses of CCA-treated wood. In this regard, the Environmental Protection Agency (EPA) has recommended limiting contact with CCA-treated lumber and using paint or sealants on the wood.

In response to this concern, the wood sealant manufacturers have voluntarily decided to phase out the use of CCAs in pressure-treated lumber. The manufacturers emphasize that no adverse health affects have been documented, but since they believe that alternative compounds can be used in place of CCAs, the manufacturers have decided to change the formula used as the preservative in pressure-treated lumber. In accordance thereby, the wood treatment manufacturers have entered into a voluntary accord with the EPA. (See "Questions & Answers Regarding the CCA Transition Process" at http://www.epa.gov/pesticides/factsheets/chemicals/cca_transition.htm.[58]) The transition to non-CCA-pressure treated lumber has begun. Any CCA-treated lumber manufactured after December 31, 2003 is to be excluded from many residential uses. There are exceptions. After that date, CCA wood may still be used for residential construction in the form of plywood, flooring, structural timbers, piles, beams, shakes, and siding. These are uses that have minimal direct contact with people and soil. CCA-treated lumber manufactured before December 31, 2003, can still be used for any purpose. Eventually, the issue of CCA exposure should become moot because of the voluntary phase-out. A builder or remodeler who is using CCA-treated wood in residential construction may wish, however, to provide a disclosure to avoid any assertion that there was a failure of a duty to warn about a potentially hazardous material. See example.

EXAMPLE

CCA Disclosure—Pressure-treated Wood

Some lumber used in the construction of this house is pressure-treated wood, treated with the CCA compound (chromated copper arsenate) as a wood preservative and pesticide. This type of treated wood has been commonly used in residential construction for more than 65 years with no discernible adverse health effects, and this builder has no knowledge that the wood is harmful in any sense. CCAs contain the elements arsenic and chromium, which are both naturally occurring and have no adverse health affects at normally encountered low levels of exposure. Very high levels of exposure are toxic and can cause a number of illnesses. The Environmental Protection Agency has, as a precaution, recommends that physical contact with unpainted or unsealed CCA lumber should be limited. CCA-treated lumber should not be burned because of the possibility of smoke inhalation, and sawing CCA-treated lumber (creating sawdust that could be inhaled) should be avoided as well. This information is provided to you, the purchaser, for the purpose of informing you about CCA-treated lumber. Additional information is available on the Environmental Protection Agency (EPA) website at http://www.epa.gov/pesticides/factsheets/chemicals/cca_qa.htm.

6

SUBCONTRACTS

RARELY WILL A BUILDING or remodeling company perform all of the construction work on a project with his/her own employees as the only labor source. Much of the labor is provided by trade contractors—people or companies that contract with builders and remodelers to provide specialized services. Sometimes the term trade contractor or subcontractor will have a specified statutory definition, such as when it used in a mechanic's lien statute. For the purposes of this section, though, a trade contractor is defined as one who has a direct contractual (as opposed to employment) relationship with a builder or remodeler to undertake a specific part of the work necessary to fulfill the builder's or remodeler's contract with a buyer or owner.

Builders and remodelers should have written contracts with their trade contractors for the same reasons that they have written contracts with their clients: to document the specifics of their agreement, to minimize misunderstandings, and to allocate risks. As to the last point, it should be noted that more and more insurance companies are insisting as a condition of general liability insurance coverage that general contractors must have written subcontracts. The complexity of the subcontract may depend in part on the builder's or remodeler's relationship with the trade contractor and on the trade contractor's level of business sophistication. In situations in which the parties have a longstanding business relationship or in which trade contractors are accustomed to making their proposals on scrap paper, the parties may want to start out with a short subcontract limited to the key provisions such as scope of the work, contract documents, contract price, payment schedule, time for performance, insurance, changes, warranty, clean-up, safety, risk allocation (indemnification), and dispute settlement (arbitration and/or mediation). As the parties become more comfortable using the written contract, they can add more complex details such as liquidated damages, lien waivers, rules and regulations regarding conduct while on the site, to name a few.

A written subcontract also may help establish the trade contractor's status as an independent contractor rather than as an employee. The determination of whether an individual is an employee or an independent contractor can have a wide range of ramifications for an employer. For example, certain labor laws such as the Fair Labor Standards Act, which provides minimum wage and over-time standards, covers employees only. Similarly, a number of state labor laws, workers' compensation laws, and unemployment insurance laws apply only to employees. An employer is liable for the wrongful acts his/her employee commits while on the job. On the other hand, with certain exceptions an employer is not liable for physical harm caused by an act or omission of the independent contractor or his/her employees or agents.

The distinction between an independent contractor and an employee is also relevant if a worker is injured. Generally, the exclusive remedy of an employee injured on the job is workers' compensation regardless of how the injury occurred. An independent contractor injured on the job may sue a negligent builder or remodeler for his or her injuries.

Employers have federal and state tax withholding obligations for their employees. Employers also face mandatory workers' compensation and unemployment insurance payments for employees. Failure to properly classify a person as an employee, as opposed to an independent contractor, can be very costly and may result in back taxes, additional insurance premiums, and penalties being imposed.

The provisions discussed below do not address every contingency, nor do they apply to all contracts with trade contractors. Thus, builders or remodelers must carefully consider the facts of each situation and use a subcontract specifically designed to fit the particulars of the project. Because subcontracts are legal documents that have great impact on builders' or remodelers' liability, builders and remodelers should have their attorneys prepare or at least review such documents before signing them.

TRADE CONTRACTOR'S PROPOSAL

The proposal is the outline of a future agreement, the offer to enter into a specific subcontract. The proposal should contain a precise description of the scope of the work to be performed by the trade contractor. It should reference the general contractor's contract with the owner or buyer by the date of their agreement and any revisions thereto.

Unless the proposal expressly states otherwise, if the builder or remodeler signs a trade contractor's proposal, it becomes a binding subcontract. Rather than signing the proposal document, a builder or remodeler may wish to incorporate the terms and conditions of the proposal into a more complete subcontract document that the parties will subsequently sign by adding the words:

"The scope of the work and the terms and conditions as stated in (trade contractor's) proposal (dated the _____ day of _____, 20_____) are incorporated by reference herein, and shall take precedence over any conflicting provisions in this contract."

Of course, the language of this or any other subcontract provision can be changed according to the wishes and bargaining strength of the respective parties (see Figure 6.1).

Figure 6.1 Sample Proposal

For:

Date _____

_____

Project _____
(name of builder or remodeler)

_____

Location _____
(street address)

_____
_____
(city, state, zip)

Phone (_____)_____
Design Professional _____
Drawings No. _____ Dated _____
Specifications Dated _____

Subject to prompt acceptance within _____ (_____) days and to all conditions stipulated below, we propose to furnish materials and labor at the price(s) stipulated below:

Price: $_____

The undersigned accepts this proposal and all its terms and conditions as a binding contract.

_____   _____
(builder or remodeler)   (trade contractor)

By _____   By _____
            (signature)   (signature)

Title _____   Title _____

Date _____   Date _____

THE SUBCONTRACT

SCOPE OF THE WORK

The clause describing the work to be performed in a subcontract between a builder or remodeler and a trade contractor must be specific. Otherwise, the builder or remodeler may expect work from the trade contractor not contemplated by the trade contractor when bidding on the job or negotiating the subcontract. The work may be crucial, and the trade contractor may take the position that additional compensation is due. This can lead to hard feelings, possible incomplete performance by the trade contractor, and project delays. If the "additional" work is done there is likely to be a demand for more money and possibly the filing of a mechanic's lien by the trade contractor if the additional payment is not then received. As previously discussed throughout this book, unmet or misaligned expectations often cause disputes. Whether between an owner or buyer, or a trade contractor and the builder or remodeler, these disputes can result in soured business relationships and can result in litigation.

Accordingly, the description of the work should contain at least three basic elements: (a) a detailed description of the work to be done and, importantly, work that will not be done by the trade contractor, (b) a designation of the relevant plans by date, and date of last revision, and (c) a statement that the work shown on the designated plans is to be done in accordance with the project specifications.[59] This section should specify whether the trade contractor is expected to provide all of the materials and supplies necessary to perform the subcontracted work. The contract also should list those instances in which the trade contractor is providing only labor. Alternatively, the contract should describe all the materials that the trade contractor will provide.

PRICE AND PAYMENT

To avoid misunderstandings, the subcontract should clearly define the payment terms. The price and payment section should state the total contract price in words and numbers (example—"Four thousand dollars [$4,000.00]"), and it should describe the method of payment with particular emphasis on when final payment is due. For example, if the trade contractor will be paid in draws, the contract should include a draw schedule showing the number of payments, the timing of each payment, and any administrative preconditions for each payment (such as submission of invoices). Similarly, if the trade contractor is to be paid monthly, the billing procedure should be clearly defined. The contract should specify whether final payment is due upon substantial completion, total completion, or some other milestone. Further, the contract should state whether the trade contractor must provide releases and lien waivers prior to payment and should also include any other mutually agreed upon terms.

Just as the general contract with the builder or remodeler may allow an owner to withhold retainage, the builder or remodeler may also want to withhold retainage from a trade contractor to assure the subcontract's completion and the correction of any defects. The contract language should provide for the retainage of a certain percentage from the funds owed to the trade contractor and should state whether these retained funds will be paid upon final payment or at some other point in time. If the retained funds are withheld until substantial completion of the entire project, retainage may be particularly unfair to those trade contractors who participated in the early stages of the project. For those trade contractors, the builder or remodeler should consider tying the release of retainage to substantial completion of the trade contractor's work rather than to substantial completion of the entire project.

> The [builder or remodeler] agrees to pay the trade contractor for the performance of this subcontract the total sum of _____ Dollars ($_____), subject to additions and deductions for such changes as may be agreed upon in writing. Progress payments will be made to the trade contractor as follows:_____
>
> Every request for a progress payment shall itemize any amount paid for any labor that is not covered by worker's compensation insurance. The premium for workers' compensation insurance for any uninsured labor shall be deducted from the amount due and paid over for necessary workers' compensation insurance coverage.

CHANGE ORDERS

A change order clause in a subcontract not only serves to avoid misunderstandings about payment for additional or modified work but also provides protection for the builder or remodeler because it can provide a mechanism to require the trade contractor to perform requested changes in the work. Because an owner or buyer may request changes or because site conditions may require changes, the builder or remodeler should also reserve the right to order changes in the subcontract. The subcontract agreement may include language that establishes a dollar ceiling, or other limits, for job changes.

It is recommended that all subcontract change orders requests be made directly through the general contractor and not by an owner or buyer. Should a trade contractor be approached by an owner or buyer for a change in the work, the subcontract agreement should require the trade contractor to first notify the general contractor and to sign a written change order with the general contractor before beginning any new work created by such a request. (The general contractor should also have the owner or buyer sign the written change order.) The written change order should specify any revisions in the price, the work, the payment schedule if necessary, and the completion date.

The subcontract should clearly identify who is authorized to approve a change order. Usually, change orders should come from the person who executed the contract (the general contractor). If someone other than the builder or the remodeler has the authority to approve a change order (architect, project manager, or foreman, for instance), that person's authority should be stated in writing and signed by the general contractor. A trade contractor should not assume that another individual has the authority to approve changes, even if that person is willing to sign a purported change order.

The [builder or remodeler] may order additional work, and the trade contractor shall perform these changes in the work. However, no alteration, addition, omission, or change shall be made in the work, or in the method or manner of the performance, except upon a written change order signed by the builder or remodeler. Any change or adjustment in the subcontract price resulting from the change in work shall be specifically stated in the change order. If the [builder or remodeler] and the trade contractor cannot agree upon a fixed price or other determination of payment, the [builder or remodeler] may direct the trade contractor to perform the requested work upon the following terms: The trade contractor will be paid for such changed work based upon the actual cost to the trade contractor for all materials, labor, equipment, and job supervision (state hourly rate for labor and supervision), plus a reasonable itemized overhead and profit [calculate as a percentage]. No change order shall vary, abrogate, void, or otherwise affect the terms, conditions, and provisions of this subcontract, except as specifically stated in the change order.

INDEMNIFICATION

One method of minimizing liability available to builders and remodelers is allocating the risk of loss to the party directly responsible for the loss. An indemnification clause (sometimes referred to as a "hold harmless" clause) in the subcontract can accomplish this allocation and help to protect the builder or remodeler from claims that may be brought by the buyer, the owner, or third parties relating to defective or nonconforming work performed by the trade contractor. For example, if the builder or remodeler is liable to the homeowner for defective construction performed by a trade contractor, an indemnification clause in the subcontract will entitle the builder to recover from the trade contractor the cost of correcting the work and any additional costs incurred (such as legal expenses or consequential damage to personal property). Increasingly, insurance companies are requiring general contractors to include an indemnification clause in their subcontracts as a condition of general liability insurance coverage.

Although builders and remodelers use several types of indemnification provisions, generally the indemnification clause provides that the trade contractor will compensate or defend the builder or remodeler against claims, loss, damage, or expenses arising out of or resulting from the trade contractor's work.

The [builder or remodeler] shall not be liable for any loss or casualty incurred or caused by the trade contractor's work. The trade contractor agrees to indemnify and shall hold the [builder or remodeler], and its agents and employees, harmless from any and all liability, claims, losses, cost of repairs and/or relocation, consequential and punitive damages, fines, penalties, taxes, assessments and expenses, including court costs and attorney's fees, that may arise out of the trade contractor's performance of work under this contract. This shall include, but not be limited to, claims of any person, entity, or governmental authority for property damage, loss of use, loss of profits, bodily injury, illness, mental anguish, death, and claims that shall include any fines, assessments, or penalties for code violations, OSHA violations, environmental regulation violations, unemployment or workers' compensation insurance premium assessments, and/or the violation of any other local, state, or federal law or regulation that relates to the performance or performance failure of the trade contractor or the trade contractor's suppliers, employees, and agents. The [builder or remodeler] may retain any and all monies due to be paid, or that may become due to be paid, to the trade contractor under this contract sufficient to save itself harmless and indemnify itself against any money judgment, fine, or assessment or asserted liability, damages, and expenses arising out of the work performed by the trade contractor under the provisions of this contract.

INSURANCE

In most jurisdictions, workers' compensation insurance is required by law, particularly for employees of the trade contractor. The subcontract agreement should always require the trade contractor to obtain the legal limits of workers' compensation insurance and to provide a certificate of insurance to the builder or remodeler (general contractor). The general contractor who fails to take these measures will soon learn that state law requires him or her to provide workers' compensation coverage for all the uninsured trade contractor's employees and may even impose a penalty on the general contractor for failure to assure that the trade contractor has the required workers' compensation coverage. Builders and remodelers should examine the trade contractor's certificate of insurance carefully. There are many unfortunate tales of builders and remodelers who thought that their trade contractor had provided a certificate of insurance only to learn that the certificate was out of date or even that the date had been altered. If there is any question as to the legitimacy of the certificate, do not hesitate to call the state commission for confirmation. If the trade contractor is exempt from workers' compensation requirements, the trade contractor should similarly be required to offer proof of the exemption prior to construction. A builder or remodeler should not allow a trade contractor to begin a job without proof of the required workers' compensation insurance, or proof of an exemption.

In addition to the workers' compensation insurance that is required by law, it is good practice to provide in the subcontract agreement that the trade contractor shall obtain the same type and same amount of coverage that is required by the general contractor in the contract with the owner. If there is no insurance requirement in the owner's contract, the subcontract agreement can specify the type and amount of coverage that the trade contractor shall obtain. These coverages may include automobile liability insurance, comprehensive general liability insurance, and property damage insurance. The contract language should again specify that, before construction, the trade contractor shall furnish to the builder or remodeler original certificates of insurance or copies of the policies showing insurance coverage of the desired types and in appropriate amounts.

As stated, the wise builder or remodeler will not allow the trade contractor to begin work until he/she provides such insurance confirmation. However, in actual practice, given time restraints and/or the high cost of coverage, trade contractors have at times been allowed by general contractors to proceed with the work without providing the insurance required by their subcontract.

This entails risk, but the risk can be lessened if the subcontract agreement provides that if the trade contractor fails to furnish or maintain the required insurance, the builder or remodeler shall have the right to (a) obtain such insurance for the trade contractor and (b) withhold from the trade contractor's payments the cost of the coverage at the applicable rate for the trade involved or any costs incurred by the builder or remodeler resulting from the trade contractor's failure to furnish or maintain such insurance. This will, of course, require the general contractor to see to it that coverage is actually obtained, for it will do no good to simply withhold an amount sufficient for a premium and then not apply it for that purpose. The subcontract should also include a clause stating:

> "All certificates of insurance and all insurance policies shall provide that the insurance may not be canceled, terminated, or modified without ___(_____) days advance written notice to the builder or remodeler. Cancellation, termination, or unauthorized modification of insurance shall constitute grounds for the builder or remodeler to order the trade contractor to stop work, and at the option of the builder or remodeler may also constitute grounds for cancellation of the subcontract agreement."

TAXES, CHARGES, AND PERMITS

This clause assigns responsibility for the taxes, fees, and other charges generated by the trade contractor's work under the subcontract. In the example below, the trade contractor must secure the necessary permits for completing his/her portion of the project.

> The trade contractor understands and agrees that he or she is an independent contractor and that he or she shall be responsible for and shall pay any and all taxes, contributions, fees, and similar expenses imposed directly or indirectly for his or her work, labor, material, and services required by or relating to this contract. The trade contractor shall at his or her own expense apply for and obtain all necessary permits and conform strictly to the laws, ordinances, and regulations applicable in the locality in which the work is performed. At no time shall the contract price increase or escalate on account of any such charge. On demand, the trade contractor shall substantiate that all taxes and other charges are properly paid.

CLEAN-UP

The contract should assign responsibility for removal of the debris generated by a trade contractor's work on the job. Clean-up is largely a matter of local custom and practice. The builder or remodeler may assume this responsibility for the entire site, or trade contractors may be required to place all of their own trash in a designated place or receptacle on the job site. Trade contractors also can be required to remove all of the debris generated by their work at the job site and be responsible for its proper disposal. Customarily, this last situation occurs more often in multifamily construction. The cost of debris disposal is a factor to be considered when negotiating the terms of the subcontract agreement.

"The trade contractor shall at all times keep the building and premises broom clean of dirt, debris, rubbish, and any other waste materials arising from the performance of this subcontract. The trade contractor is responsible for removal of all debris created by his or her work and the disposal thereof at a designated spot at the job site."

CASE STUDIES

Case 1. Perry Avenue Fund 88, Ltd., hired J. R. Slaught Construction Company to supervise the construction of 58 single-family dwellings on property owned by Perry in California. The parties' contract provided for binding arbitration of all disputes. Thereafter, Slaught hired several trade contractors and suppliers. A dispute arose between Slaught and the owner, and the matter was submitted to arbitration. In response to Slaught's demand for arbitration, the owner counterclaimed that the work was improperly performed or contained defective material. Slaught demanded that the trade contractors join in the arbitration between Slaught and the owner, but they declined. The California Court of Appeal relied on the following clause in the subcontracts to compel the trade contractors to participate in the arbitration:

5. ASSUMPTION OF PRINCIPAL CONTRACT: The work to be done hereunder is a portion of the work required of Contractor under the General Contract referred to in the Special Conditions hereof. Insofar as applicable, trade contractor shall be bound by all of the terms and conditions of the Contract Documents, and shall strictly comply therewith. All rights and remedies reserved to Owner under the Contract Documents shall apply to and be possessed by Contractor in its dealings with trade contractor."

The court concluded that because the construction contract required Slaught to submit to arbitration, the arbitration provision as incorporated into the subcontracts through paragraph 5 also required the trade contractors to submit to arbitration.[60]

Case 2. The Alaska State Housing Authority awarded a contract to Wick Construction Company to build a courthouse and office building. Wick subcontracted all work relating to the fabrication and erection of the curtainwall to Kenai Glass Company. The building was completed and accepted 414 days late. Wick attributed the delay to Kenai, and it withheld the final payment due Kenai under the subcontract. Kenai sued for the retainage, and Wick counterclaimed that Kenai breached the subcontract by failing to perform in a timely manner. The trial court awarded Wick $765,654 in total damages, and Kenai appealed on the grounds that the subcontract limited Wick's recovery for its damages to $400 per day of delay. The Alaska Supreme Court, finding for Kenai, held that a conduit clause in the subcontract incorporated a liquidated damages clause in the contract between the Housing Authority and Wick, limiting liability for delay to $400 per day.[61]

CONDUIT CLAUSE

The conduit clause, also known as the flow-down clause, allows the builder or remodeler to shift risks downward in the contractual chain. The clause binds the trade contractor to the builder or remodeler as the builder or remodeler is bound to the buyer or owner. This provision should state that the builder or remodeler has the same rights and privileges against the trade contractor as the construction contract gives to the buyer or owner against the builder or remodeler.

This type of clause is particularly useful where the prime contract is dictated by the owner and the builder or remodeler has little input into the terms of the contract. If a dispute between the buyer or owner and the builder or remodeler results in arbitration, this clause may enable the builder or remodeler to join the trade contractor in the arbitration with the owner and avoid a separate action against the trade contractor.

Of course, if the builder or remodeler attempts to bind the trade contractor to the provisions of the general contract, he/she should be prepared for a request from the trade contractor for rights, remedies, and redress corresponding to those the builder or remodeler has against the owner. If a conduit clause is used in the subcontract, the trade contractor is entitled to a copy of the agreement between the buyer and the builder or the owner and the remodeler before signing any agreement with the builder or remodeler. The trade contractor also should inspect all plans and specifications and all contract documents.

> The trade contractor shall assume toward the [builder or remodeler] all the obligations and responsibilities that the [builder or remodeler] assumes toward the [buyer or owner] under the general contract, and the [builder or remodeler] shall have the same rights and privileges against the trade contractor as the [buyer or owner] in the general contract has against the [builder or remodeler] insofar as these obligations, responsibilities, rights, and privileges pertain to the trade contractor's work.

CONCEALED CONDITIONS

Just as the prime contract addresses the possibility of changed or differing conditions, the contract between the builder or remodeler and the trade contractor should also address this issue (see Differing Site Conditions in Chapters 2 and 3). Generally, if the subcontract contains no differing site conditions clause but imposes a site inspection requirement on the trade contractor, the subcontract places the risk of uncertainty of subsurface conditions on the trade contractor. Thus, the subcontract might expressly provide that the trade contractor has inspected the site and that in arriving at the contract price the trade contractor has assumed the risk that unforeseen conditions may make the job more expensive.

STOP WORK—TAKEOVER BY GENERAL CONTRACTOR AND TERMINATION OF AGREEMENT

There can be circumstances when a builder or remodeler may wish to order the trade contractor to stop work pending the correction of work or the furnishing of certain requirements, such as certificates of insurance or a contractor's license. The language of the subcontract agreement can specify the circumstances under which a stop work order can be issued and provide for indemnification to the builder and remodeler for any costs or penalties associated with the resulting delay. If the situation is not rectified within a certain period of time, the contract can call for termination and takeover by the general contractor.

Termination is a remedy for a material breach of contract. The subcontract should spell out the circumstances (cause) under which the subcontract agreement may be terminated. Additionally, the subcontract should clearly state the rights, duties, and obligations of the parties in the event of termination. The termination clause should provide that the builder or remodeler has the right to take over the job of the trade contractor and to complete the job themselves or to hire another trade contractor to complete. The clause should provide that the terminated trade contractor shall be responsible for all costs and expenses associated with the completion of the work and costs and expenses associated with the removal, repair, and correction of any defective work of the terminated trade contractor.

Conversely, some subcontracts may provide for cancellation by the builder or remodeler without cause. Such a clause is likely to be used by a builder or remodeler whose contract with the owner allows the owner to terminate the contract at any time.

For Cause. In the event the trade contractor should at any time fail to perform the work with competence, promptness, or diligence, the [builder or remodeler] shall have the right to terminate this agreement for cause after ___(_____) days notice to the trade contractor (unless within said ___(_____) day period the trade contractor begins to remedy such failure). Upon termination, the contractor shall have the right to take over and to remove or repair any defective work, to complete unfinished work, and to hire any additional trade contractors for the purpose of these tasks. Said terminated trade contractor shall be responsible for all costs of removal, repair, and/or completion and shall indemnify the contractor for any and all costs and expenses incurred in that regard. The contractor may retain any and all amounts due to the terminated trade contractor and may apply such amounts to the cost of removal, repair, and/or completion. Any excess due over and above the above-described costs and expenses will be paid over to the terminated trade contractor after final completion of the defective or uncompleted work.

Without Cause. The [builder or remodeler] has the option to terminate this agreement without cause. In the event of termination by the [builder or remodeler], the [builder or remodeler] shall pay to the trade contractor any amount due for work already completed and for the loss of anticipated profits under the subcontract.

NO LIEN

The lien waiver clause typically provides that the builder, remodeler, or trade contractor will not file any liens against the property on account of labor, material, or equipment furnished under the contract. A lien waiver clause may be sought by an owner or a lender, but it offers little, if any, benefit to a builder, remodeler, or trade contractor. A blanket provision in the contract documents waiving any lien rights whatsoever should be avoided. In some states, waivers before the performance of work are prohibited by statute. Lien waivers or releases should ideally relate only to payments received.

SAFETY

The subcontract should provide that the trade contractor will cooperate with the builder or remodeler to prevent injuries to any workers employed and any other individuals present on the job site. In addition, the subcontract should confirm the trade contractor's obligation to observe and comply with applicable federal, state, and local safety and health rules and regulations, specifically including the Occupational Safety and Health Act (OSHA).

> In the course of its work the trade contractor shall initiate, maintain, and supervise all safety precautions and programs against injury to persons and property. The trade contractor shall provide safe working conditions for its employees, other employees, and other persons and entities on the site.
>
> In furtherance thereof, the trade contractor shall give all notices and comply with all applicable federal, state, and local laws bearing on the safety of persons or property or their protection from damage, injury, or loss on or about the premises where the work is being performed.
>
> Establishment of a safety program by the [builder or remodeler] shall not relieve the trade contractor from its safety responsibilities. The trade contractor shall indemnify the [builder or remodeler] for any fines or penalties imposed upon the [builder or remodeler] to the extent caused by the trade contractor's failure to comply with applicable safety requirements and for attorneys' fees and costs incurred in defending any citations for noncompliance by the trade contractor.

WARRANTY

The warranty is another risk-allocation device, similar to the indemnification clause, that allows the builder or remodeler to minimize his/her liability. Prudent builders and remodelers will obtain warranties from their trade contractors to cover the quality of the their work and the materials they furnish for the period of time required under the builder's or remodeler's warranty to the owner or purchaser. The warranty should explicitly state what is covered and what is not covered, and it should refer to certain standards of construction, such as NAHB's *Residential Construction Performance Guidelines for Professional Builders & Remodelers.*[62]

> The trade contractor warrants his or her work under this subcontract against all deficiencies and defects in materials and/or workmanship. Unless otherwise specified in this subcontract, all materials and equipment furnished shall be new. Substitutions not properly approved or authorized and unauthorized deviations from plans, specifications, manufacturer's installation instructions, or building codes shall be deemed to be defects in workmanship covered by this warranty, whether or not there shall be actual resulting damage. The trade contractor agrees to repair or replace at [his or her] own expense and pay any damages resulting from any defect in materials or workmanship that appear within one (1) year from [the date of occupancy by the owner, completion of the subcontract work, or acceptance or use by the (builder or remodeler)]. Warranty work must be completed promptly within ___(_____) days after receipt of a written request from either the [builder or remodeler] or the [buyer or owner]. If the trade contractor does not promptly complete the warranty work, the [builder or remodeler] or the [buyer or owner] may have the defective work corrected by a third-party contractor. All costs and expenses associated with such work, and any additional professional services, to include inspectors, remediators, architects, engineers, or consultants, will be paid by the trade contractor. In case of an emergency, as defined in the [builder's or remodeler's] limited warranty, the trade contractor shall respond within _____ hours after receiving notice of the emergency. Emergency service may be requested by telephone with a written service order to follow.

INDEPENDENT CONTRACTOR STATUS

As discussed at the beginning of this chapter, a written subcontract may help establish the trade contractor's status as an independent contractor rather than as an employee. Actions speak louder than words, however. Courts and the government agencies may disregard the pronouncement of independent contractor status declared in a subcontract agreement if the parties conduct their affairs as if they actually have an employer-employee relationship.

Employment status and its affect on insurance and taxes is of particular concern to builders and remodelers. Builders and remodelers who cannot demonstrate that their workers are in fact independent trade contractors may end up paying insurance premiums as if those persons were employees. During their annual audit, insurance companies will request certificates of insurance for trade contractors, showing the dates and amounts of the trade contractors' own insurance. Because premiums are calculated as a percentage of payroll, if these certificates are not produced, the insurance company will add the labor costs paid to trade contractors to the builder's or remodeler's payroll and increase their insurance premium accordingly. This is another reason why builders and remodelers should require that their trade contractors provide them with valid certificates of insurance prior to construction.

Figure 6.2 IRS's 20 Factors Affecting Independent Contractor Status

1. **Instructions.** A worker who is required to comply with other persons' instructions about when, where, and how he or she is to work is ordinarily an employee. The right to control, not actual control, is all that is required to establish control.
2. **Training.** Training an employee is indicative of an employer-employee relationship.
3. **Integration.** Integration of the worker's services into the business operations generally shows that the worker is subject to direction and control.
4. **Services Rendered Personally.** Indicative of an employer-employee relationship because presumably the person for whom the services are performed is interested in the methods used to accomplish the work as well as in the results.
5. **Hiring, Supervising, and Paying Assistants.** An independent contractor should have the right to hire and fire assistants.
6. **Continuing Relationship.** A continuing relationship between the worker and the employer is indicative of an employer-employee relationship.
7. **Set Hours of Work.** The establishment of set hours of work by the person for whom the services are performed is a factor indicating control.
8. **Full-Time Required.** An independent contractor is free to work when and for whom he or she chooses.
9. **Doing Work on Employer's Premises.** While this factor depends on the nature of the service involved, control over the place of work is indicated when the person for whom the services are performed has the right to compel the worker to work at specific places as required.
10. **Order of Sequence Set.** An independent contractor is free to follow his own work pattern and need not follow the established routines and schedules of the person for whom the services are performed.
11. **Oral or Written Reports.** An independent contractor should not be required to submit regular oral or written reports to the person for whom the services are performed.
12. **Payment by the Hour, Week, Month.** Payment made by the job or on a straight commission generally indicates that the worker is an independent contractor.
13. **Payment of Business and/or Traveling Expenses.** An employer generally pays the employee's business and/or traveling expenses.
14. **Furnishing of Tools and Materials.** An independent contractor furnishes his or her own tools and materials.
15. **Significant Investment.** Independent contractors invest in facilities that they use in performing services.
16. **Realization of Profit and Loss.** Independent contractors can realize a profit or suffer a loss as a result of the work they perform.
17. **Working for More Than One Firm At A Time.** An independent contractor performs more than de minim services for a multiple of unrelated persons or firms at the same time.
18. **Making Service Available to the General Public.** An independent contract makes his or her services available to the general public.
19. **Right to Discharge.** An independent contractor cannot be fired so long as he or she meets his or her obligations under the contract.
20. **Right to Terminate.** Generally, an employee may terminate the employment relationship without incurring liability.

Figure 6.2 IRS's 20 Factors Affecting Independent Contractor Status (Continued)

Three Categories of Control
(These categories are to be used in conjunction with the 20 factors)

1. **Behavioral Control.** This includes the type of instructions that the business (builder or remodeler) gives to the worker, such as when and where to do work, and the training provided to the worker. The key consideration is whether the business retains the right to control the details of the worker's performance or has relinquished that right.
2. **Financial Control.** This addresses the builder's or remodeler's right to control the business aspects of the worker's job.
3. **Relationship of the Parties.** The nature of the relationship may be evidenced by:
   a. A written contract
   b. Benefits provided, such as a paid vacation or health coverage
   c. The permanency of the position
   d. The extent to which the services performed are a key aspect of the builder's or remodeler's regular business

Rev. Ruling 87-41 (1987).

Federal tax withholding obligations differ depending on the classification of a worker. Companies hiring employees generally must withhold unemployment tax, Social Security tax, and income tax. In addition, employers may have state unemployment and income tax withholding obligations similar to those imposed under federal law. The failure to properly classify an "independent contractor" as an employee may result in the assessment of back taxes and penalties.

The Internal Revenue Service (IRS) identifies 20 factors it considers in determining whether an individual is an employee or an independent contractor and three categories of control factors. No one of the 20 factors governs the determination, but the degree of control exercised by, or granted to, the employer is generally conceded to be a more significant factor, hence the significance of the three categories of control. The subcontract should incorporate as many of these factors as may be feasible (see Figure 6.2).

If the IRS concludes that a worker is an employee, all is not necessarily lost, however. Congress created a statutory "safe harbor," which overrides the common law determination of the 20 IRS factors. If certain conditions are met, the Revenue Act of 1978 530(a), 26 U.S.C. 3401, note (1989) allows employers to treat workers as independent contractors, even though under common law they might be considered employees. To take advantage of the safe harbor provision, the employer must have (a) consistently treated the worker (and any individual holding a substantially similar position) as an independent contractor and (b) had a reasonable basis for not treating the worker as an employee.

ATTORNEY'S FEES, ARBITRATION, MEDIATION

It is a general rule in this country that each party to a lawsuit pays their own attorney's fees—win or lose. The prevailing party in a lawsuit may pay out a considerable portion of the monetary judgment to his/her attorney. Builders and remodelers can avoid paying legal expenses for valid claims by including a clause in the subcontract agreement that awards attorneys fees and costs to the prevailing party in a legal dispute between the trade contractor and the builder or remodeler (see Chapters 2 and 3 on attorney's fees).

Alternative dispute resolution, arbitration or mediation, is another method of resolving disputes between builders/remodelers and trade contractors without resorting to costly and time-consuming litigation. Builders and remodelers can choose to include an arbitration clause or a mediation clause in their subcontract agreements (see Chapters 2 and 3 on arbitration and mediation).

7

INSPECTIONS

INSPECTIONS

ALL THE CONTRACT PROVISIONS in the world will not benefit a builder or remodeler as much as nurturing a good relationship with a buyer or owner. One way a builder can nurture the relationship is to have the buyer visit the site often so that he/she can see the difficulties and complexities that the builder must go through. These visits can be formalized as inspections. The same process is somewhat built into a remodeling project because the owner is usually living on the premises. But even so, remodelers should incorporate formal owner inspections into the remodeling process.

Experience demonstrates that improved communication between the parties to a construction contract lessens the chance that the consumer will file a lawsuit. Problems can arise if buyers or owners have unrealistic expectations or simply do not understand the complexities of new home construction or remodeling. To reduce the prospects of misconstrued expectations leading to unreasonable demands, the construction or remodeling contract, the limited warranty, the statement of nonwarrantable conditions, and all of the other documents involved in the construction or remodeling process should be comprehensive and set out in simple and understandable terms. A builder or remodeler can further assure a harmony between expectations and performance and can reduce the likelihood of claims by thoroughly inspecting the property with the buyer or owner and recording the process. To avoid any surprises or possible delays at final inspection, builders and remodelers should consider having the owner or the owner's agent conduct interim inspections of the work at various stages of completion. Remember, payment for a job may hinge on acceptance of the work.

BUYER ORIENTATION AND HOME MAINTENANCE

Before a buyer moves into a new house, the builder or the builder's representative should walk through the house with the buyer and explain what has been done and how the equipment, appliances, and other items work. During this home buyer orientation, the builder should explain to the buyer how to maintain and take care of the items for which the buyer is responsible. Educating the buyer and completing the checklist in Figure 7.1 may prevent future problems with the home resulting from the owner's poor maintenance that may otherwise be blamed (or tried to be blamed) on the builder. At the very least, the buyer will see and will have in writing the items that are his/her responsibility. This may deter the homeowner from trying to blame the builder, and it will make it difficult for the owner to claim ignorance and to assert a breach of a duty to inform on the builder's part.

A remodeler should hold the same type of orientation for the owner of a remodeling project and provide similar instruction on maintenance and owner responsibility.

Figure 7.1 lists the items that the builder should discuss with the buyer. It also serves as a record of the builder's disclosures to the buyer. This sample may not include all of the items that should be addressed by the builder for any particular house, and any particular house may not be equipped with every item on this list. The builder should develop and use a format and list that works best for his/her construction and each particular situation.

The remodeler should also adapt this list to suit the owner orientation for a particular project. Should a dispute arise, the remodeler likewise will benefit from a record of the disclosures made to an owner and in having the owner sign the checklist.

NEW HOME PUNCHLIST

While the builder demonstrates the various items in the house to the buyer or subsequent to those demonstrations, the buyer must inspect the house for defects, problems, or any aspects of construction with which the buyer is dissatisfied. The construction contract should require the buyer to make this inspection before the closing (see Inspection, Acceptance, and Possession in Chapter 2).

As the builder walks through the house with the buyer prior to closing, the buyer fills out the punchlist (Figures 7.2 and 7.3). The buyer should be required to (a) initial every single item that he/she approves, (b) specifically identify items that require improvement, and (c) spell out what is wrong. These items should be corrected before closing and before the buyer is allowed to move into the house. Special provisions should be made for corrections that will require more time (e.g., if the builder needs to order parts).

The buyer and the builder should agree on a timetable for the improvements and write them on the punchlist. They should also set a date—30 days or so after the closing—for a final inspection so that the builder can check on the minor adjustments that are warranted for a 30-day period (such as dripping faucets and sticking doors).

To avoid the problem of a buyer repeatedly calling a builder to report minor problems in the days or weeks after moving in, the builder might suggest that the buyer keep a record of all minor problems and present it to the builder at one time.

Figure 7.1 Sample Home Maintenance Instruction Checklist

[Both builders and remodelers would need to adapt this form to their particular homes or projects. For a particular job, a remodeler might use only what was applicable to that job. This form is designed for a single owner or buyer; if more than one owner or buyer is involved, the form should be adapted to accommodate the initials and signature of each of the owners or buyers.]

Date _____

Buyer's or owner's name _____

Property street address _____

Buyer's or Owner's Initials _____

Plumbing

1. Instruction on use of faucets (emphasize cleaning of aerator); show water cutoffs; and explain how to change washers or cartridges (if used).

   _____

2. Instruction on use of shower and tub drains and care of fiberglass surfaces; show water cutoffs.

   _____

3. Instruction on adjustment of toilet tank mechanism.

   _____

4. Explain care of hot water heater:

   _____

   A. Periodically check pop-off valve and line.

   _____

   B. If water is not hot, check the pilot first.

   _____

   C. Always turn off pilot (or circuit breaker with electric water heaters) before draining tank completely.

   _____

   D. Periodically flush tank.

   _____

5. Show location of water meter, main cutoff, and sink and sewer cleanouts. (In case of an emergency, remove cap and allow sewer to overflow outside.)

   _____

6. Show location of any plumbing access panels and their purpose.

   _____

7. Show location of well and septic tank (if any), provide instruction on taking care of well pump, tank, and field and explain pumping of tank.

   _____

Electrical

8. Show buyer which outlets are switch-controlled.

   _____

9. Explain correct bulb size for lighting fixtures.

   _____

Figure 7.1 Sample Home Maintenance Instruction Checklist (Continued)

10. Show location of main entrance panel.

_____

11. Explain circuit breakers and ground-fault circuit breakers and how to operate them.

_____

12. Explain operation and testing of smoke detectors.

_____

13. Explain operation of security system, intercom, telephone, doorbells, and cable connection for television (if any of these are installed). Show all electrical outlets.

_____

Heating and Air Conditioning

14. Explain warranty.

_____

15. Show location and operation of thermostats.

_____

16. Show location of filters and explain when they should be changed.

_____

17. Explain how to balance forced-air systems in heating and cooling seasons.

_____

18. Explain operation of heat pump (if installed) and back-up electric resistance heat.

_____

19. Explain operation of hot water heating system and zones or electric baseboard heating (if installed).

_____

20. Explain that if problems with heating or cooling develop, buyer should do the following in the order listed:

_____

   A. Check thermostat setting.

   _____

   B. Check circuit breaker box to be sure circuit breaker is on (explain that a tripped circuit breaker should be turned all the way off first, then turned back on).

   _____

   C. Reset circuit breaker.

   _____

21. Furnish name of company to call for service.

_____

Appliances

22. Instruction on use and care of all appliances.

_____

23. Explain limited warranties and give buyer other literature.

_____

24. Explain maintenance of range hood and cleaning or changing of range hood filter.

_____

_____

Figure 7.1 Sample Home Maintenance Instruction Checklist (Continued)

25. Explain how to clean dryer vent pipe and filter.

_____

26. Explain steps to follow if appliances do not operate:
    A. Check to be sure they are plugged in.

    _____

    B. Check circuit breakers (see item 20).

    _____

    C. Reset circuit breakers.

    _____

27. Furnish names, addresses, and phone numbers of service companies to call for direct service.

_____

General Interior

28. Explain care, cleaning, and treatment of floors: wood, carpet, tile. Suggest use of casters under furniture. Explain that damage caused by neglect is not warranted.

_____

29. Explain care of paint (not warranted) and that builder does not do touch ups. Remind buyer not to scrub latex-painted interior walls. Give buyer names and color numbers of paints used.

_____

30. Explain use of spackling for normal cracks in sheetrock and nail pops (often repaired by builder after 1 year with owner doing the painting).

_____

31. Explain use of caulk for cracks in tile and to reseal tub when required (not warranted).

_____

32. Explain care of counter tops and that knives will cut the surface.

_____

33. Explain care of doors.
    A. Clean weep holes in sliding glass door thresholds.

    _____

    B. Replace weatherstripping when it wears out or is damaged.

    _____

    C. Oil hinges if doors squeak.

    _____

    D. Avoid paint buildup on door and window sash edges to keep them from sticking.

    _____

34. Explain operation of fireplace (if installed), use of seasoned wood to prevent creosote build-up, and the necessity of having flue cleaned regularly.

_____

35. Explain types of cleaning products, such as nonabrasive materials to be used on counter tops, wood finishes, bathroom tile, fiberglass showers and tubs, porcelain, marble and cultured marble, and other products (if used).

_____

36. Explain that bathroom and privacy locks can be unlocked from the outside with small screwdriver, nail, or coat hanger.

_____

Figure 7.1 Sample Home Maintenance Instruction Checklist (Continued)

37. Demonstrate removal of window sash for cleaning.
_____

38. Explain operation of exterior door and window locks.
_____

39. Explain hairline shrinkage cracks in concrete floors and walks.
_____

40. Explain possible future condensation on cool basement walls and floor if warm, moist air comes in contact with them. Explain avoidance through heating and dehumidification. Warn against trying to dry house out too quickly with excessive heat.
_____

41. Explain how to use bathroom and kitchen exhaust fans to avoid moisture buildup, condensation, and mold.
_____

General Exterior

42. Show location of and explain secondary air conditioning drain.
_____

43. Explain hairline shrinkage cracks in concrete surfaces.
_____

44. Explain that sunken utility lines and washed-out areas are not warranted.
_____

45. If shrubs are not warranted, explain this fact to the owner. (Be certain that grass and shrubs are alive during inspection.) Explain need for fertilizer and plenty of water.
_____

46. Light fixtures (bulbs not warranted).
_____

47. Explain that hairline cracks in concrete pad and puddles of 1/4 inch are normal.
_____

48. Explain that treated lumber used in wood decks, steps, or railings should weather 1 year prior to staining.
_____

49. Provide warranties on garage door openers and name, address, and phone number of trade contractor.
_____

50. Wood siding (if used) must be repainted or stained every 4 to 5 years. Mildew can be removed by scrubbing with weak water-and-bleach solution. Aluminum siding can be painted. It will dent if struck. Vinyl siding can crack or break if struck.
_____

51. Explain how to take care of brick.
_____

52. Provide limited warranties on asphalt or other roofing.
_____

53. Explain care of windows and operation of window locks.
_____

54. Provide limited warranties on glass in windows and sliding glass doors.
_____

Figure 7.1 Sample Home Maintenance Instruction Checklist (Continued)

55. Other _____

[For Builders—I have discussed each of the items listed above with a representative from (name of builder) and I understand them. I have been instructed in the use and care of the above-listed items in my new home and find my home completed in a manner satisfactory and acceptable to me].

[For Remodelers—I have discussed each of the items listed above with a representative from (name of remodeler) and understand them. I have been instructed in the use and care of the above-listed items in the [remodeling, renovation, rehabilitation, restoration of or addition to] my house. I find this project completed in a manner satisfactory and acceptable to me.]

_____   _____
(buyer's or owner's signature)   (builder or remodeler)

By _____

Title _____

Date _____

Figure 7.2 Sample Punchlist Instruction Letter

The builder presents this letter to the buyer along with the Buyer's Checklist at the time of the pre-settlement buyer orientation to prepare the punchlist. A remodeler would need to develop a letter appropriate to his or her specialty that could be adapted to a particular type of job.]

[Date]

[homebuyer's name]

[street address]

[city, state, and zip code]

Dear [homebuyer's name]:

(builder's name) is proud to welcome you to your new home. Attached to this letter you will find a checklist to help you inspect your new home. A separate sheet has been provided for each room and area of construction.

Please go through your new home, room by room, and carefully check to see whether all items are in satisfactory condition. Initial the space provided after you have satisfied yourself that the item's condition meets with your approval. If any repairs or adjustments are needed, describe the problem in the Improvement Needed column, using the back of the page if necessary. Be sure to write in any additional items that are not listed and describe their condition fully. If a listed item does not apply, put an X in the space for your initials.

Before you occupy your home, we will do our best to bring the items that require improvement up to satisfactory condition, consistent with the standards of construction in (city, state) and with our builder's limited warranty. You will be required to make a second inspection at that time, and you will have the opportunity to check all the items to make sure they meet with your approval.

Sincerely,

_____
(name of builder or builder's representative)

_____
(title)

Figure 7.3 Buyer's or Owner's Checklist for Developing the Punchlist

[The items listed under Improvement Needed will serve as the punchlist. In adapting this sample form, both builders and remodelers should provide more space for writing, especially under Improvement Needed, so the buyer or owner has room to explain what needs to be done. Remodelers probably will want to use only the items that are appropriate for a specific job. For instance, if a kitchen was not involved in a remodeling project, the remodeler would eliminate the kitchen items from the owner's list for that job.]

Date_____

Item_____

Initials_____

Improvement Needed

Bathroom

Vanity	Floor
Sink	Walls
Medicine cabinet	Ceiling
Bathtub	Light fixture (not bulbs)
Shower	Windows
Shower curtain bar or door	Doors
Toilet	Woodwork
Towel bars	Baseboard heater or air vent
Paper holder	Other

Kitchen

Sink	Cooktop

Figure 7.3 Buyer's or Owner's Checklist for Developing the Punchlist (Continued)

Oven, range	Hood and exhaust fan
Microwave	Freezer
Mixer	Disposal
Dishwasher	Trash compactor
Refrigerator	

Item_____
Location_____
Initials_____
Improvement Needed

Cabinets	Light fixture (not bulbs)
Drawers	Windows
Countertops	Doors
Floor	Woodwork
Walls	Baseboard heater or air vent
Ceiling	Other

Living Room, Dining Room, Den, Family Room, Bedroom

Floor	Walls

Figure 7.3 Buyer's or Owner's Checklist for Developing the Punchlist (Continued)

Ceiling

Light fixtures (not bulbs)

Doors

Windows

Shades

Woodwork

Ceiling fan

Baseboard heater or air vent

Closets

Closet rods and shelving

Other

General Interior

Interior doors

Hardware

Paneling

Insulation

Wallpaper, paint

Fireplace(s)

Cabinets

Bookcases

Woodwork

Tile work

Electrical switches

Electrical outlets

Glass

Figure 7.3 Buyer's or Owner's Checklist for Developing the Punchlist (Continued)

Hallway

Walls
_____

Floor
_____

Ceiling
_____

Light fixture (not bulbs)
_____

Doors
_____
_____

Closets
_____

Windows
_____

Shades
_____

Woodwork
_____

Basement or Utility Room

Washer
_____

Dryer
_____

Water heater
_____

Furnace or heat pump
_____

Closets
_____

Walls
_____

Floor
_____
_____

Ceiling
_____

Light fixture (not bulbs)
_____

Light switches
_____

Doors
_____

Other
_____

Baseboard heater or air vent
_____

Figure 7.3 Buyer's or Owner's Checklist for Developing the Punchlist (Continued)

General Exterior

Paint

_____

_____

Siding, brick

_____

_____

Chimney

_____

_____

Roof

_____

_____

Doors

_____

_____

Garage

_____

_____

Walkways

_____

_____

Balcony

_____

_____

Light fixtures (not bulbs)

_____

_____

Light switches

_____

_____

Electrical outlets

_____

_____

Vents (dryer, range, hood, bathroom fan)

_____

_____

Other

_____

_____

I understand each of the items on the preceding pages and have discussed each item with a representative of (builder's name). I have been instructed in the use and care of the items listed on the preceding pages of this punchlist. With the sole exception of the items listed under Improvement Needed, I find my [new home or project] to be completed in a manner satisfactory and acceptable to me. I understand that, with the exception of those items that I have listed under Improvement Needed, I am purchasing the [house or project] as is, and I understand that the [builder or remodeler] makes no other guarantees or warranties other than those that are clearly stated in the contract and the other contract documents.

Punchlist completion date _____

Re-inspection date _____

_____   _____
(buyer's or owner's signature)   (builder or remodeler)

Date _____

By _____
(signature)

Title _____

As items on the "improvement needed" part of the checklist are corrected, the buyer should initial and date each item. The builder should keep this punchlist on file until the statute of limitations has expired. If used properly, the punchlist is good evidence of the condition of the house and of the buyer's satisfaction with the condition of the house. Used with the limited warranty, the punchlist provides further limitations on a builder's liability if the warranty is designed to exclude liability for damage or defects that the buyer should have discovered and listed for correction during the inspection.

The list may also serve as evidence that the buyer was satisfied with the items in the house at one time. It also demonstrates the builder's efforts to identify and correct problems.

The punchlist format presented here is merely a suggestion. The builder may prefer to use a final acceptance or completion report format (Fig. 7.4). Different items may apply to other houses, and the builder should consider carefully what format works best in a given situation. The builder could provide a separate punchlist for each room in the house. The list for each room should bear the name of the room to which it applies, and the same format should be used before and after the closing.

QUALITY CONTROL CHECKLIST

Although a remodeling project does not involve a settlement, a pre-completion punchlist is equally crucial in a remodeling project. The pre-completion checklist signed by the homeowner helps to prevent unrelated problems from being blamed on the remodeler. Remodelers could adopt the builders' procedures outlined above and suit them to individual projects.

FINAL INSPECTION AND ACCEPTANCE

When an owner or the owner's architect or engineer formally accepts work after final inspection, the builder or remodeler will normally not be liable thereafter to the owner for any nonlatent defects in the work. The builder or remodeler should record the names of the persons participating in the inspection as well as the scope of the inspection and have the parties sign that record. The sample final inspection/acceptance form shown in Figure 7.4 is geared for builders. A similar form can be used by remodelers with a more specific list for inspected items and features that are pertinent to a particular remodeling project.

Figure 7.4 Sample Final Inspection and Acceptance Form

Owner	_____
Builder	_____
In re-contract dated	_____
Construction site address	_____
Date and time of inspection	_____
Persons present at inspection	_____

A check mark in the box of a listed item indicates acceptance by the owner. Any deficiencies in material or workmanship will be indicated on the line next to a listed item and may be supplemented in the spaces for additional remarks.

BOX	ITEM	Comment Line
❑	Appliances	_____
❑	Attic/steps	_____
❑	Basement	_____
❑	Bathroom fixtures	_____
❑	Cabinets	_____
❑	Carpets	_____
❑	Ceilings	_____
❑	Ceramic tile	_____
❑	Countertops	_____
❑	Doors	_____
❑	Driveway-Walkways	_____
❑	Drywall	_____
❑	Electric switches/outlets	_____
❑	Exterior light fixtures	_____
❑	Exterior wood trim	_____
❑	Fireplace/chimney	_____
❑	Floors (wood/linoleum)	_____
❑	Garage/garage door	_____
❑	Grading/landscaping	_____
❑	Heating/air conditioning	_____
❑	Interior hardware	_____
❑	Interior light fixtures	_____
❑	Interior trim	_____
❑	Masonry	_____
❑	Mirrors	_____
❑	Painting/wallpaper	_____
❑	Plumbing/sinks	_____
❑	Roof/gutters	_____
❑	Sash	_____
❑	Siding	_____
❑	Water heater	_____
❑	Windows/screens	_____
❑	Vents/hoods/fans	_____

_____

Figure 7.4 Sample Final Inspection and Acceptance Form (Continued)

Other items and additional remarks

_____

_____

_____

The undersigned owner(s) hereby affirm(s) that they have conducted a final inspection of the above-stated premises on the date and at the time so indicated. Except as may be indicated, the owner(s) has (have) found the home and indicated items to be in good condition and accepts the home, the listed items, and the builder's performance as being in full compliance with the terms and conditions of the above-stated contract. The owner(s) do(es) release the builder from any and all subsequent damage or failure and the consequences thereof of the home and/or its fixtures, appliances, and components, except as is provided for and stated in the builder's warranty. The owner(s) acknowledge(s) and understand(s) that cracks in masonry, concrete, walls, and other components may develop in the ordinary course of new construction settling/expansion and contraction, and the standard for the right to warranty repair of such cracks shall be governed by NAHB's _Residential Construction Performance Guidelines._ The owner(s) grant(s) permission for the builder to re-enter the premises after owner(s) occupancy to correct any indicated items.

Owner_____   Date _____

Owner_____   Date _____

Builder_____   Date _____

Witness_____   Date _____
                    (optional)

The owner(s) do(es) hereby acknowledge that all of the listed deficiencies in workmanship and materials as indicted above have been corrected by the builder to my (our) satisfaction, and I (we) do hereby accept the home as fully completed in accordance with the contract and do further release the builder from responsibility and liability from all future damage or failure and consequences thereof, except as may be provided in the builder's warranty.

Owner_____   Date _____

Owner_____   Date _____

Builder_____   Date _____

DESIGN-BUILD CONTRACTS USED BY
REMODELERS AND CUSTOM BUILDERS

DESIGN-BUILD DESCRIBES A project in which the custom builder or remodeler both designs a job specifically for a particular client and then constructs the job based on that design. The design and construction functions are undertaken by the same entity, as opposed to the traditional method of construction in which the owner contracts with an independent architect for construction plans and blueprints and then separately contracts with the builder or remodeler for actual construction of the project. Discussing the pros and cons of the design-build arrangement is beyond the scope of this book. However, this chapter does provide guidance to custom builders and remodelers on how to avoid two common pitfalls that can await the uninitiated design-build company—specifically, practicing architecture without a license and offering design services without adequate liability protection.

PRACTICING ARCHITECTURE

Custom builders or remodelers who offer design services to their customers must verify that they are properly licensed to do so. Depending on the individual state license requirements, design work for residential and commercial structures must be performed by a properly licensed architect. All states have regulations governing the practice of architecture. Almost all states prohibit unlicensed persons from offering architectural services and often impose civil or criminal sanctions against violators. In addition to potential criminal and civil penalties, practicing architecture without a license may be particularly costly because in many courts a contract performed by a person unlicensed to perform those services is unenforceable. This could mean that a design builder who lacks an architectural license will not be paid on a design-build contract.

States can differ as to what services constitute the practice of architecture. The majority of states hold that design services, such as the preparation of schematics, working drawings, plans, and specifications are architectural services and may be performed only by licensed architects.

Builders generally may prepare preliminary sketches for use as the basis for the architect's schematics, drawings, and floor plans but, unless excepted by the licensing statute, not as part of the final plan of construction. The prudent builder or remodeler should consult an attorney experienced in construction law before offering design services. Figure 8.1 lists licensing issues that design builders and design-build remodelers should discuss with their attorneys.

EXEMPTIONS

Some states' architectural licensing laws provide exemptions for the design of certain types of construction, but these exemptions can differ widely. Depending on the state, structures with certain uses (often single-family homes) and of a limited height or size may be exempted. Unless you are certain that an exemption covers your specific undertaking, however, you should not offer design services without having a licensed architect on staff or independently contracted. Builders and remodelers must look to their own state's architectural licensing laws to see what exemptions, if any, their state permits.

STAMPING OR SEALING PLANS

The architectural licensing laws cannot be circumvented by having an architect affix a seal or a stamp to plans that are not prepared by that architect but are in fact prepared by an unlicensed design builder or design-build remodeler. This practice is illegal in most states. A builder or remodeler who obtains such a stamp or seal for his/her plans may be guilty of a civil or even a criminal offense.

Figure 8.1 Licensing Issues Design-Builders and Design-Build Remodelers Should Discuss with Their Attorneys

---

- Is design-build specifically addressed by statute?
- Must a design-build joint venture get a special license or will the individual licenses of the designer and the builder or remodeler meet the statutory requirements?
- Do the licensing statutes for architects, engineers, and contractors indicate how the design-build entity needs to be structured to comply with the statutory licensing requirements?
- Will a licensed architect on staff meet the licensing requirements for design by a design-build firm?
- Can a homeowner contract for design-build services directly with a licensed designer who does not have a contractor's license or directly with a licensed contractor who does not have an architect's license?
- Will the requirements for a licensed architect be satisfied by subcontracting the architecture to a licensed architectural firm if the design-builder or design-build remodeler is not licensed as an architect or as an engineer and does not have an employee who is licensed as such?

Source: Reprinted with permission from Thomas H. Asselin and L. Bruce Stout, "Legal Exposure of the Design/Build Participants: The View of the General Contractor," *The Construction Lawyer,* Vol. 15, No. 3 (August 1995), p. 8–28.

STAFF ARCHITECTS AND INDEPENDENT CONTRACTORS

A licensed architect can provide his/her services as an employed member of a design-build company's staff or as an independent supplier of design services under contract to the design builder or design-build remodeler. When the designer is an independent contractor to or engaged in a joint venture with the builder or remodeler, these parties should have a written contract specifying their respective responsibilities and liabilities. As an example, in addition to standard contract provisions discussed in Chapter 6 (cost of the work, the payment terms, time for performance, and so on), the service contract might also provide that the independent designer (architect) shall be solely responsible for stamping relevant contract drawings, drafting the accompanying specifications, and indemnifying the design builder or design-build remodeler for any damages or legal expenses that they may incur as the result of design errors.[63]

PROTECTION AGAINST LIABILITY FOR DESIGN ERRORS

Design errors may *not* be covered under a builder's or remodeler's general liability insurance policy for construction activities. In fact, the general liability policy may specifically exclude coverage for professional (architectural) services. If the policy is silent on professional service coverage, it is possible that the insurance company could decide to voluntarily pay a claim based on design error, or it is possible that a court could rule in favor of coverage because the policy did not expressly exclude professional design services. Neither prospect is certain, however, so the wise design builder or design-build remodeler will investigate the extent of his/her insurance coverage for design services before any problem occurs. Read the insurance policy, and check with your insurance agent to determine your coverage.

To fill any gap in insurance coverage for professional design services, design builders and design-build remodelers could consider obtaining an errors and omissions policy. However, these policies are often difficult to obtain and may be prohibitively expensive for builders and remodelers who are not licensed architects.

Alternatively, builders and remodelers might consider allocating this risk to a third-party architect or an engineer hired as a consultant to review the plans and specifications. The consulting agreement could provide for indemnification of the design builder or design-build remodeler for damages and legal expenses resulting from a negligent consultation review. If this course is taken, the design builder or design-build remodeler should obtain the consultant's malpractice insurance certificate or a copy of their insurance policy to make certain that the consultant has the means to provide for indemnification. The design builder or design-build remodeler could also ask to be listed as an insured on the consultant's insurance policy.

Of course, one of the best ways of protecting a design builder or design-build remodeler from potential liability for design errors is to only perform those design services that the builder or remodeler is capable of undertaking. For example, if the builder or remodeler is working with an unusual or unfamiliar structural design or is uncertain about the structural sufficiency of the design, the design plans should be reviewed by a structural engineer or architect qualified in structural design.

DESIGN-BUILD CONTRACTS

A design builder or design-build remodeler may need three contracts to protect his/her interests adequately: a contract for a feasibility study, a design contract, and a construction contract. Sometimes the feasibility and design phases are included in one contract. Other times, the design and construction phases are combined. This section focuses on the design contract. For tips on drafting a design-build construction agreement, consult chapters 2 and 3.

DESIGN CONTRACT

The design contract, sometimes called a preliminary design-build agreement or a preconstruction services contract, covers the scope of the design work to be performed, the cost of the design service, and the rights and duties of the parties. This contract serves the following purposes:

- Sets forth the names of the parties to the contract, their addresses, phone numbers, and any other identification or contact information
- Briefly describes the type of project and location
- Specifies the scope of the design. These specifications may take the form of a phase schedule. For example:
  Phase 1. Schematics
  Phase 2. Preliminary design and floor plan
  Phase 3. Working drawings and specifications
- Specifies the cost of design services, including the amount, manner, and time of payment. If the work is to be done in phases, payment may be linked to the start of a new phase. It also may be tied to levels of service. For instance:
  Level 1. Production of thumbnail sketches and one site visit might be at no cost
  Level 2. Any out-of-pocket expenses for engineering or other fees will be paid by the client
  Level 3. All remaining services, including production of working drawings, for a specific fee or hourly rate, plus out-of-pocket expenses

In another example, the initial schematics for a $2,000 design job might be priced at $400. The relatively low initial fee may allow the design itself to entice the customer into deciding to proceed on the whole job:

Phase 1. Schematics $400

Phase 2. Preliminary design and floor plan $800

Phase 3. Working drawings and specifications $800

- Explains how outside services, such as engineering, will be handled and charged to the client

- Provides a method of payment in the event the contract is terminated during the various phases of preconstruction

- May include a liquidated damages clause

- Explains what will happen if the client materially changes the scope of the work or the manner of its execution

- Includes a completion date for the design phase. It may make the date contingent on the owner (a) providing necessary information and (b) making necessary decisions within a reasonable time.

- Specifies whether the design fee will be credited against the construction contract price in the event the client uses the firm for construction

- Explains who owns the drawings, specifications, and other documents and how they can be used. For example, the contract might specify that the plans remain the sole property of the builder or remodeler and that the purchaser may use them only for construction, repair, alteration, or other improvement by the builder or remodeler.

- Discusses the client's dual rights of rescission and cancellation. (A sample design contract appears in Figure 8.2.)

Figure 8.2 Sample Design Contract

This preconstruction agreement is made this _____ day of _____, 20___, between _____, the client, who resides at _____, and _____, the [builder or remodeler], whose principal place of business is at _____. The client and the [builder or remodeler] agree as set forth below:

   Project: (describe in detail) This project is designed to fall within a budget range of $_____ to $_____ for construction.

1. **Furnishing Design.** The [builder or remodeler] shall furnish the design of the project in accordance with the following schedule:

   Phase 1. Based on the client's project requirements, the [builder or remodeler] will provide design schematics, including field measurements. These schematics are to assist the client in determining the feasibility of the project.

   Phase 2. On approval of the design schematics, the [builder or remodeler] will proceed with preliminary design development, floor plan, and elevations. Unless otherwise noted, drawings will be to scale.

   Phase 3. From approved preliminary design documents the [builder or remodeler] will provide working drawings and specifications. These working drawings will serve as the basis for the [builder's or remodeler's] estimate of the cost of construction and for the construction of the project.

2. **Payment Schedule.** In return for the foregoing services, the client agrees to pay the [builder or remodeler] as follows:

   Phase 1. Compensation for phase 1 shall be in the amount of dollars ($_____), and the payment is due on _____.

   Phase 2. Compensation for phase 2 shall be in the amount of dollars ($_____), and the payment is due on _____.

   Phase 3. Compensation for phase 3 shall be in the amount of dollars ($_____), and the payment is due on _____.

3. **Engineering and Other Extra Fees.** The [builder or remodeler] anticipates that the scope of the project will require the services of an engineer. The client shall pay the engineering fees at _____ dollars ($_____) per hour, up to a maximum cost of _____ ($_____). The [builder or the remodeler] shall not be responsible for the payment of any engineering fees.

4. **Failure to Proceed.** If the client elects not to proceed after any phase, the [builder or remodeler] is entitled to payment in accordance with paragraph B.

5. **Change in Work.** If the scope of the work or the manner of its execution is materially changed, the additional work shall be billed on an hourly basis at the following rates: [builder or remodeler] @ _____ dollars ($_____); engineer @ _____ dollars ($_____); others [list them] @ _____ dollars ($_____).

6. **Ownership of the Documents.** The preliminary design documents, working drawings, and specifications are for the sole use of the [builder or remodeler] in connection with this project, and they shall remain the property of the [builder or remodeler]. They are not to be used by the client or any third party on other projects without the written consent of the [builder or remodeler]. The client will be liable to the [builder or remodeler] for all losses arising out of the unauthorized use or sale of these copyrighted documents.

7. **Client Cooperation.** Client will provide full information regarding the owner's requirements for the project and make necessary decisions required for completion of design documents in a timely manner.

Figure 8.2 Sample Design Contract (Continued)

8. **Delivery of Estimated Costs.** The [builder or remodeler] shall complete the design phase and provide the client with the cost to construct the project by the _____ day of _____, 20_____.

9. **Client's Right to Cancel.** Pursuant to federal law you have three (3) days from [signature date] to cancel this contract. See the attached form for an explanation of this law.

10. **Client's Right of Rescission.** Pursuant to federal law you have three (3) days from [signature date] to rescind this agreement. Client acknowledges receipt of two (2) copies of the notice of the right of rescission.

_____   _____
(buyer's or owner's signature)   (name of builder, remodeler, or corporate name where applicable)
_____   By _____
(buyer's signature)   (authorized signature)

Date _____
Title _____

Date _____
This contract is dated, and becomes effective,

_____
(month, day, year)

_____
(buyer's initials)

9

CONTRACTS WITH OTHER TEAM MEMBERS

D<small>URING THE COURSE OF</small> a construction or remodeling project, the builder or remodeler may work with other professionals such as attorneys, in-house real estate salespeople, real estate brokers, suppliers, and lenders, to name a few (Figure 9.1). This chapter highlights some of the legal issues that may arise when working with these individuals and entities.

ATTORNEYS

Throughout this book, builders and remodelers have been advised not to use the included forms or procedures without the review and approval of an attorney, preferably one experienced in construction contract law. The list in Figure 9.2 explores some of the ways in which attorneys can assist builders and remodelers with their contracts.

Of course, the role of the attorney is not limited to contract review or drafting. A builder or remodeler may call upon an attorney to provide a number of other services. For example, the attorney may:

- Advise the builder or remodeler regarding compliance with federal, state, and local regulations
- Assist in obtaining a building permit
- Provide support during presentations to planning and zoning boards
- Represent the builder or remodeler in financial transactions
- Represent the builder or remodeler in situations in which an owner or trade contractor breaches a contract (such as when an owner refuses to pay or a trade contractor refuses to perform)
- Defend a builder or remodeler in the event of a breach of contract or negligence action

Figure 9.1 Other Parties With Whom Builders and Remodelers May Contract

- Accountant
- Architect
- Engineer
- Interior designer
- Experts, consultants, and specialists
  — Demolition experts
  — Environmental experts
  — Hazardous waste removal specialists (indoor and outdoor)
  — Risk management specialists

- Draft contracts

- Assist the builder or remodeler in filing a mechanic's lien

- Represent the builder or remodeler in alternative dispute resolution proceedings

When hiring an attorney, builders and remodelers should consider these issues:

- Does the attorney charge hourly, by the case (fixed fee), or on a contingency basis? A contingency fee (a fixed percentage of a money judgment award due only upon recovery) is traditionally offered to plaintiffs primarily in personal injury cases, and less frequently in property damage cases.

Figure 9.2 Ways Attorneys Can Assist Builders or Remodelers in Preparing Contracts

- Advise the builder or remodeler about particular provisions that should or should not be inserted in the contract and explain why so that an astute businessperson can understand what each contract provision means at least in general terms.
- Tailor the contract to reflect state and local laws.
- Assist in drafting the contract so that it clearly and unambiguously expresses the parties' rights and obligations.
- Explain the potential legal ramifications—both positive and negative—that may arise from the contract.
- In preparing documents and in other legal matters, consult with other experts on the builder's or remodeler's behalf.
- Prepare or assist in the preparation of any documents that should accompany the contract, such as a notice of the right of rescission or a notice of the contractor's lien rights (in those states where the notice must be delivered before work is performed).
- Give advice on a regular basis. Once the attorney is familiar with the contract, he or she will be able to provide quick and accurate answers should questions arise.

- If the charge is hourly, what is the rate, and what is the rate for other attorneys and legal staff in the office who may work on the case?

- The builder or remodeler should insist on a written employment contract with the attorney specifying the attorney's fees, the basis for all charges of fees and expenses, and the terms of payment. Itemized statements are recommended. Some attorneys require a retainer to be paid initially. The retainer is placed on deposit in a special trust account and may be drawn by the attorney only when the fees have been earned or expenses incurred, and only for the amount of earned fees and expenses.

- Does the attorney offer a mechanism for resolving client disputes?

- Under what circumstances may the parties terminate the relationship, and how will fees and costs be handled in such an event?

IN-HOUSE REAL ESTATE AND REMODELING SALES AGENTS

Determining whether an in-house sales agent is an employee or an independent contractor is a significant issue for builders and remodelers. At the federal level an employer is required to withhold income and Social Security taxes from employees wages and to pay the employer's share of Social Security taxes. At the state level the employer is liable for unemployment insurance tax and for workers' compensation insurance.

Independent contractor status depends on the actual relationship between the parties as determined on a case-by-case basis. (See Chapter 6, Independent Contractor Status). The actual relationship (often viewed in terms of the degree of control over activities) between the builder or remodeler and an in-house sales agent is more important to the Internal Revenue Service than what their contract for services may state. However, if the working relationship will be structured to meet the independent contractor test, the contract for services should definitely reflect that status as an independent contractor.

The sales agent provides services to the business community as an independent contractor and is engaged by [builder or remodeler] solely for the services outlined in the scope of work. Nothing in this agreement shall be interpreted or construed as creating an employer-employee relationship between the sales agent and [builder or remodeler].

The sales agent is responsible for all federal and state income taxes resulting from any contract payments paid by [builder or remodeler]. The sales agent will receive an IRS form 1099 for all earnings. [Builder or Remodeler] will not have any responsibility for withholding or paying income taxes or Social Security payments on behalf of any individuals employed for work under this agreement by the sales agent.

REAL ESTATE BROKERS

In today's competitive market, more new home builders are using the services of real estate brokers to sell their homes. This relationship offers advantages to both parties: It provides the builder with access to a larger market and it allows the broker to increase his/her inventory. A builder's use of a broker, as distinct from an in-house sales staff, would involve (a) a real estate salesperson employed by a real estate firm working on the site or (b) a builder-broker cooperative program. A builder-broker cooperative program may involve one real estate firm or many of them. In either case, however, the real estate firm does not work exclusively for the builders, and none of its employees work on the site.

A key issue under the single-firm arrangement is broker loyalty, and it should be addressed in the parties' contract. The contract should provide that any prospect inquiring by mail, telephone, or in person belongs to the builder and may not be solicited by the broker or referred by the broker to another broker. For example, if a couple walks in off the street, the broker may not offer to show the couple other persons' properties on his/her day off or refer the couple to another broker for that purpose.

Builders who enter into a cooperative program with outside brokers should resolve the following matters at the outset and include their understandings in the contracts with the real estate brokers.

- What is expected of the broker?
- What is the commission rate? Will it be based on the home's gross sales price or on the base sales price (the price without any options)?
- Under what terms will a commission be paid? For example, if the broker's commission depends in part on him/her accompanying the prospect to and registering him/her at the builder's development on the prospect's first visit to the site, this condition should be clearly spelled out in the contract.
- Similarly, will the builder honor the broker's registration of the prospect for a specified period of time (say 30 to 60 days)? Because the broker will be entitled to a commission during that time if the builder sells the property, a builder often will list names of his/her current active prospects in the contract with the broker and exclude sales to those prospects from commissions.
- If a dispute arises, how will it be settled? The agreement should spell out the dispute resolution procedures to be followed.
- What sales and marketing services will the real estate broker provide and which ones will the builder perform?

- Some builders and brokers subscribe to builder and broker codes or guidelines that cover important matters such as those discussed in the preceding list. For example, the Southern Arizona Home Builders Association and the Tucson Association of Realtors® have adopted the Builder-Broker Code of Mutual Understanding. The builder and broker agree to subscribe to the code and to operate in accordance with its provisions.

These two groups can be contacted at the addresses listed below:

Southern Arizona Home Builders Association
2840 N. Country Club Road
Tucson, Arizona 85716
(520) 795-5114

Tucson Association of Realtors®
1622 N. Swan Road
Tucson, Arizona 85712
(520) 327-4218

SUPPLIERS

A supplier provides builders, remodelers, and trade contractors with the materials, supplies, or equipment they use in their work. Suppliers sell building materials, and builders and trade contractors use the materials to erect and construct a building on the site.[64] Builders and remodelers should have written contracts with their suppliers for the same reasons that they have written contracts with their clients and their trade contractors: to document their agreements, to minimize misunderstandings, and to allocate risks.

If the parties fail to address an item in the contract or the contract does not adequately cover the item, the provisions of the Uniform Commercial Code (UCC) will apply. The UCC has been adopted by all fifty states and governs commercial transactions involving personal property, including supplies and materials. The statutory provisions of the UCC can be modified by contract. Builders or remodelers may wish to identify the key terms of their supply arrangement and commit them to a written contract rather than solely rely on the UCC (unless, of course, you are aware of applicable UCC provisions and are fully agreeable to those terms). A contractor who objects to a term in an offer from a supplier should provide an additional or different term (not merely delete the objectionable term from the acceptance) because silence may not be deemed to be a sufficient rejection, as was seen in the illustrative case cited below.

The supply contract should identify the material necessary to complete the work, including accessories, and when appropriate it should note that certain materials are not included. If necessary, the contract should state that the products supplied and the work accomplished under the contract will conform to the plans and specifications. The material should be identified by brand name, size, quality, quantity, and other similar descriptive information. The contract should include the cost of the material (including any discounts) and the payment terms (including any deposits and retainage). Shipping terms, delivery dates, location, and conditions should be addressed in the contract. For example, if the parties have agreed that the supplier will uncrate the material and set it in place, these terms should be in the contract. The contract should provide for insurance, the return of defective and surplus materials, the supplier's warranties, and a method for resolving disputes.

CASE STUDY

Jorgensen made a written offer to sell certain goods to Mark Construction by issuing its signed quotation form, which conspicuously included a limitation of warranty liability clause. Mark accepted this offer by issuing a signed purchase order based on and including reference to Jorgensen's quotation. Mark's purchase order described the goods to be furnished, the purchase price, the terms of payment, and the time and place of delivery, as contained in Jorgensen's quotation, but the purchase order made no reference to the limitation of warranty liability provision.

When Jorgensen sued Mark for breach of contract, Mark counterclaimed against Jorgensen for breach of warranty, and Jorgensen claimed that its liability was limited under the contract. Finding for Jorgensen, the court concluded that submission of the purchase order constituted acceptance of all of the terms of the offer made in the quotation, and that Mark's silence was not an effective rejection or a counteroffer.[65]

10

LIABILITY AND CONTRACT ENFORCEMENT

THERE IS NEVER AN absolute guarantee that builders and remodelers will not be sued or will not end up in arbitration or mediation proceedings, no matter how carefully they construct their buildings and renovations and no matter how diligent they may be in their business practices. However, builders and remodelers can reduce the potential for liability in numerous ways throughout the construction process and afterwards. Some of the actions that have successfully reduced liability for builders and remodelers are listed in Figure 10.1. Of these, experience has shown that two of the more important measures are to use well-written contracts and to make a strong commitment to customer service. A well-written contract is always the best protection, but a good relationship with the customer will often save the day when all else has failed.

GROUNDS OF LIABILITY

Homebuilders and remodelers may face liability to an owner or a purchaser under several legal theories of recovery. Because each theory has met with some success in various cases, a typical construction complaint often alleges several of these causes of action. Some of the more popular grounds for lawsuits brought by homeowners, particularly against builders or remodelers, include:

- Breach of contract
- Breach of express warranty
- Breach of implied warranty
- Negligence
- Fraud and misrepresentation
- Consumer Protection Act violation—deceptive trade practices

Figure 10.1 Actions to Prevent Liability Problems

- Use a well-written contract for all transactions in the sales and construction process. All parties to the contract should read and understand all provisions before signing the document.

- Make a strong commitment to customer service. Such a commitment involves conscientious customer relations, quick follow-up on punchlists and callbacks, and correcting the problem promptly in some cases (even when the remodeler or builder is not at fault) because that course probably will prove less expensive than litigating the matter later.

- Regularly examine your insurance program to make sure it is comprehensive. Fill in any gaps in insurance coverage.

- Develop realistic construction schedules that allow enough time to do the work well, for any interruptions that might be caused by the anticipated weather, and for minor unexpected problems with deliveries.

- Emphasize safety in all aspects of the business. Insist on safe procedures and use of safety equipment.

- Follow all building codes and other regulations to the letter. Avoid cutting corners.

- Use reputable subcontractors, design professionals, and real estate brokers; establish sound working relationships with them and all parties in the construction process; promote a cooperative attitude; and avoid polarizing the parties to all contracts.

- During the sales and construction process, make only promises you can keep and keep those you make. Review brochures, advertising, and other marketing devices for unintended promises or warranties.

- Treat prospects', owners', and buyers' concerns seriously.

- Obtain signed change orders (showing the price) for any alterations to the original construction plans, specifications, or other aspects of the job.

- Comply with all laws prohibiting discrimination based on race, religion, creed, color, national origin, sex, marital or family status, age, arrest record, or disability. Review employment policies, practices, and materials as well as brochures, advertising, and other marketing devices for unintended discrimination.

- Use indemnity clauses in contracts with design professionals and subcontractors.

- Disclaim and/or limit the duration of implied warranties or obtain waivers of such warranties in states where waivers are permissible.

- Consider alternative dispute resolution techniques, such as arbitration or mediation, in lieu of litigation.

- Operate a building or remodeling business in an ethical, legal, and carefully organized way with an emphasis on customer service to greatly reduce your exposure to liability.

- Retain an attorney knowledgeable about construction for review of contracts and periodic review of operations. However, in the event of a dispute, builders and remodelers can seek the assistance of some local builders associations or Remodelers™ Councils.

BREACH OF CONTRACT

A failure to carry out an obligation of the contract may constitute a breach of contract. Each party to a contract is entitled to receive the product or compensation they contracted for. A builder or remodeler cannot unilaterally (without the consent of the other party) provide a lower-quality product or refuse to perform in accordance with the contract terms, nor can a customer unilaterally refuse to pay the agreed price. All these acts constitute breaches of contract. There are different kinds of breaches. A material breach of contract is a breach that goes to the essence of the agreement. The nonbreaching party has the option to void the contract and be excused from performance or to perform the contract and in both instances to assert a claim for damages. A minor breach, however, will not excuse performance by the nonbreaching party.

EXAMPLE

Clause in contract states that house must be completed by July 1, and time is of the essence—Contractor is unable to start construction until July 7—This is a material breach—purchaser has option to consider contract void.

SECOND EXAMPLE

House is completed by July 1, except for installation of shutters—This is not a material breach—essence of the contract was completion of house and not completion with all decorative accessories—Purchaser is not permitted to avoid the contract but may be permitted to claim damages.

CASE STUDY

Kaiser contracted with Fishman for the construction of a beach-front dwelling. Fishman knowingly deviated from the plans and specifications provided by Kaiser. The original plans called for 20 pilings, but Fishman placed only 14 pilings, and 6 of them were drilled in incorrect locations. The court determined that the resulting dwelling was inferior to that called for by the plans and specifications. The court concluded that Fishman deliberately failed to comply with the contract terms, so it awarded Kaiser "cost to cure" damages, which would give him with the house he bargained for, rather than the repair damages argued for by Fishman.[66]

BREACH OF EXPRESS WARRANTY

Express warranties are any statements (oral or written) that the work will meet certain standards. Breach of warranty occurs when such a statement proves to be false. Express warranties often are limited to specific responses for a stated period of time, excluding other occurrences. (Example—An express limited warranty may state that the builder will fix and repair construction defects to the walls, flooring, and foundation for a period of one year but will not be responsible for consequential damages arising out of any construction defect. This warranty is limited in duration to one year. It is limited in coverage to walls, flooring, and foundation [it doesn't cover roofs, for example]. Recovery under this warranty is also limited to the cost of repair [for instance, it excludes recovery for personal property damaged as a consequence of a covered construction defect].)

CASE STUDY

A prospective purchaser, who wanted to build a home with a view of a valley, contracted with a designer to look at a lot to determine its suitability as a homesite. The designer advised the prospective purchaser that the lot was suitable, that the home would fit properly on the lot, and that the house would have a view. However, the house could not be placed in the position chosen by the purchaser because of zoning restrictions and restrictive covenants.

The court held that in assuring the purchaser that the lot selected was a suitable site and that the house could be placed on it properly and have a view, the designer warranted that certain facts existed, which in fact did not. Accordingly, the purchaser was entitled to compensation for those damages that the designer had reason to foresee as a probable result of his breach of express warranty.[67]

BREACH OF IMPLIED WARRANTY

Implied warranties are imposed on builders by state court decisions and statutes. They exist in addition to any express warranties, without the occurrence of an oral or written promise made by the builder. The rationale is that since the purchase of a new home represents such an enormous investment for most purchasers, and since there is a perceived disparity between the expertise of a professional builder and an ordinary home purchaser, it is declared to be the public policy (in most states) for a builder/vender of a new home to warrant by implication that the house is habitable and that it has been built in a workmanlike manner. This implied warranty is deemed to be a part of the home purchase or construction contract, even though it is not stated in the contract documents, and it covers both materials and workmanship. Many states permit the disclaimer of implied warranties, but most states will enforce a disclaimer only if it is clear, unambiguous, and (often) conforms to strict requirements of specified language and format.

The time an implied warranty remains in effect can vary from state to state, from as little as one year to ten years and beyond. Some states set the time of duration for an implied warranty in the statute that created the implied warranty. Other states limit the duration for an implied warranty through a statute of limitations or a statute of repose for bringing claims involving improvements to real property. Other states set no particular time limit except to rule that the implied warranty will remain in effect for a "reasonable length of time." Some states hold that implied warranties extend only to the original purchaser, but other states declare that implied warranties extend to subsequent purchasers as well.

Some states also subject remodeling contracts to implied warranties of habitability and workmanlike construction.

CASE STUDY

The Eriksons purchased a spec house from builder Reynolds. The exterior of the house was synthetic stucco. After living in the house for a while, the Eriksons received a "stucco inspection report." The report asserted that the stucco installation was defective and would inevitably result in water intrusion behind the water barrier, then in structural decay, and ultimately in a compromise to the structural integrity of the building. The Eriksons sued Reynolds alleging a breach of the implied warranties of habitability and workmanlike construction.

Addressing first the implied warranty of habitability, the court stated that this warranty is breached by egregious defects in the fundamental structure of the home. Mere defects in workmanship do not breach the implied warranty of habitability. The gist of this warranty is whether the structure is fit for habitation. A condition in the dwelling that does not presently impact on its structural soundness but may in the future is not one that renders the house unfit for habitation. Accordingly, the court dismissed the claim based on the implied warranty of habitability.

Next addressing the implied warranty of workmanlike construction, the court stated that this warranty arises in contracts for the construction of a dwelling. Since the contract between the Eriksons and Reynolds was for the purchase of a completed spec house, there was no contract for construction, and the implied warranty of workmanlike construction did not apply. Case dismissed.[68]

NEGLIGENCE

Negligence is the failure to use such care as a reasonably prudent and careful person would use under the same or similar circumstances. Negligence deals with the law of torts. A tort action seeks to remedy a civil wrong. It is based on public policy, whereas a contract action is based on the mutual promises of the parties. Negligence is the breach of an individual's duty to exercise reasonable care so as not to cause unreasonable risk of harm to another.

Generally, the elements necessary to establish an action for negligence are:

- A legal duty owed by one person to another to exercise the degree of care demanded by the circumstances to protect the other person from foreseeable harm
- A breach of that duty
- A direct causal connection between the breach and the resulting injury
- Actual loss or damage

Negligence may be asserted as the basis of a damage claim in combination with claims involving breach of contract or warranty. Negligence may provide a basis of recovery even when the contract has been properly fulfilled and no defective construction is evident.

> ### CASE STUDY
>
> ABC Builders, Inc., built a house at the foot of a hillside in 1968. In 1978, heavy rains caused the hillside to slide down and push against the house. The slide destroyed the house. The homeowners sued ABC on the grounds of negligence. The court held that ABC had a duty to furnish a safe location for a residential structure and that the duty did not depend on whether the damage might arise within the confines of the lot boundaries or from forces originating beyond its limits. ABC was liable to the homeowners for negligence in selecting the site because the evidence established that ABC was an experienced builder, had extensive knowledge about the location, and should have known of the potential dangers of selecting this lot as a building site.[69]

FRAUD AND MISREPRESENTATION

The elements necessary to establish an action for fraud and misrepresentation include:

- A false representation of a material (important) fact

- Knowledge or belief on the part of the speaker (or writer) that the representation is false or that he or she does not have sufficient information to make the claim

- Intent to induce the other person to act or refrain from acting based upon the misrepresentation

- Justifiable reliance on the representation on the part of the injured party

- Damage to the plaintiff resulting from such reliance

Under certain circumstances builders and remodelers have a duty to disclose facts regarding a known condition of the property that a prospective buyer or homeowner could not discover upon a reasonable inspection, particularly a dangerous condition or a condition that could likely change a buyer's mind about acquiring the property. In such a case, silence constitutes misrepresentation.

CONSUMER PROTECTION ACTS—DECEPTIVE TRADE PRACTICES

Many states have enacted some form of consumer protection law prohibiting unfair or deceptive trade practices in the furnishing of goods and services to consumers. A few specifically include real estate transactions, including home sales and construction (see New Jersey Statutes Annotated 56:8–2[70]). Other states' laws have been interpreted by courts to exclude the sale of homes because the definition of consumer goods does not include real property but have been interpreted to include contracts to construct homes because these are defined as services. (See Keiber v. Spicer Const. Co., 1107 (Ohio Ct. App. 1993) interpreting Ohio Revised Code chapter 1345.[71]) Still

---

CASE STUDY

Home buyers sought damages from a builder-developer because the new homes that they bought in Vorhees Township, New Jersey, were constructed near a hazardous waste dumpsite known as the Buzby Landfill. The families alleged that, although the developers were aware of the existence and hazards of the landfill, they did not disclose those facts to the families when they bought their homes.

The court observed that in the case of on-site conditions, courts have imposed affirmative obligations on sellers to disclose information materially affecting the value of property and "there is no logical reason why a certain class of sellers and brokers should not disclose offsite matters that materially affect the value of the property."

Thus, in New Jersey a builder-developer of residential real estate or a broker representing the builder may be liable for not disclosing off-site physical conditions that they knew of but were not known nor readily observable by the buyer provided that the conditions are sufficiently material to affect the habitability, use, or enjoyment of the property so as to render the property substantially less desirable or valuable to the reasonable buyer.

---

other consumer protection laws specifically exclude the sale or construction of homes from the definition of consumer transactions (see Virginia Code Annotated s. 59.1-196, et seq.[72]).

In those states that apply consumer protection laws to home construction contracts, a builder may be in violation and liable for acts set out in the statute that are deemed to be unfair, false, misleading, or deceptive. Some examples may include failure to disclose important facts, such as construction on expansive soils or other subsurface fault, providing low cost estimates with the knowledge that the actual cost of construction will be much higher, or failing to provide components of the kind or quality that was promised or advertised. There are key advantages from the customer's perspective in asserting a violation of the consumer protection law in a suit involving a construction dispute. Consumer protection laws usually permit the recovery of attorney's fees (not available in suits for breach of contract, breach of warranty, or negligence), and several consumer protection laws also provide for the recovery of treble damages.

ENFORCEMENT TOOLS FOR BUILDERS AND REMODELERS

Of course, contracts have two sides. Just as often it is not the builder's or remodeler's liability that is at issue but instead the liability of the purchaser, owner, trade contractor, or supplier. Builders and remodelers need to be aware of the remedies available to them and the processes of enforcement of their contract rights to protect their interests.

UNIFORM COMMERCIAL CODE

Builders and remodelers should have familiarity with the Uniform Commercial Code (UCC). The UCC is a body of statutory law governing a wide variety of commercial transactions, including

---

CASE STUDY

Prospective home buyer Cox visited a model home at the subdivision of builder/developer Falcon Associates, Inc. Based on this visit, Cox entered into a contract with Falcon Associates to construct a two-story home in the subdivision. The completed home had many visible defects and was not of like quality to the model home Cox had visited. In addition, Falcon Associates failed to install R-19 insulation throughout the home as promised. Cox sued on the grounds that Falcon Associates had violated the provisions of the Illinois Consumer Fraud and Deceptive Practices Act. Falcon Associates moved for dismissal on the basis that any deficiencies were not intentional.

The court held that Falcon Associates was liable under the Consumer Act when it intended purchasers to rely on the model home as an indicator of quality and also was liable on its failed promise to install R-19 insulation, even if Falcon Associates did not intend to deceive Cox. The court stated that the buyer need not show that the seller intended to deceive but need only show that the seller intended the buyer to rely on its acts or information. Even an innocent or negligent misrepresentation may be actionable under the Act.[73]

---

the sale of goods. The same statutes have been adopted and apply in all fifty states. The UCC does not pertain to the sale of real estate, nor to transactions primarily involving the provision of services. Typically, construction contracts involve the performance of services, and the UCC does not apply. However, the UCC does apply to contracts for the purchase of building materials and supplies. Should these components used in construction be defective or fail to perform, the UCC contains specific warranties that are implied in the sales contract. Just as the builder impliedly warrants that his or her work is habitable and performed in a workmanlike manner, the supplier of building materials impliedly warrants to the buyer that the goods are merchantible (UCC s.2-314). Another implied UCC warranty, fitness for a particular purpose (UCC s. 2-315), arises when the seller furnishes goods knowing that the buyer is relying on the seller to provide goods suitable for a particular purpose. Breach of these warranties by the manufacturer or supplier may entitle the buyer of goods to recover incidental and consequential damages.

MECHANIC'S LIENS

Every state has some form of mechanic's lien law. The purpose of these laws is to protect the contractors, laborers, suppliers, and frequently the design professionals who contribute labor or materials to real estate improvements. Building and selling a house is not like selling a car. The house is permanently affixed to the real estate and cannot be repossessed and carried off in the event of nonpayment. The mechanic's lien laws provide contractors and other contributors to the improvement with a secured interest in the real property in return for the services they performed and the materials they supplied and affixed to the property. The laws also provide priority for me-

CASE STUDY

A roofing contractor brought an action against the manufacturer/supplier of roofing material to recover losses incurred from having to re-roof a community college building because leaks had developed. The roofer's cause of action was based on breach of an implied warranty of fitness for a particular use, pursuant to UCC s. 2-315. The particular use envisioned by the contractor was that the manufacturer/supplier's membrane when used in conjunction with a particular substrate would produce a 20-year bonded roof. An expert witness testified that the membrane supplied had a tensile strength of only 50 pounds per lineal inch, whereas a membrane with a tensile strength of 110 pounds per lineal inch would be required to create a 20-year bond. The court held that the manufacturer/supplier knew about the contractor's expectations, but supplied a membrane that was not fit for that particular use, that subsequently failed, and that caused the roof to leak The roofing company was entitled to recover for the cost of re-roofing and for the interest it paid on funds it borrowed to replace working capital consumed in the course of the re-roofing job.[74]

chanic's lien claims over and above other claims against the property owner and the real estate, often including priority over mortgage interests in the real estate.

The terms "frequently" and "often" are being used because every state has a different body of mechanic's lien laws with different terminology, different coverage, and very different procedures. The lien laws of each state are statutory. The procedures required to obtain a mechanic's lien are spelled out in the statutes, and these procedural steps must be followed carefully, otherwise the ability to acquire the mechanic's lien and to obtain security in the real estate and priority over other claims may be lost.

Typically, mechanic's lien laws provide that in the event of nonpayment the contractor, or other contributor to the improvement, has the right to file a mechanic's lien at the court or recorder's office where real property deeds are recorded as public records. The mechanic's lien serves as notice to all subsequent purchasers and creditors that there is a lien against the real estate and that the property interests or secured indebtedness interests of these persons or entities will be subject to, or subordinate to, the mechanic's lien. The mechanic's lien is not a judgment, however, nor does it last forever. At some point, designated in the statutes, the holder of a mechanic's lien (if still unpaid) must file a lawsuit to obtain a civil judgment on the debt owed (a process called foreclosure) or the mechanic's lien will be automatically dissolved.

In some states, the process for filing the lien is relatively simple. Go to the court house, fill out a claim form that states the amount owed, the name and address of the property owner, and a legal description of the real estate, pay the filing fee, and you have your mechanic's lien. In other states, however, the process can be very complex. The process may require the filing and serving within specified periods of time of preliminary notices when construction commences and with additional notices required at the time the mechanic's lien is filed or is to be filed. Every state has a specific time limit for filing a mechanic's lien (Figure 10.2). A failure to file the mechanic's lien within the prescribed time frame will result in a loss of the right to make an enforceable mechanic's lien claim. This does not mean that you have lost your right to sue for the debt owed, but it does mean that you have lost the security and the priority that the mechanic's lien provides.

CASE STUDY

The George F. Robertson Plastering Company filed suit against the property owner, Altman, to enforce a mechanic's lien that had been filed more than five years after the work had been performed. Altman objected on the grounds that the filing of the mechanic's lien was not timely. The plastering company asserted that Altman had waived the time limit through a clause in the contract for the plastering job. The Supreme Court of Missouri held that the Missouri mechanic's lien statute then in effect required the claim of lien to be filed with the clerk of court within four months from the time that material or labor was last furnished. The court stated that the mechanic's lien is a creature of statute and not of contract. The requirement of filing the lien on time is not something that can be enlarged or waived by contracting parties. By failing to file the mechanic's lien within the statutorily required four-month period, the plastering company lost the right to sue to enforce the lien.[75]

METHODS OF SETTLEMENT OR OBTAINING JUDGMENT

MEDIATION

Mediation, a form of alternative dispute resolution, is an attempt to reach a settlement utilizing the services of a neutral facilitator, called a mediator. The effort to mediate is always a voluntary one. If either party objects to the process, it will not go forward. On occasion a court will order litigants to participate in a mediation process before the court will permit a case to be set for trial. But the court cannot order the matter to be resolved through mediation. Resolution always requires the cooperation and agreement of the disputing parties. If the parties do agree on a settlement, that agreement is written down and signed as a contract. This contract can then be enforced by court order, if necessary. For more information on mediation, please refer to Chapter 2.

ARBITRATION

Arbitration is also a form of alternate dispute resolution, but it is not a settlement process. It is an abridgment of a civil trial with an arbitrator taking the place of a judge and jury and with streamlined rules of discovery, evidence, and procedure. The advantages lie in savings, savings of time through a process that normally takes less time than court proceedings and savings of money through less legal expenses being incurred. Some also believe that arbitration proceedings are less likely to result in runaway jury awards or punitive damage assessments. Disadvantages include the possibility that because of procedural irregularities the case will not be finally resolved by arbitration and that the case will ultimately have to be re-heard in a court of law, thereby resulting in everything actually

Figure 10.2 Time Period for Original or General Contractors to File Mechanic's Liens by Jurisdiction

JURISDICTION	STATUTE	TIME LIMIT TO FILE
District	38-102	Contractor shall file within 3 months after completion.
Alabama	35-11-215	Original contractor shall file within 6 months after the last item of work or labor has been performed.
Alaska	34.35.068	If a notice of completion is not recorded by the owner, contractor must file claim of lien within 90 days after the completion of construction.
Arizona	33-993	If a notice of completion is not recorded by the owner, original contractor must file lien within 90 days after completion.
Arkansas	18-44-117	Contractor shall file within 120 days after the work or labor is done.
California	Civil Code s. 3115	If a notice of completion is not recorded by the owner, original contractor must file 90 days after completion.
Colorado	38-22-109(5)	Lien statement to be filed before the expiration of 4 months from the day last labor was performed or material furnished.
Connecticut	49-34	Contractor shall file within 90 days after last furnishing of materials or labor.
Delaware	25-2711	Contractor shall file no sooner than 90 days from date of completion, but must file within 30 days thereafter.
Florida	713.08(5)	Original contractor must file within 90 days after final furnishing of materials or services.
Georgia	44-14-361.1(a)(2)	Claim of lien must be filed within 3 months after completion of work.
Hawaii	507-43(b)	Notice of claim must be filed not later than 45 days after the date of completion.
Idaho	45-507	Claim of lien to be filed within 90 days after last furnishing of materials or labor.
Illinois	60/7	Contractor shall file within 4 months after completion.
Indiana	32-8-3-3	Contractor shall file within 90 days after performing labor or furnishing materials.
Iowa	572.9	Principal contractor shall file within 90 days from date last material or labor was furnished.
Kansas	60-1102	Contractor shall file within 4 months after completion.
Kentucky	376.080	Contractor shall file within 6 months after ceasing work or furnishing materials.
Louisiana	4822(C)	Statement of claim shall be filed within 60 days after completion of work.
Maine	10-3253	Claimant shall file within 90 days after ceasing labor or furnishing materials.
Maryland	9-105(a)	A person entitled to a lien shall file within 180 days after work has finished and materials have been furnished.

Figure 10.2 Time Period for Original or General Contractors to File Mechanic's Liens by Jurisdiction (Continued)

JURISDICTION	STATUTE	TIME LIMIT TO FILE
Massachusetts	254-8	If a notice of completion is not recorded by the owner, the contractor shall file not later than 120 days after last furnishing materials or labor.
Michigan	570.1111	A contractor shall file within 90 days after last furnishing materials or labor.
Minnesota	514.08	A contractor shall file within 120 days after last furnishing materials or labor.
Mississippi	85-7-141	A contractor shall file within 12 months after the time that the indebtedness is due.
Missouri	429.080	Original contractor shall file within 6 months after the indebtedness shall have accrued.
Montana	71-3-535	Lien to be filed not later than 90 days after final furnishing of services or materials.
Nebraska	52-137	Lien to be recorded within 120 days of last furnishing of materials or labor.
Nevada	108.226	If notice of completion is not filed by owner, a contractor shall record lien within 90 days after completion or last furnishing of labor and materials.
New Hampshire	447:9, 10	Attachment to be filed within 120 days after services are performed or materials furnished.
New Jersey	44A-6	Contractor shall file lien within 90 days of time when last work was done or materials were furnished.
New Mexico	48-2-6	Original contractor shall file lien within 120 days after completion.
New York	NY Lien Law s. 10	For improvements involving single family dwellings, the notice of lien must be filed within 4 months after completion.
North Carolina	44A-12	Claims of lien must be filed within 120 days after the last furnishing of materials or labor.
North Dakota	35-27-13	Every person desiring to perfect a lien shall file within 90 days after all his contribution is done.
Ohio	1311.06	A contractor shall file within 60 days of last labor or work if lien involves a one- or two- family dwelling or a residential unit of a condominium.
Oklahoma	42-142	Any person claiming a lien shall file within 4 months after last furnishing labor or materials.
Oregon	87.035	A contractor shall file a claim for liens within 75 days after ceasing to provide labor or materials.
Pennsylvania	49 P.S. s. 1502	Claimants must file within four months after completion.
Rhode Island	34-28-4	Notice of intention to be filed within 120 days after doing work or furnishing materials.
South Carolina	29-5-90	Statement of account must be filed within 90 days after ceasing labor or furnishing materials.

Figure 10.2 Time Period for Original or General Contractors to File Mechanic's Liens by Jurisdiction (Continued)

JURISDICTION	STATUTE	TIME LIMIT TO FILE
South Dakota	44-9-15	Lien must be filed within 120 days after completion of work or furnishing of material.
Tennessee	66-11-117	Statement of account to be filed within 90 days after completion.
Texas	Property Code 53.052	Person claiming the lien must file an affidavit s. not later than the 15th day of the 4th calendar month after the day on which the indebtedness accrues.
Utah	38-1-7	Claim must be filed within 90 days from the date that labor and material was last furnished.
Vermont	51-1923, 1924	No specific time is set for filing the memorandum of lien, but filing the memorandum is necessary, and an action to perfect the lien must then be filed within 3 months from the time that the memorandum of lien is filed.
Virginia	43-4	Contractor shall file a lien not later than 90 days from the last day of the month in which material is last furnished or labor is last performed.
Washington	60.04.091	Claim shall be filed within 90 days after ceasing to furnish material or labor.
West Virginia	38-2-8	Notice of lien shall be filed within 90 days after completion of work.
Wisconsin	779.06	Lien must be filed within 6 months from the date that materials and labor were last furnished.
Wyoming	29-2-106	Lien statement to be filed within 120 days after last work was performed or materials were furnished.

Caution. This table is intended for informational purposes only. Statutory provisions can change. Requirements vary from state to state. Some states require preliminary notices before liens can be filed and also require notices after liens have been filed. Time periods for filing can vary depending on the type of construction and on the relationship with the property owner. Always review the mechanic's lien laws for the state where the work is being performed to determine what is required to file and preserve a mechanic's lien.

taking more time and being more expensive than if the case had originally been brought in a court. Some also believe that arbitrators tend to seek compromise (equity) at the expense of the technicalities of law and may ignore or downplay a strong legal position by one party in favor of making everyone happy. For more information on arbitration, please refer to Chapter 2.

THE COURTS

The most common dispute between builders/remodelers and owners is over payment, although there are many other issues that can form the basis of a dispute, from copyright infringement of design plans to defamation of character. If all else fails—negotiation, filing the mechanic's lien, mediation efforts—the builder/remodeler can file suit in a court of law. Every state has a system of trial courts, and there also is a system of federal courts.

Most lawsuits involving ordinary construction contracts are filed in state court. Generally, the locality where the work was performed or where the owner resides determines the location of the place to bring suit. This is called venue. Each location has a number of courts from which to choose. The one to use (the one with proper jurisdiction to hear the case) depends usually on the amount of money involved. (Federal jurisdiction, if available at all, may also involve certain technical requirements, such as the diversity of citizenship of the litigants.)

Small Claims Court. Available in most states, small claims courts have limited jurisdiction involving minor amounts of money. Some states limit claims to $1,000. Others have limits up to $15,000 (Figure 10.3). Small claims procedures usually prohibit lawyers from participating. Evidence is presented to the court, but the rules of evidence are modified or eliminated to streamline the proceedings and to prevent technical objections. The case is often heard and decided in a single court appearance. Most states publish brochures with step-by-step instructions on filing suit and presenting a small claims case. Builders and remodelers who are owed small amounts of money will find that small claims courts are user friendly (no attorneys—no or few legal objections to evidence), take relatively little time from their busy schedules, and are inexpensive to use.

County Court. Sometimes called district court or municipal court, it is a court not of record with a limited jurisdiction. Not of record means that few written pleadings are used, and the proceedings are usually not transcribed. Jurisdiction is limited to claims of generally not more than $10,000 to $25,000, depending on the state. Pre-trial discovery applies but is often limited in scope. Normal rules for the admissibility of evidence do apply. The parties can be represented by attorneys, if they so desire. Usually there are no juries. The judge hears the evidence and decides the case. It often takes more than one court appearance before the case is decided. Builders and remodelers who have experience and knowledge of court proceedings may be able to utilize this court without legal assistance. However, builders and remodelers who face an opposing party who is represented by counsel are likely to be at a disadvantage. Cases can be won or lost on the basis of "legal technicalities" (which are simply the knowledge of rules, procedures, and legal precedent that the other party may not be aware of), even if the merits of the case lie on the other side.

Superior Court. Sometimes called circuit court, it is a court of record with an unlimited monetary jurisdiction (although superior courts generally have a minimum amount that must be claimed before this court will assume jurisdiction). All actions are initiated by written pleadings, such as

Figure 10.3 Small Claims Court Jurisdictional Limit by State

State	Maximum Amount of Claim	State	Maximum Amount of Claim
Alabama	$3000	Montana	$3000
Alaska	$7500	Nebraska	$2400
Arizona	$2500	Nevada	$5000
Arkansas	$5000	New Hampshire	$5000
California	$5000	New Jersey	$2000
Colorado	$7500	New Mexico	$7500
Connecticut	$3500	New York	$3000
Delaware	$15000	North Carolina	$4000
District of Columbia	$5000	North Dakota	$5000
Florida	$5000	Ohio	$3000
Georgia	$15000	Oklahoma	$4500
Hawaii	$3500	Oregon	$5000
Idaho	$4000	Pennsylvania	$8000
Illinois	$5000	Rhode Island	$1500
Indiana	$3000	South Carolina	$7500
Iowa	$4000	South Dakota	$8000
Kansas	$1800	Tennessee	$10000
Kentucky	$1500	Texas	$5000
Louisiana	$3000	Utah	$5000
Maine	$4500	Vermont	$3500
Maryland	$2500	Virginia	$1000
Massachusetts	$2000	Washington	$4000
Michigan	$3000	West Virginia	$5000
Minnesota	$7500	Wisconsin	$5000
Mississippi	$2500	Wyoming	$3000
Missouri	$3000		

motions or petitions. A court reporter frequently transcribes all the court proceedings to create a record. Extensive pre-trial discovery is used, including oral depositions, requests for admissions, motions for production of documents and exhibits, and written interrogatories. A jury can be impaneled to decide evidentiary issues. Many court appearances are generally required before the case is finally decided. This can take many months, or even years. Lawyers are a necessity because of the technical and procedural requirements that a layman cannot be expected to know and that this court will strictly enforce.

Appeals. Every trial court has an avenue of appeal to a higher court. Decisions of a small claims court or a county court are usually appealable to the superior court, often as a matter of right (which means that no reason for the appeal—such as an erroneous ruling—need be given). The appeal normally takes the form of a new trial in the superior court. Decisions of a superior court arc appealable to a court of appeals or supreme court. These are appellate courts, not trial courts. These appeals are discretionary—only given for good cause, such as for an erroneous ruling affecting the outcome of the trial. The appeal is limited to specific issues of law. The case is not retried in the appellate court.

Judgment. If the builder/remodeler prevails in the lawsuit against the owner for payment, the builder/remodeler will be awarded a money judgment. The money judgment can then be collected as provided by state law. This may include a voluntary payment by the owner or the owner's lender, the garnishment of judgment debtor's wages or other monetary deposits, an attachment and sale of the judgment debtor's personal property, or the foreclosure sale of the judgment debtor's real property.

NOTES

Chapter 2. Contract Between Builder and Buyer (Owner)

1. *Batter Building Materials Co. v. Kirschner,* 110 A.2d 464 (Conn. 1954).
2. Interstate Land Sales Full Disclosure Act, 15 United States Code sec. 1701 et seq. (1982) (see 24 Code of Federal Regulations parts 1700–1730).
3. *Surety Development Corp. v. Grevas,* 42 Ill. App.2d 268, 192 N.E.2d. 145 (1963).
4. *Winn v. Aleda Construction Co., Inc.,* 315 S.E.2d 193 (Va. 1984).
5. McNeil Stokes, *Construction Law in Contractor's Language,* 2nd ed. (N.Y.: McGraw-Hill, 1990), p.54.
6. K. Collier, *Construction Contracts.* (Englewood Cliffs, N.J.: Prentice Hall, 1987), p.151.
7. *Naylor v. Siegler,* 613 S.W.2d 546 (Tex. Civ. App. 1981).
8. *Grubb v. Cloven,* 601 S.W.2d 244 (Tex. Civ. App. 1981).
9. Steven Stein, *Construction Law,* vol. 1. ¶5.07[1] [b][v] (New York: Matthew Bender, 1995).
10. *Old Post Office Plaza Limited Partnership v. Goodwin,* No. CVN-8910-889, 1991 WL 270281 (Conn. Sup. Ct. Nov. 18, 1991).
11. *V. L. Nicholson Co. v. Transcon Investment and Financial Ltd., Inc.,* 595 S.W.2d 474 (Tenn. 1980).
12. *Barlet v. Frazer,* 218 N.J.Super.106, 109 (1987).
13. Maryland Real Property Code Annotated, § 10-506(a) (1988).,
14. See 16 Code of Federal Regulations §460.16 (1992).
15. *Hudson v. D&V Mason Contractors, Inc.,* 252 A.2d 166 (Del. Super. Ct. 1969).
16. Magnuson-Moss Warranty Act, 15 United States Code, sec. 2301 et seq. (see also 16 Code of Federal Regulations sec. 107).
17. James Acret, *Construction Litigation Handbook.* (Colorado Springs: Shepards/McGraw-Hill, 1986) p. 78.

Chapter 3. Contract Between Remodeler and Owner

18. *Sites v. Moore*, 79 Ohio App.3d 694, 607 N.E.2d 1114 (1992).

19. *Walsh Services v. Feek*, 45 Wash.2d 289, 274 P.2d 117 (1954).

20. McNeil Stokes, *Construction Law in Contractor's Language*, 2nd ed. (New York: McGraw-Hill, 1990) p. 311-312.

21. K. Collier, *Construction Contracts*. (Englewood Cliffs, N.J.: Prentice Hall, 1987), p.151.

22. *Hanrahan v. Audubon Builders, Inc.*, 614 A.2d 748 (Pa. Super. 1992).

23. *Welch v. Fuhrman*, 496 So.2d 484 (La. App. 1986).

24. Steven Stein, *Construction Law*, vol. 1, ¶5.07 [1][b][v] (New York: Matthew Bender, 1995).

25. *Kaufman v. Gray*, 135 A.2d 455 (D.C. 1957).

26. McNeil Stokes, *Construction Law in Contractor's Language*, 2nd ed. (New York: McGraw-Hill, 1990), p.192.

27. *Markway Construction Company, Inc. v. Kirchenbauer*, 769 S.W.2d 836 (Mo. Apps 1989).

28. California CA BUS & PROF S 7159; Connecticut C.G.S.A S 20-429; Florida F.S.A. S 520.73; Hawaii HRS S 444-25.5; Illinois 815 ILCS 513/20; Indiana IC 24-5-11-10; Maryland MD BUS REG S 8-501; Massachusetts M.G.L.A. 142A S 2; Minnesota M.S.A. S 514.011; Nevada N.R.S. 597.719; New York NY GEN BUS S 771; Tennessee T.C.A. S 62-37-110; Texas TX PROPERTY 41.007 and 27.007.

29. 16 Code of Federal Regulations, Part 429 (1992) (Cooling Off Period for Door-To-Door Sales).

30. 12 Code of Federal Regulations, Part 226 (1992), (Regulation Z, Truth in Lending); *What Builders and Remodelers Should Know About Right of Rescission Provision in the Truth in Lending Act* (Washington, D.C.: Consumer Affairs Dept., National Association of Home Builders, 1987).

31. *Einhorn v. Ceran Corporation*, 177 N.J. Super. 442, 426 A.2d 1076 (1980).

32. *Denice v. Spotswood I. Quinby, Inc.*, 248 Md. 428, 237 A.2d 4 (1968).

33. Adapted from "Contract for Repairs or Alterations," Clause 8, model contract (Louisville, Ky.: Home Builders Association of Louisville, 1993).

34. Adapted from "Term and Conditions," Clause 13 model contract (San Antonio, Texas: Greater San Antonio Builders Association, 1981).

Chapter 4. Warranties and Disclaimers

35. *Bridges v. Ferrell*, 685 P.2d 409 (Okla. App. 1984).

36. *Residential Construction Performance Guidelines for Professional Builders and Remodelers, 2nd ed.* (Washington, D.C.: BuilderBooks, 2000).

37. *Breckenridge v. Cambridge Homes, Inc.*, 246 Ill. App.3d 810, 616 N.E.2d 615 (1993).

38. Exclude consumer products," *A Primer for Builders. . .* p. 6.

39. Exclude consumer products," *A Primer for Builders. . .* p.6.

40. Conform whole warranty," *A Primer for Builders. . .* p.6.

41. *Warranties and Disclaimers for Remodelers* (Washington, D.C.: BuilderBooks, 1998) p. 72.

42. *Warranties and Disclaimers for Remodelers* (Washington, D.C.: BuilderBooks, 1998) p. 72.

43. *Warranties and Disclaimers for Builders* (Washington, D.C. BuilderBooks 1999) 72 pp.

44. Alaska – AS 09.45.881 – 09.45.899; Arizona – A.R.S. s 12-1363; California – CA CIVIL s 895 – 945.5; Colorado – C.R.S. 13-20-802 – 13-20-807; Florida – SB 1286 – signed 5/27/03; Idaho – I.C. 6-2501 – 6-2504; Indiana – IC 32-27-3; Kansas – HB 2294 – signed 4/14/03; Kentucky – HB 289 - signed 3/18/03; Montana – s 27-2-208, MCA; Nevada – N.R.S. 40.645; Texas – V.T.C.A. Property Code s. 27.007; Virginia – Va. Code Ann. 55-70.1; Washington – WA ST 64.50.020; West Virginia – W. Va. Code s. 21-11A-1 – 21-11A-8.

Chapter 5. Environmental Clauses and Liability Issues

45. www.cdc.gov/nceh/airpollution/mold/stachy.htm

46. *Get the Facts on Mold.* (Washington, D.C.: BuilderBooks, 2002).

47. "A Citizen's Guide to Radon: The Guide to Protecting Yourself and Your Family (4th ed.)" *Home Buyer's and Seller's Guide to Radon* (2002).

48. "Model Standards and Techniques for Control of Radon in New Residential Buildings" or EPA's "Consumer Guide to Radon Reduction, revised February 2003."

49. 40 Code of Federal Regulations, §61.141 (National Emission Standard for Asbestos).

50. 29 C.F.R. 1926.62 App B.

51. 40 C.F.R. s. 745.227.

52. 16 C.F.R. s. 1304.

53. *Protect Your Family From Lead In Your Home,* EPA.

54. 29 C.F.R. 1926.62 App B.

55. 40 C.F.R. s. 745.227.

56. EPA fact sheet, "Hazard Summary—Arsenic Compounds" at www.epa.gov/ttn/atw/hlthef/arsenic.html.

57. Minnesota Department of Health, *Arsenic in Minnesota's Well Water* or Michigan Department of Community Health, *Arsenic in Well Water.* The EPA also has publications, such as *Drinking Water from Household Wells,* January 2002.

58. "Questions & Answers Regarding the CCA Transition Process" at http://www.epa.gov/pesticides/factsheets/chemicals/cca_transition.htm.

Chapter 6. Subcontracts

59. Adapted from N. Schemm, "Subcontract Forms from the Subcontractor's Perspective." Reprinted with the permission of *The Practical Real Estate Lawyer.* Subscription rates $35/year; $8.75/issue. This article appeared in the September 1986 issue of *The Practical Real Estate Lawyer.*

60. *Slaught v. Bencomo Roofing Co.,* 30 Cal. Rptr. 2d 618, 25 Cal. App. 4th 744 (1994).

61. *Industrial Indemnity Co. v. Wick Construction Co.*, 680 P.2d 1100 (Alaska 1984).

62. *Residential Construction Performance Guidelines for Professional Builders & Remodelers, 2nd ed.* (Washington, D.C.: BuilderBooks, 2000).

Chapter 8. Design-Build Contracts Used By Remodelers and Custom Builders

63. Christopher C. Whitney, "An Evolving Perspective on Design/Build Construction: A View from the Courthouse." *The Construction Lawyer*, Vol. 15, No. 2 (April 1995), p.97, n.29.

Chapter 9. Contracts With Other Team Members

64. Duluth Steel Fabricators, Inc. v. Commissioner of Taxation, 237 N.W. 2d 625 (Minn. 1975).

65. Earl M. Jorgensen Co. v. Mark Construction, Inc., 540 P.2d 978 (Hawaii 1975).

Chapter 10. Contract Liability and Enforcement

66. *Kaiser v. Fishman*, 187 A.D.2d 623, 592 N.Y. S2d 230 (1992).

67. *Quagliana v. Exquisite Home Builders, Inc.*, 538 P.2d 301 (Utah 1975).

68. *Erickson v. Reynolds*, 114 Wash. App. 1044 (2002).

69. *ABC Builders, Inc. v. Phillips*, 632 P.2d 925 (Wyo. 1981).

70. See, e.g., New Jersey Statutes Annotated 56:8-2.

71. *Keiber v. Spicer Const. Co.*, 1107 (Ohio Ct. App. 1993). interpreting Ohio Revised Code chapter 1345.

72. Virginia Code Annotated s. 59.1-196, et seq.

73. *Falcon Associates, Inc. v. Cox*, 298 Ill.App.3d 652 (1998).

74. *Certain-Teed Product Corp. v. Goslee Roofing and Sheet Metal, Inc.*, 339 A.2d 302 (Md. App. 1975).

75. *George F. Robertson Plastering Company v. Altman*, 430 S.W.2d 169 (1968).

APPENDIX

CONSTRUCTION AND SALES CHECKLIST

THE SAMPLE CONSTRUCTION AND sales checklists (Figures A.1 and A.2) provide a format for working with the home buyer or homeowner throughout the construction and sale of a home or during a remodeling project. The checklists are intended to remind builders and remodelers of the tasks that ordinarily should be performed to satisfy legal and professional requirements. Use of the checklists should be started at the beginning of the builders' or remodelers' relationships with their buyers or homeowners. They will serve as permanent records of the parties' actions and decisions.

The checklists merely suggest an approach to recording approvals by the buyer or the homeowner and the activities that are accomplished. Before using the checklists, builders and remodelers should tailor them to fit the needs of their individual businesses and construction projects.

Most of the items in Figure A.1 will apply only when builders are (a) constructing homes on lots already owned by the home buyers or (b) custom-building homes. Other items in Figure A.1 apply solely to the more common situation in which builders own the lots on which they are building. Still others apply to both situations. Some actions or methods necessary for a particular builder or product may not be included in the checklist.

A number of the items found in Figure A.1 will also be found in the checklist for remodelers in Figure A.2. Other items apply solely to a remodeling project. The left side of each checklist provides space to record the date and (if applicable) for the parties to initial the items. The right side of each checklist contains space for comments by the builder or remodeler. Each checklist is cross-referenced to the other parts of *Contracts and Liability for Builders and Remodelers*.

The checklist is an inexpensive way of avoiding litigation. If builders and remodelers take time before the project begins to compile a list of tasks that should be performed to satisfy legal and professional requirements and they review their lists during the course of a project, they are less likely to miss a deadline, fail to deliver a notice, or forget to advise or discuss warranties, disclaimers, or other important information with the owner. For example, under the 1968 Federal Truth in Lending Act, a consumer who enters into a remodeling contract may have three days to rescind (terminate) the contract. The remodeler must deliver two copies of the notice of the right to rescind to each consumer entitled to rescind. The notice of rescission must be in a separate document.

If a remodeler ignores this law or does not comply fully, the contract can be canceled while the work is in progress, and the remodeler might have to refund money paid for work completed. By making the right of rescission a standard item on the checklist, the remodeler will reduce the firm's exposure to the great financial risk associated with failing to comply with this law (see Mandatory Clauses in Chapter 3).

One of the major advantages of keeping such a checklist is to assist the builder or the remodeler in the event of litigation. Cases often reach the evidence-gathering stage long after a project is completed and the parties have difficulty recalling what happened or verifying their memories of events. A clear record kept in the form of a checklist, log, or diary will assist builders and remodelers in reconstructing events and proving not only what they did but also demonstrating that the other party was kept informed. The existence of such a record may help to deter groundless litigation.

Figure A.1 Sample Construction and Sales Checklist for Builders

[The builder can draft a shorter list of only items that the buyer actually needs to initial. The buyer should see and initial only the items that pertain to him or her. The buyer and the builder should both sign that list.]

Dates	Builder's Initials	Owners' or Buyer's Initials	Item	Comments
____	____		Verify that necessary state and/or local contractor's license and any ther necessary legal documents are up to date.	____ ____ ____
____	____		Determine buyer's financial capabilities and method of payment.	____ ____
____	____		Hold pre-bid conference.	____
____	____		Submit bid.	____
____	____	____	Submit initial construction documents to buyer (see Chapter 2).	____ ____
____	____	____	Obtain certificate of title or other evidence of buyer's ownership of lot or land if appropriate.	____ ____
____	____		Obtain performance bond (if required by buyer).	____
____	____		Obtain labor and material payment bond (if required by buyer).	____ ____
____	____	____	Deliver bonds to buyer (if required by buyer).	____
____	____	____	Deliver certificates of insurance to buyer.	____
____	____		Make all necessary payments.	____

Figure A.1 Sample Construction and Sales Checklist for Builders (Continued)

Dates	Builder's Initials	Owners' or Buyer's Initials	Item	Comments
___	___	___	Notify buyer of list of trade contractors (see Chapter 6).	___
___	___	___	Provide buyer with estimated progress schedule.	___
___	___		Obtain copies of all property insurance policies from owner of lot or land.	___
___	___		Determine whether hazard insurance policies are necessary.	___
___	___	___	Discuss warranties on personal property with buyer. Make specific warranties available for buyer's examination (see Chapter 4).	___
___	___		Prepare construction or sales contract (see Chapter 2).	___
___	___		Review contract with attorney before executing it.	___
___	___		Receive certificate of insurance or other evidence of insurance from home buyer (including evidence of increase).	___
___	___		Review contract and all contract documents with the home buyer line by line at the contract-signing meeting (see Chapter 4).	___
___	___	___	Present builder's limited warranty and list of nonwarrantable items to buyer.	___
___	___	___	Execute contract with buyer (see Chapter 2).	___
___	___	___	Give the home buyer a list of trade contractors who will be working on the project (see Chapter 6).	___
___	___	___	Conduct preconstruction conference with home buyer; review contract, plans, specifications to ensure that home buyer has no confusion about work to be done.	___
___	___		Obtain utility (water, gas, electric) permits in lot owner's or buyer's name.	___
___	___		Submit regular (weekly, monthly) statements to buyer for payment per contract.	___
___	___	___	Consult with buyer regarding changes in plans or specifications.	___
___	___	___	Obtain home buyer's signature on written change orders with costs specified and change in completion date, if any.	___
___	___		Keep dated written records of discussions with home buyer (or architect) regarding progress of work.	___

Figure A.1 Sample Construction and Sales Checklist for Builders (Continued)

Dates	Builder's Initials	Owners' or Buyer's Initials	Item	Comments
_____	_____		Keep dated records of any delays. (These records will prove useful if the contract contains a liquidated damages clause; see Chapter 2).	_____
_____	_____		If a dispute arises because an incident occurs on the site, record what happened (for example, take photographs, make video recordings, have witnesses write down what they saw or heard).	_____
_____	_____		For significant issues, provide the home buyer or architect with a memo concerning the matters discussed orally.	_____
_____	_____		Respond promptly in writing to correspondence from home buyer or architect, particularly if the correspondence accuses the builder of failing to perform in accordance with the contract. Silence may be deemed to be acquiescence.	_____
_____	_____	_____	Conduct home buyer orientation; walk through house with home buyer and fill out the home maintenance checklist (see Figure 7.1).	_____
_____	_____	_____	Walk through house with home buyer and fill out punchlist. Assist home buyer in identifying all items that need improvement and establish timetable for completion.	_____
_____	_____	_____	Complete punchlist items (see Figure 7.3).	_____
_____	_____		Have home buyer initial completed punchlist items previously listed as needing improvement (see Figure 7.3).	_____
_____	_____		After final payment, set up appointment for any necessary warranty work and do work promptly.	_____
_____	_____		If payment is withheld, file a lien; check local lien law (see Chapter 10).	_____
_____	_____		Execute certificate of completion with home buyer (see Chapter 3).	_____
_____	_____		Send a short letter to home buyer 30, 45, or 60 days after move-in to acknowledge the beginning of the warranty period and to solicit a list of warranty items that need attention. Alternatively, arrange a follow-up meeting with the home buyer 4 to 6 weeks after move-in.	_____
_____	_____		Shortly before the end of the warranty period, advise the buyer in writing that the warranty is nearing expiration and invite the owner to submit a final list of items that require warranty attention.	_____

Figure A.2 Sample Construction and Sales Checklist for Remodelers

[The remodeler can draft a shorter list of only items the owner actually needs to initial. The owner should see and initial only the items that pertain to him or her. The remodeler and the owner should both sign that list.]

Dates	Remodeler's Initials	Owners' or Homeowner's Initials	Item	Comments
___	___		Verify that necessary state and/or local contractor's license and any other necessary legal documents are up to date.	___ ___ ___
___	___		Determine whether the homeowner actually owns the property. Check local land records. Request certificate of title from owner's title insurance company.	___ ___ ___ ___
___	___		Determine the homeowner's financial capabilities and methods of payment.	___ ___
___	___	___	Educate the homeowner on the nature of remodeling and the company's method of doing business.	___ ___ ___
___	___		Hold pre-bid conference.	___
___	___		Submit proposal.	___
___	___	___	Submit initial construction documents to homeowner.	___ ___
___	___	___	Deliver certificate of insurance or other evidence of insurance to homeowner.	___ ___
___	___	___	Provide homeowner with estimated progress schedule.	___ ___
___	___	___	Discuss manufacturer's warranties on personal property with homeowner. Make specific warranties available for homeowner's examination (see Chapter 4).	___ ___ ___ ___ ___
___	___		Consult with the homeowner regarding plans and specifications.	___ ___
___	___	___	Present remodeler's limited warranty and list of nonwarrantable items to homeowner.	___ ___ ___
___	___		Prepare a construction contract (see Chapter 3).	___ ___
___	___		Review contract with attorney before executing it.	___ ___
___	___		Receive certificate of insurance or other evidence of insurance from homeowner (including evidence of increase).	___ ___ ___

Figure A.2 Sample Construction and Sales Checklist for Remodelers (Continued)

Dates	Remodeler's Initials	Owners' or Homeowner's Initials	Item	Comments
___	___		Review contract and all contract documents with the homeowner line by line at the contract-signing meeting.	___ ___ ___
___	___		Execute contract with homeowner (see Chapter 3).	___ ___
___	___		Give the homeowner any required notices, such as the notice of rescission or the notice of the remodeler's lien rights (see Chapter 3).	___ ___ ___ ___
___	___	___	Give the homeowner a list of trade contractors who will be working on the project (see Chapter 6).	___ ___ ___
___	___		Conduct preconstruction conference with homeowner; review contract, plans, specifications to ensure that homeowner has no confusion regarding work to be done.	___ ___ ___ ___ ___
___	___		Obtain necessary permits.	___
___	___		Submit regular statements (tied to contract terms) to homeowner for payment.	___ ___
___	___		Consult with homeowner regarding changes in plans or specifications.	___ ___
___	___		Obtain labor and material payment bond (if required by owner).	___ ___
___	___		Obtain homeowner's signature on written change orders with costs specified and new completion dates, if necessary.	___ ___ ___
___	___		Keep dated written records of discussions with homeowner (or architect) regarding progress of work.	___ ___ ___
___	___		Keep dated records of any delays. (These records will prove useful if the contract contains a liquidated damages clause (see Chapter 3)).	___ ___ ___ ___
___	___		If a dispute arises because an incident occurs on the site, record what happened (for example, take photographs, make video recordings, have witnesses describe what they saw or heard in writing).	___ ___ ___ ___ ___

Figure A.2 Sample Construction and Sales Checklist for Remodelers (Continued)

Dates	Remodeler's Initials	Owners' or Homeowner's Initials	Item	Comments
___	___		For significant issues, provide the homeowner or architect with a hand-written memo concerning the matters discussed orally.	___
___	___		Respond promptly in writing to correspondence from homeowner or architect, particularly if the correspondence accuses the remodeler of failing to perform in accordance with the contract. Silence may be deemed to be acquiescence.	___
___	___	___	Conduct home buyer orientation; walk through house with homeowner and fill out the home maintenance checklist (see Figure 7.1).	___
___	___	___	Walk through house with homeowner and fill out punchlist. Assist homeowner in identifying all items that need improvement and establish timetable for completion.	___
___	___	___	Complete punchlist items (see Figure 7.3).	___
___	___		Have homeowner initial completed punchlist items previously listed as needing improvement (see Figure 7.3).	___
___	___		After final payment, set up appointment for any necessary warranty work and do work promptly.	___
___	___		If payment is withheld, file a lien; check local lien law (see Chapter 10).	___
___	___		Execute certificate of completion with homeowner (see Chapter 3).	___
___	___		Send a short letter to homeowner 30, 45, or 60 days after move-in to acknowledge the beginning of the warranty period and to solicit a list of warranty items that need attention. Alternatively, arrange a follow-up meeting with the owner 4 to 6 weeks after move-in.	___

Figure A.2 Sample Construction and Sales Checklist for Remodelers (Continued)

Dates	Remodeler's Initials	Owners' or Homeowner's Initials	Item	Comments
____	____		Shortly before the end of the warranty period, advise the owner in writing that the warranty is nearing expiration and invite the owner to submit a final list of items that require warranty attention.	____ ____ ____ ____ ____

GLOSSARY

alternative dispute resolution procedure (ADR)—in noncriminal matters, liability is determined by an arbitrator or some other neutral third party.

caption—the caption is the heading or introductory part of a legal document. It should include the names of all persons listed as property owners. The caption should also give a legal description of the property.

closing costs—refers to many fees and expenses.

cost of work—costs necessarily incurred in the builder's proper performance of the work contained in the contract documents, including wages, salaries, payments to trade contractors, materials, supplies, equipment, and rental charges.

differing site conditions—a physical characteristic of the property that materially changes the construction techniques from those reasonably expected at the time of the contract.

draw schedule—a schedule for making payments at certain specified points in the construction process.

equitable adjustment—payment of any increased costs necessitated by the differing site condition.

express warranty—a warranty in words, either spoken or written. Courts view an express warranty like any other agreement. When an express warranty is breached by the builder or remodeler, the courts see that as a breach in contract.

Federal Trade Commission (FTC)—enforces federal consumer protection laws that prevent fraud, deception, and unfair business practices.

implied warranty—courts have ruled that it is understood within a contract that there is a promise to provide a house that is reasonably free from defects in workmanship or materials and, in the case of a new home, that it is habitable even if a builder or remodeler hasn't made a specific written or oral promise.

indemnity—shifting financial loss from the one required to pay to the party that caused the loss.

liability—legal responsibility, either civil or criminal, as determined by a judge or jury.

liquidated—refers to damages that are agreed to in advance.

liquidated damages clause—provides for the payment of a predetermined amount of money in the event that there is a breach of contract.

material breach of the contract—a party may not terminate the contract without liability unless the other party defaults and the default goes to the root of the contract.

mechanic's lien laws—also called construction lien laws in some states—ensure that participants in the construction process get paid for their work by granting them a specific interest in real property that has been improved by their labor or materials.

mediation—process whereby the conflicting parties meet voluntarily to negotiate a private and mutually satisfactory agreement aided by a neutral third party. A key difference between mediation and arbitration is that unlike an arbitrator, a mediator does not make a decision in favor of one party or the other.

mutuality of performance—statement in the contract that provides a description of the work you are to provide and provisions for payment in return.

per diem—payments decided on a day-to-day basis.

perfecting the lien—the process whereby the claimant must provide one or more forms of notice before the lien can be effective.

quit-claim deed—releases ownership rights that the seller may have in the property.

retainage—the percentage of the contract price that is withheld by the owner until completion. For example, when the project is substantially completed and all potential mechanic's liens have been waived or released, if retainage is provided for, the contract should specify when (under what circumstances) the retainage will be disbursed.

statute of limitations—the period of time during which a lawsuit can be timely filed. The purpose of a statute of limitations is to require that suits be brought during a period of time when witnesses and supporting evidence are more likely to be fresh and available and to provide a final cut-off to potential claims.

trade contractor—has a direct contractual relationship with a builder or remodeler to undertake a specific part of the work to fulfill a builder's or remodeler's contract with a buyer or owner.

Uniform Commercial Code (UCC)—uniform body of law that governs a wide variety of business transactions, including the sale of goods.

warranty of habitability or fitness—a promise made that requires that the new home be fit for its intended use.